Irish STEM lives

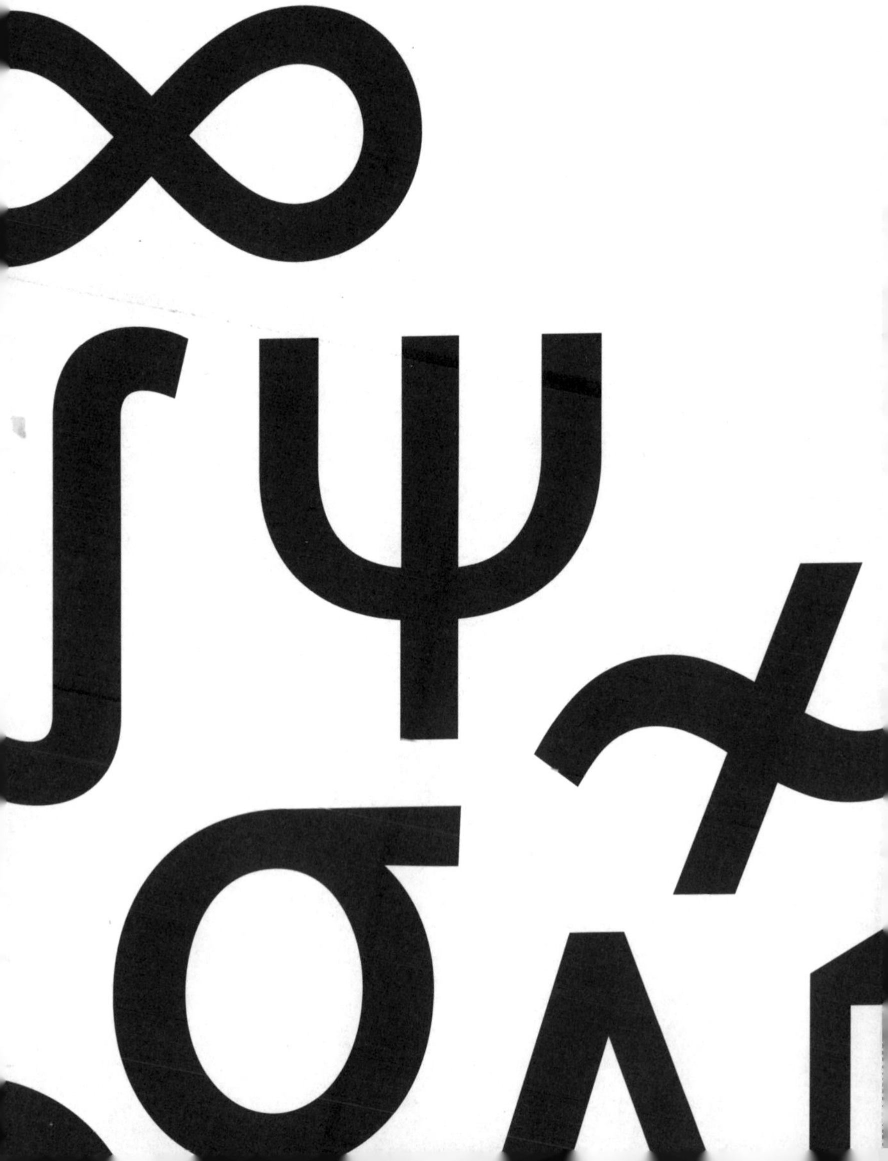

Irish STEM lives

EDITED BY Turlough O'Riordan and Jane Grimson

Acadamh Ríoga na hÉireann
Royal Irish Academy

Irish STEM lives
First published 2025
Royal Irish Academy, 19 Dawson Street, Dublin 2
ria.ie

The biographies in this book are selected from the Royal Irish Academy's *Dictionary of Irish Biography* (© Royal Irish Academy 2009, 2018; published by Cambridge University Press, reproduced with permission), a comprehensive, scholarly biographical reference work for Ireland, treating the lives of persons from the earliest times to the present day, and encompassing every sphere of human activity. Access to the online version of the *Dictionary* is freely available at dib.ie.

Every effort has been made to locate and credit the copyright holders of all images reproduced in this publication. The publisher welcomes information to correct any oversight in future editions.

ISBN 9781802050325 (PB)
ISBN 9781802050332 (pdf)
ISBN 9781802050349 (epub)

All rights reserved. The material in this publication is protected by copyright law. Except as may be permitted by law, no part of the material may be reproduced (including by storage in a retrieval system) or transmitted in any form or by any means; adapted; rented or lent without the written permission of the copyright owners or a licence permitting restricted copying in Ireland issued by the Irish Copyright Licensing Agency CLG, 63 Patrick Street, Dún Laoghaire, Co. Dublin, A96 WF25.

British Library Cataloguing in Publication Data. A CIP catalogue record for this book is available from the British Library.

Design: Fidelma Slattery
Index: Eileen O'Neill

Printed in Poland by L&C Printing Group

This product is made of material from well-manager FSC®-certified forests and other controlled sources.

MIX
Paper | Supporting responsible forestry
FSC® C152082

General Product Safety Regulation (GPSR): For any safety queries, please contact us at productsafety@ria.ie

To offset environmental impacts during the production of our books and journals we will plant 45 trees with Easy Treesie in 2025.

Royal Irish Academy is a member of Publishing Ireland, the Irish book publishers' association

5 4 3 2 1

Contents

Acknowledgements	vii
Abbreviations	viii
Introduction	x
ROBERT BOYLE	1
NICHOLAS CALLAN	9
GEORGE BOOLE	14
WILLIAM ROWAN HAMILTON	24
WILLIAM DARGAN	37
MARY WARD	47
ROBERT MALLET	51
JOHN TYNDALL	57
GEORGE FRANCIS FITZGERALD	70
GEORGE GABRIEL STOKES	74
AGNES CLERKE	85
WILLIAM THOMSON	89
BINDON BLOOD STONEY	93
OSBORNE REYNOLDS	97
JOHN HOLLAND	101
MARGARET HUGGINS	105
PERCY LUDGATE	110
WILLIAM AND CHARLES ALGERNON PARSONS	115
THOMAS AND HOWARD GRUBB	121
WILLIAM 'STUDENT' GOSSET	127
ALICIA BOOLE	131
ALICE EVERETT	135
MAUDE DELAP	138
HARRY FERGUSON	142
ERWIN SCHRÖDINGER	150
EMILY ANDERSON	156
KATHLEEN LONSDALE	163

MARY GOUGH	169
JOHN STEWART BELL	173
PETER RICE	177
GERRIT VAN GELDEREN	182
HILARY STEVENSON	186
JOHN LIGHTON SYNGE	189
ERNEST WALTON	195
HELEN MEGAW	202
EVA PHILBIN	207
KAY MCNULTY	210
DAN BRADLEY	216
SHEILA TINNEY	223
JAMES DOOGE	226
JOHN SCOTT	235
MARY MULVIHILL	241
JOHN BYRNE	247
ANNE KERNAN	253
Index	258

Acknowledgements

While we were compiling *Irish STEM Lives*, many people offered support and kindly shared their advice. Ruth Hegarty, head of RIA Publications, and Dr Eoin Kinsella, managing editor of the *Dictionary of Irish Biography*, were early supporters, as were Dr James Quinn and Professor P. Gerry McKenna. Professor Iggy (Ignatius) McGovern, Dr Linde Lunney and Professor James Lunney offered sage advice and guidance that was essential to the overall shape of this collection. Bruce Misstear assisted us, as did the two anonymous peer reviewers, whose perceptive observations have improved the shape of the introduction to this collection.

In the quest to source images to accompany this collection we would like to thank the staff at the Cambridge Central Library, the Archives and Library of the Royal Astronomical Society, the Shelby White and Leon Levy Archives Centre at the Institute of Advanced Study at Princeton, the Special Collections Research Centre at the University of Chicago Library, Dara Mac Dónaill, the *Irish Times* and the Valentia Island Heritage Centre. Jim Moore and Dr Jackie Uí Chionna graciously allowed us to use incredibly rare images of Mary Gough and Emily Anderson, while Dr Eimer Philbin Bowman and Professor Orla Feeley kindly assisted us in locating a photo of Eva Maric Philbin. Konstantin Ermolin and Rebecca Cairns and the staff of the Library of the Royal Irish Academy were continually helpful and supportive.

Turlough would like to thank Eve, whose sagacity and inquisitiveness are a joy to behold. We dedicate this collection to future generations of STEM practitioners.

Abbreviations

AI	Artificial Intelligence
Annual Reg., 1758 [etc.]	*The Annual Register, 1758* (1759–)
BA	Bachelor of Arts
BE	Bachelor of Engineering
BL	British Library
B.Sc.	Bachelor of Science
Burke, *IFR*	*Burke's Irish family records* (1976)
CBS	Christian Brothers' School
CERN	Conseil Européen pour la Recherche Nucléaire/European Organization for Nuclear Research
Crone	J. S. Crone, *A concise dictionary of Irish biography* (2nd ed., 1937)
DIAS	Dublin Institute for Advanced Studies
DIH	D. J. Hickey and J. E. Doherty, *A dictionary of Irish history since 1800* (paperback ed., 1987)
DNB	Sir Leslie Stephen and Sir Sidney Lee (eds), *The dictionary of national biography* (66 vols, 1885–1901; reprint with corrections, 22 vols, 1908–9; supplementary vols for 1901 and after)
D.Sc.	Doctor of Science
Dublin Hist. Rec.	*Dublin Historical Record* (1938–)
ESB	Electricity Supply Board
FRIBA	fellow of the Royal Institute of British Architects
FRS	fellow of the Royal Society
IBL	*The Irish Book Lover* (1909–57, 32 vols)
ICE	Institution of Civil Engineers
ICEI	Institution of Civil Engineers of Ireland
Ir. Builder	*The Irish Builder and Engineer* (1867–; formerly *The Dublin Builder*, 8 vols, 1859–66)
ITWW	*Who's who, what's what and where in Ireland in association with the Irish Times* (1973)
JP	justice of the peace
LLD	Doctor of Laws
MA	Master of Arts

McRedmond	Louis McRedmond (ed.), *Modern Irish lives: dictionary of 20th-century Irish biography* (1996)
ME	Master of Engineering
MICE	member of the Institution of Civil Engineers
MP	member of parliament
MRIA	member of the Royal Irish Academy
MRIAI	member of the Royal Institute of the Architects of Ireland
M.Sc.	Master of Science
Newmann	Kate Newmann, *Dictionary of Ulster biography* (1993)
NUI	National University of Ireland
OBE	officer of the Order of the British Empire
ODNB	*Oxford dictionary of national biography* (2004–)
Ph.D.	Doctor of Philosophy
Proc. Roy. Soc. (Lond.)	*Proceedings of the Royal Society (of London)*
QC	queen's counsel
QCB	Queen's College, Belfast
QCC	Queen's College, Cork
QCG	Queen's College, Galway
QUB	Queen's University Belfast
RBAI	Royal Belfast Academical Institution
RDS	Royal Dublin Society
RHA	(member of the) Royal Hibernian Academy
RI	Royal Institution of Great Britain
RIA	Royal Irish Academy
RIA Proc.	*Proceedings of the Royal Irish Academy* (1836–)
RIBA	Royal Institute of British Architects
RTÉ	Raidió Teilifís Éireann
RUI	Royal University of Ireland
STEM	science, technology, engineering and mathematics
TCD	Trinity College Dublin
UCC	University College Cork
UCD	University College Dublin
UCG	University College Galway
UCL	University College, London
UV	ultraviolet
WWW	*Who was who ... 1897–1916* (1920–)

Introduction

On 16 October 1843 William Rowan Hamilton was walking from Dublin's Dunsink Observatory to a meeting at the Royal Irish Academy (RIA) when he was hit by a sudden flash of inspiration:

> I then and there felt the galvanic circuit of thought close; and the sparks which fell from it were the fundamental equations between i, j, k; ... I felt a problem to have been at that moment solved – an intellectual want relieved – which had haunted me for at least fifteen years before.

Compelled to record his equation on the spot, Hamilton etched it into the stone of Brougham Bridge on the Royal Canal (better known today as Broom Bridge). Though that original etching is no longer visible, the moment is commemorated by a plaque installed in 1958, a physical testament to a moment of profound intellectual importance.

Hamilton (p. 24) is one of the forty-six lives collected in this volume, all of whom are united by their inquisitiveness. Together they offer a panoply of engineering ingenuity, scientific discoveries, technological advances and mathematical insights achieved by Irish women and men, or by those born elsewhere whose achievements occurred while living in Ireland. From the development of the 'scientific method' in the circle surrounding Robert Boyle (p. 1), to the large-scale particle physics experiments undertaken by John Stewart Bell (p. 173) and Anne Kernan (p. 253) at CERN, *Irish STEM lives* traces the evolution of the pursuit of knowledge over the past four centuries.[1] In that time the people gathered in this volume have influenced our lives in ways both fascinating and varied: the evolution of our built environment, which has in part developed as a result of their complex and intricate engineering ingenuity; the imperatives of mass food production and our deep understanding of nutrition and food safety, which are essential to health and longevity; and our utilisation of electricity and electromagnetism, of induction coils and semiconductors, which together underpin the digital infrastructure that enables our knowledge economy and our media consumption. The computational approaches and communications infrastructure these technologies facilitate have, in less than a century, transformed our lives.

STEM

The phrase 'science, technology, engineering and mathematics' was first used in engineering and educational contexts as far back as 1968. Though the term 'STEM' has been widely adopted across the English-speaking world, use of the acronym is comparatively recent – it was first coined in 2001 by scientific administrators at the US National Science Foundation.[2]

---

[1] The European Organization for Nuclear Research (CERN) is based near Geneva on the border between Switzerland and France. CERN is probably best known as the site of the large hadron collider, the world's largest and highest-energy particle collider.

[2] See the *Oxford English dictionary* headword at https://www.oed.com/dictionary/stem_n?tab=meaning_and_use (accessed 1 Nov. 2024); https://www.britannica.com/topic/STEM-education.

The disciplines that comprise STEM are at the forefront of some of the most exciting advances in human knowledge, and indeed of the global economy. Across areas such as artificial intelligence (AI), climate change, modelling the trajectory of pandemics and food safety, STEM is integral to modern society. Despite the term's widespread usage, defining the boundaries of STEM is somewhat problematic. Should the social sciences be included? What about the emerging fields of digital humanities, bioengineering and the biosciences? Or the better-established natural science disciplines? For this collection we have adopted what might best be described as the 'traditional' definition of STEM – science, technology, engineering and mathematics. Yet the boundaries between disciplines are becoming increasingly blurred, and in some cases they are breaking down entirely. There is a growing emphasis on the importance of inter- and trans-disciplinarity, which runs contrary to the drive towards increased specialisation.

Consider the rapidly developing field of AI, where tools such as ChatGPT and DeepSeek are based on large language models that require an understanding of linguistics, the structure of language, statistical methods and computing. Training such systems often makes use of neural networks inspired by the functioning of the human brain. While AI (and indeed other emerging fields) are too recent to be reflected in this volume, we have included Percy Ludgate (p. 110), Kay McNulty (p. 210) and John Byrne (p. 247), each of whom made significant contributions to computational methods that underpin research across a multitude of disciplines today. William Rowan Hamilton formulated quaternions in 1843; now, when utilised to describe multidimensional space, they serve the ongoing refinement of 'deep learning' approaches that drive significant developments in AI.

Polymaths

At a time when 'science' itself was being defined, Robert Boyle was multidisciplinary long before such an approach was (re)conceived. The engineer and seismologist Robert Mallet (p. 51) also investigated glaciation, alloys, geology and magnetism. George Gabriel Stokes (p. 74) undertook deep research in physics and mathematics, which served his foundational work in physiology. John Tyndall's (p. 57) prowess across engineering, physics and chemistry informed his investigation of gases and vapours, while work on meteorology, infra-red analysis and spectroscopy imbued his foundational identification of the greenhouse effect. Tyndall's 'light pipe' is a clear precursor to modern fibre optics, while his work on sterilisation also situates him as an important figure in bacteriology and microbiology.

Emily Anderson's (p. 156) career demonstrates the complementary nature of artistic scholarship and intelligence work to cryptography, foregrounding the creative aspects of the STEM domain. Anderson's rigorous application of pattern recognition and cryptographical analysis underpinned both her public (musicologist) and covert (leading cryptanalyst and code breaker in both the first and second world wars) careers. Charles Parsons (p. 116) excelled as a scientific engineer and inventor, and as a manufacturer and businessperson – an 'entrepreneur' in later parlance. Such behaviours and approaches are more commonplace today.

This collection also presents us with waypoints in the evolution of computational thinking and methods. The mathematician George Boole's (p. 14) Boolean algebra was posthumously harnessed by Claude Shannon in elucidating information theory, which underpins the electronic circuitry that serves modern communications networks across the world today. President of the Royal Society William Parsons (p. 115) supported the development of Charles

Babbage's 'difference engine', while a few decades later in Dublin the lone genius Percy Ludgate designed a novel computational device of impressive significance. Long unheralded, McNulty's contribution to the development and operation of the world's first general-purpose computer saw her introduce subroutines to computer programming.

Alongside Boole and Hamilton are two important mathematicians. Stokes, a hugely gifted teacher, made such fundamental contributions to hydrodynamics, light theory, fluorescence and the ultraviolet (UV) spectrum that his name is assigned to important equations, theorems and formulae. John L. Synge's (p. 189) geometrical investigation of Einstein's theory of relativity (he was also an editor of Hamilton's papers) drove his stellar career across North American academia. At the Dublin Institute of Advanced Studies, Synge's work on black holes drew students from around the world. Both Stokes and Synge deployed mathematics in the pursuit of physics research, following in George Fitzgerald's (p. 70) illustrious footsteps. J. S. Bell's vocational route into experimental and mathematical physics led him to CERN, where he postulated his famous theorem, integral to quantum mechanics. Dan Bradley (p. 216) experienced a similarly circuitous route into academia; initial work on spectroscopy led him to research lasers.

Singular inventions – Nicholas Callan's (p. 9) induction coil, John Holland's (p. 101) submarine and Harry Ferguson's (p. 142) tractor – have their equivalents in ideas, methods and processes. The Guinness brewer and statistician William Gosset's (p. 127) t distribution is a foundational statistical tool. Osborne Reynolds (p. 97), a versatile and skilled engineer, established the Reynolds number and the Reynolds equation, both widely known and frequently deployed across engineering fields.

Gender

Historically, women did not have access to a 'scientific' education. Moreover, the achievements and contributions of those who did succeed in overcoming such barriers were not recognised or were ascribed to male family members or research partners. That many of the careers and achievements of the STEM women collected here are clustered in a small number of fields, principally in astronomy, astrophysics and mathematics, points to the accessibility of those domains to women with both the means and opportunity to pursue their intellectual interests. It also makes clear how those fields were amenable to independent scholarship undertaken outside formal or institutional settings. Crucially, and especially in mathematics, such disciplines were regarded as safe for women to immerse themselves in. Pondering abstract principles left the patriarchy, and the social structure it relied upon, unquestioned.[3]

Agnes Clerke (p. 85), Margaret Huggins (p. 105) and Mary Ward (p. 47) were all STEM communicators. Their careers, undertaken for the most part in the nineteenth century, demonstrate how they overcame, in different ways, the implicit and explicit barriers women then faced. As gender barriers finally began to recede (though not to disappear) in the twentieth century, chemists Kathleen Lonsdale (p. 163) and Helen Megaw (p. 202) both worked on crystallography, a domain at the forefront of subsequent leading-edge STEM developments, while Eva Maria Philbin (p. 207) rose to the top of the chemistry profession in Ireland. Lonsdale and Megaw indicate how the study of the structure and properties of crystals, while requiring institutional support and specialist apparatus, was open to

---

[3] Dale DeBakcsy, *A history of women in mathematics: exploring the trailblazers of STEM* (2023), p. x.

women by the early- to mid-twentieth century. It's possible that Lonsdale, Megaw and other women gravitated towards crystallography due to the creation of distinctly egalitarian laboratory cultures, while facets of the Froebel kindergarten pedagogy (alongside that educational movement's practice of exposing girls to scientific education) also influenced many women crystallographers.[4]

In the twentieth century there are several women who, it is generally accepted, deserved to receive a Nobel prize for their work. Instead, the award went to their male, more senior, collaborators or supervisors. As a Doctor of Philosophy (Ph.D.) student at Cambridge University, Irish physicist Jocelyn Bell Burnell discovered pulsars. However, the 1974 Nobel prize in physics went to her supervisor, Antony Hewish, together with Martin Ryle. Other examples abound, notably Rosalind Franklin, Lise Meitner and Chien-Shiung Wu.[5] The lives collected here include many

---

[4] Georgina Ferry, 'Women in crystallography', *Nature*, 505 (30 Jan. 2014), 609–11, https://doi.org/10.1038/505609a; Bart Kahr, 'Broader impacts of women in crystallography', *Crystal Growth & Design*, vol. 15, no. 10 (Oct. 2015), 4715–30, https://doi.org/10.1021/acs.cgd.5b00457.

[5] Franklin's work on X-ray crystallography was integral to the research establishing the double helix structure of DNA, yet James Watson, Francis Crick and Michael Watkins were awarded the 1962 Nobel prize for physiology or medicine. Although her 1958 death precluded her inclusion in the 1962 award, if anyone in the scientific community had recognised her significant contribution and nominated her before her death (the relevant Nobel archives were opened in 2008 and record no such nomination) she could have shared the 1962 award.

Meitner was an Austrian physicist who was the first woman in Germany to be appointed to a full professorship in physics. Together with Otto Hahn, she discovered nuclear fission, for which Hahn was awarded a Nobel prize in 1944. Despite being nominated forty-nine times for both physics and chemistry, Meitner never received a Nobel prize. Element 109 was named Meitnerium in her honour.

Chien-Shiung Wu was a Chinese-American physicist. Following a request by physicists Tsung-Dao Lee and Chen Ning Yang, she successfully provided the experimental evidence to prove their theory regarding the 'handedness' of particles. (A particle is right-handed if the direction of its spin is the same as its direction of motion. It is left-handed if they are opposite.) Lee and Yang were awarded the Nobel prize in physics in 1957 for their part, but Wu's vital contribution to the work was ignored.

women whose significant contributions to STEM failed to receive due recognition. The careers of women STEM practitioners were often conditioned by men, as with Margaret Huggins (her husband) or Lonsdale and Alicia Boole (their collaborators). Despite making significant contributions to their fields, many STEM women were presented and perceived as adornments to male colleagues. Relegated to routine roles, as with Alice Everett (p. 135), opportunities for institutional or career advancement, or professional recognition from learned societies, were either impossible or exceedingly rare.

It was not until the latter part of the nineteenth century that women began to be admitted to universities or to learned societies, an important sign of peer recognition. Yet change was slow; in the spring of 1945 the Royal Society for the first time elected women to its fellowship, including Kathleen Lonsdale.[6] Though the RIA admitted Princess Ekaterina Romanovna Dashkova as its first female honorary member in April 1791, it only began admitting women as full members for the first time in 1949, including mathematical physicist Sheila Power (later Tinney) (p. 223), as well as Phyllis Clinch, Françoise Henry and Eleanor Knott.[7]

Societal norms also inhibited progress. Mathematician Alicia Boole (p. 131), whose famous father died when she was four years old, endured relatively straitened circumstances. After her marriage a friend introduced her to polytopes (multidimensional geometry), on which she

[6] Joan Mason, 'The admission of the first women to the Royal Society of London', *Notes and Records: the Royal Society Journal of the History of Science*, vol. 46, no. 2 (1992), 279–300, https://doi.org/10.1098/rsnr.1992.0027.
[7] Royal Irish Academy minutes, SR 16/1/C, 23 April 1791, vol. 1, 70; Angela Byrne, 'Princess Ekaterina Romanovna Dashkova: the woman who broke through the "august sanctuary" of the male-dominated Russian Academy', RIA library blog, 10 Jan. 2019, https://www.ria.ie/blog/princess-ekaterina-romanovna-dashkova-the-woman-who-broke-through-the-august-sanctuary-of-the-male-dominated-russian-academy/.

published important papers. Family life then intervened for two decades, after which she re-engaged fruitfully, producing important work in the final decade of her life. The significant contribution of Kay McNulty and her female colleagues to the development of ENIAC, the first general-purpose computer, was demeaned by their public presentation as mere 'hostesses' or 'operators'. After her 1948 marriage to one of the engineers with whom she had worked on ENIAC, McNulty 'noted without comment that her new husband gave her a cookbook on their honeymoon, and that she was thereafter expected to be the family cook; she left paid scientific work on her marriage' (p. 213).

The role of women in STEM history in Ireland was until very recently almost completely overlooked.[8] Of the 118 lives in a collection published in 2007, accounting for the origins and development of Irish science and technology, just five (4.24 per cent) were women.[9] This is despite the important work of the STEM communicator Mary Mulvihill (p. 241). Mulvihill, a science journalist, was integral to the publication of *Stars, shells and bluebells* in 1997, honouring fifteen women STEM practitioners from the eighteenth, nineteenth and early twentieth centuries. *Lab coats and lace* (2009) followed, focusing on women active in the late nineteenth and twentieth centuries.[10] Published by the Women in Technology and Science Ireland (WITS) group, which she founded, Mulvihill's two volumes are the cornerstone of the history of women in STEM in Ireland

---

[8] Ken Houston (ed.), *Creators of mathematics: the Irish connection* (2000) comprises eighteen biographical essays, all on male mathematicians.

[9] Charles Mollan, *It's part of what we are: some Irish contributors to the development of the chemical and physical sciences* (2 vols, 2007).

[10] Mary Mulvihill, *Stars, shells and bluebells: women scientists and pioneers* (1997); eadem (ed.), *Lab coats and lace: the lives and legacies of inspiring Irish women scientists and pioneers* (2009).

and were instrumental in kick-starting a sustained response to the dearth of research on the subject.[11]

Class, education and institutional connections

The networks and institutions in which the people in this collection lived and worked emphasise the importance of familial units, which often proved advantageous in certain social and educational contexts – particularly so in the nineteenth century. Osborne Reynolds benefitted from his father's mathematical knowledge, as did Alicia Boole from her father, George, while her mother Mary was also a maths tutor and renowned pedagogical innovator. Maude Delap's (p. 138) father, a clergyman posted to Valentia Island, off the coast of Co. Kerry, spurred her interest in natural history. Robert Mallet's father – a skilled plumber, engine maker and ironmonger – prefigured his own early interests. Thomas and Howard Grubb (p. 121) and William and Charles Parsons demonstrate how familial networks, as much as academic or institutional ones, often encourage STEM advances.[12]

George Gabriel Stokes advised Howard Grubb and collaborated with William Thomson, Lord Kelvin (p. 89), illustrating the close-knit nature of the Irish STEM world

---

[11] See for example Juliana Adelman and Éadaoin Agnew (eds), *Science and technology in nineteenth-century Ireland* (2011); Jackie Uí Chionna, *Queen of codes: the secret life of Emily Anderson, Britain's greatest female codebreaker* (2023). Published under open access by University College London in 2023, *Women in the history of science* collects a range of primary materials with accompanying detailed commentaries. The book richly documents the contribution of women to the evolution of STEM, and we hope the growing interest in the important role women played in STEM history in Ireland will generate similar endeavours (Hannah Wills, Sadie Harrison, Erika Jones, Farrah Lawrence-Mackey and Rebecca Martin (eds), *Women in the history of science: a sourcebook* (2023), https://doi.org/10.14324/111.9781800084155.

[12] Though each Parsons and Grubb father and son have individual entries in the *DIB*, they have been combined into a single 'family' entry for this collection.

in the late nineteenth century. This proximity also generated tension. Tyndall and Thomson interacted on a number of scientific topics and took opposite sides on broad issues of the philosophy of nature, including the impact of Darwinian evolution. Their shared political unionism, however, salved some of their differences.

That only four of the lives presented here emerged from relatively humble origins (Alicia Boole, Ludgate, Gough and Bell) marks the historical importance of socio-economic status in determining both educational and professional development. Five had clergymen fathers (Stokes, Reynolds, Delap, Walton and Fitzgerald) and nine were born to professionals (Megaw, Clerke, Huggins, Kernan, Dooge, Byrne, Mallet, Rice and Scott). Three were born to the clerical class (Holland, Bradley and Philbin), two from the military (Gosset and Lonsdale) and four from families engaged in commerce (Hamilton, McNulty, Howard Grubb and Mulvihill). That four of those hailing from professional families were women further emphasises the importance of social and educational capital. The centrality of land and the rural economy to Irish history is marked by the presence of five children of 'strong' farmers (Callan, Dargan, Thomas Grubb, Ferguson and Stevenson). Four lives hailed from landowning families of varying stature (Stoney, Tyndall, Ward and Synge). Boyle and the two Parsons highlight the singular benefits of aristocratic wealth, privilege and leisure to those interested in the world.

Another striking thread to emerge in this volume is the role of the academic parent in shaping careers, particularly in the case of women. Alice Everett was the child of a professor of natural philosophy, as were Emily Anderson and William Thomson. Furthermore, both Sheila Tinney and Alicia Boole were the daughters of professors of mathematics. Here the contrast between the origins of

Tinney and Mary Gough (p. 169), both mathematicians, offers insights. Tinney's elevated socio-economic privilege emerges in her primary and secondary education in Galway, and then Dublin, by the elite-leaning Dominican Order, and her undergraduate career in those same cities. Tinney went on to have a superb postgraduate and academic career in mathematics. The daughter of a labouring smallholder farmer, Gough was raised in impoverished surroundings. Her emigration as a young adult to Texas, to enter a religious teaching congregation, enabled her to become in 1931 the first Irish woman known to have earned a Ph.D. in mathematics. By then a long-serving teacher in various primary and secondary schools, and later at an undergraduate college, Gough's doctorate was intended to augment her teaching impact. These contrasting experiences and careers exemplify the variable role of social capital.

Institutional contexts also have considerable relevance. Trinity College Dublin (TCD) and the Royal Dublin Society (RDS) were the educational and scientific outposts of the Anglo-Irish protestant ascendancy. The three Queen's Colleges – established in Belfast, Cork and Galway from 1845 – broke this hegemony.[13] The Department of Science and Art, established in 1853 to inculcate industrial education in the working and middle classes across Ireland, and the Museum of Irish Industry, established in 1854, marked the beginning of state-funded scientific and technical education in Ireland.[14] While TCD and the RDS continued to embody the (declining) dominance of the protestant ascendancy, the Queen's Colleges – due to their secular constitution – were

---

[13] Enda Leaney, 'Missionaries of science: provincial lectures in nineteenth-century Ireland', *Irish Historical Studies*, vol. 34, no. 135 (May 2005), 267.

[14] Leaney, 'Missionaries of science', 275–6. University College Dublin emerged out of the Catholic University of Ireland, which merged with the Museum of Irish Industry's successor, the Royal College of Science.

disdained by the Roman catholic hierarchy. However, these colleges did inculcate scientific engagement across provincial Ireland, both intellectually and culturally.[15]

Thus family, class, culture, religion and educational institutions together influenced, in a variety of ways, the lives in this collection. So too did geography. Many had to travel to further their education or professional careers, often to universities in Britain for postgraduate studies or professional advancement. Holland, Gough, Anderson, McNulty, Bell and Kernan were all émigrés, as were others collected here in a variety of ways. Ernest Walton (p. 195), initially educated at TCD, was drawn to work with Ernest Rutherford at Cambridge. There, with John Cockcroft, he 'succeeded in effecting nuclear disintegration by artificial means' (in essence, splitting the atom) in 1931; Walton and Cockroft were awarded the 1951 Nobel prize in physics for this work. Walton returned to TCD in 1934. Gosset, Schrödinger (p. 150) and van Gelderen (p. 182) came to Ireland as adults. Gosset gained employment in a major business in Dublin which exported internationally. Schrödinger and van Gelderen migrated in response to the ravages Nazi Germany wrought on Europe.

Our world today

Important advances across the STEM realm, evident throughout the lives presented here, have transformed society in recent centuries. The emergence of railways in Ireland, for which William Dargan (p. 37) was the essential catalyst, and the invention of the steam turbine by Charles Parsons, exemplify the enormous advances in transport and

---

[15] Juliana Adelman, 'Communities of science: the Queen's Colleges and scientific culture in provincial Ireland, 1845–1875' (Ph.D. thesis, NUI Galway, 2006), 71–8.

mechanisation since the early nineteenth century. The agricultural revolution and advances in food safety are evidenced in engineer Ferguson's invention of the modern tractor, scientist Hilary Stevenson's (p. 186) major contribution to food safety, and in biochemist John Martin Scott's (p. 235) work on human nutrition and reproductive health.

Rigorous engineering underpins our built environment. Bindon Blood Stoney's (p. 93) contributions to Dublin's built environment and international construction technology are mirrored in Peter Rice's (p. 177) integral contribution to Sydney Opera House and the Centre Pompidou in Paris, two of the world's most iconic twentieth-century buildings. Their careers illustrate how so much of the infrastructure we take for granted is based on rigorous and creative engineering.

In addition to Mary Mulvihill, two other important STEM communicators are included in this volume – Mary Ward and Gerrit van Gelderen. Ward, a cousin of the pre-eminent astronomer William Parsons, enthusiastically deployed the microscope – now commonplace, but in the mid-nineteenth century a specialised apparatus – in pursuit of knowledge. Her ensuing publications (impressive early examples of the 'popular science' genre) situate her as an early STEM communicator. The Dutch artist and naturalist van Gelderen, drawn to Ireland's avian environment, then unblemished by industrialisation, made impactful television programmes examining Ireland's rich natural history, habitats and landscapes. His broadcasting did much to engender interest in nature and animal life across Irish society.

Recent scholarship has also enhanced this collection. New biographical research on Ward, cryptologist Emily Anderson and computing pioneer Percy Ludgate has expanded our knowledge and understanding of their fascinating lives and careers. Our research for this collection also spurred the commissioning of new biographical entries that, as well as being published here, are now also included in the RIA's *Dictionary of Irish Biography* (*DIB*).[16]

In presenting this collection we considered various ways of sequencing the lives, each of which gave rise to various tensions. We considered organising them by discipline, or STEM field, or alphabetically by surname. In the end, we opted to order them chronologically by year of death. This approach has the added benefit of melding with our broad conception of the Irish STEM experience, bounded by Boyle and Kernan.

Editorial note – choosing lives

Our selection is intrinsically partial, but one that we hope draws together fascinating figures from Irish STEM history. While their research, insights and discoveries vary, what unites them is a sense of deeply committed, purposeful enquiry. When we began work on this collection in January 2022, our first task was to establish the broad criteria for the selection of lives from amongst the 600 or so STEM-related lives in the *DIB*. Our decision to adopt the traditional definition of STEM – science, technology, engineering and mathematics – meant excluding the social sciences and medicine. Diversity was one of the most important criteria: of the disciplines to be represented within the collection, of the period the lives chosen inhabited, and in terms of gender.

---

[16] Mary Gough and Helen Megaw were what the *DIB* regards as 'missing persons', i.e., people who were not included when the *DIB* was first published in 2009 but whose candidacy has been reconsidered in light of recent scholarship. Recent scholarship also led to the substantial expansion of the existing *DIB* entries for Emily Anderson and Percy Ludgate, while vital context on the personal life of Erwin Schrödinger has also been added to his entry. The *DIB* entry on Mary Ward was completely rewritten for this volume. All are available at www.dib.ie.

Gender was at the forefront of our considerations when initial planning for this collection commenced. From the outset, we decided to ensure that women would comprise at least one-third of the lives collected. This reflects our aim to ensure that the contribution of women is recognised and celebrated. However, this threshold is more than symbolic. Across organisations and institutions, when the participation of an under-represented group reaches 25–30 per cent, a tipping point is reached, engendering more inclusiveness, benefitting everyone.[17] We have also decided to only include images of women.

As with the *DIB*, this collection features only the dead. To qualify for inclusion, each individual must also have been born or have spent part of their career in Ireland. Many emigrated to Britain or the United States (a defining factor in the wider Irish experience over the nineteenth and twentieth centuries), where, during the first wave of globalisation, opportunities abounded. The distinct Irish experience – as a colony of sorts, then a constituent of the British empire, and subsequently as an independent state for over a century – is the overarching context governing the lives collected here.

With regard to disciplinary coverage, some individuals do not fall neatly into a particular (sub-)discipline. We include polymaths such as Tyndall (optics; sterilisation; meteorology and climate science), Everett (astronomy; optics;

---

[17] For a wide-ranging analysis of the nature, source of and possible solutions to gender disparity across STEM, see Tessa E. S. Charlesworth and Mahzarin R. Banaji, 'Gender in science, technology, engineering, and mathematics: issues, causes, solutions', *Journal of Neuroscience*, vol. 39 (2019), 7728–43, http://dx.doi.org/10.1523/JNEUROSCI.0475-18.2019. Gender disparities, which vary globally, are persistent. For a recent discussion of this under-representation see Sapna Cheryan, Ella J. Lombard, Fasika Hailu, Linh N. H. Pham and Katherine Weltzien, 'Global patterns of gender disparities in STEM and explanations for their persistence', *Nature Reviews Psychology*, vol. 4 (2025), 6–19, https://doi.org/10.1038/s44159-024-00380-3.

photometry; wireless engineering; television) and Stokes (hydrodynamics; geodesics; spectroscopy; physiology). Jim Dooge (p. 226), known mostly in Ireland as a politician, was also an engineer of international eminence who made foundational contributions to the field of hydrology. The Nobel laureate Erwin Schrödinger, who became an Irish citizen, spent seventeen years living and working in Dublin. Despite recent work showing Schrödinger to have been a sexual predator, we have included him because of his singular scientific contribution to the quantum physics revolution.[18] It has nonetheless given us the opportunity to update the *DIB* entry on Schrödinger to include his predatory sexual history.

Those we chose to leave out include the polymath and academician Robert Lloyd Praeger (1865–1953), perhaps Ireland's greatest naturalist; the eminent biochemist Edward Conway (1894–1968); and the polymath John Desmond Bernal (1901–71). We were also unable to include a cohort of Irish chemists whose lives and careers embody the transformation of chemical research – in academic and industrial contexts – from the eighteenth century onwards.[19] Their exclusion in no way seeks to diminish their importance or influence. Instead, our selection represents our deliberate intention to reach across the STEM domain to collect a range of interesting, and especially previously less prominent, lives.

TURLOUGH O'RIORDAN AND JANE GRIMSON
February 2025

---

[18] Joe Humphreys, 'How Erwin Schrödinger indulged his "Lolita complex" in Ireland', *Irish Times*, 11 Dec. 2021; John Gribbin, *Erwin Schrödinger and the quantum revolution* (2012), 200; John Moore, *Schrödinger: life and thought* (1989), 89, 223, 363–4.

[19] Biographical entries on Richard Kirwan (1733–1812), Bryan Higgins (*c.* 1737–*c.* 1818), William Higgins (*c.* 1762/3–1825), Peter Woulfe (1727?–1803) and James Muspratt (1793–1886) are available at www.dib.ie.

Robert Boyle

(1627–91)

Natural philosopher

Robert Boyle was born on 25 January 1627 at Lismore Castle, fourteenth child and seventh son of Richard Boyle, 1st earl of Cork, and his second wife, Catherine Fenton. Robert was brought up in Ireland until he was sent to Eton College, aged eight, in 1635. His father withdrew him from Eton in 1638 and, after a year in which he was educated privately at his father's English seat, Stalbridge House in Dorset, he set out on a continental tour under the tutelage of the Huguenot savant Isaac Marcombes; he visited France and Italy and continued his education during a stay in Geneva from 1642 to 1644.

Returning to England, he initially settled on the estate at Stalbridge, which by this time had been bequeathed to him, and it was here that his career as a writer began. Initially, he devoted himself not to natural philosophy but to compositions written in a self-consciously literary style in which he advocated the pursuit of moral rectitude. Some of Boyle's writings from this period were published by him in modified form later in his life, while others were first published in the late twentieth century.

In 1649 Boyle's preoccupations changed dramatically when he erected a laboratory at Stalbridge and began to experiment for the first time. His writings from the years that follow display an acute sense of the value of such experimental knowledge in the defence of religion, which was to remain with him for the rest of his life: this is perhaps seen most clearly in his 'Of the study of the book of nature' (*c.* 1650), which has recently been published for the first time in vol. xiii of the new edition of his *Works*.

In the early 1650s, Boyle came into contact with the American chemist George Starkey, alias Eirenaeus Philalethes, and it is clear that this liaison had a profound effect on Boyle. Through Starkey, Boyle was introduced to the work of J. B. van Helmont – whose influence on Boyle is now known to have been far greater than was once thought – and to more sophisticated chemical experimentation than he had practiced previously. Boyle pursued similar interests in conjunction with contacts made through the 'intelligencer' Samuel Hartlib, with whom he carried out an extensive correspondence at this time. From this period onwards, Boyle retained a deep interest in alchemy, as recent study has made clear.

Between June 1652 and July 1654, Boyle spent all but about three months in Ireland. Towards the end of his stay, he fell seriously ill of a dropsy that permanently affected his eyesight. Although his profuse income remained substantially based on his Irish landholdings, he never visited Ireland again.

A new phase in Boyle's career opened with his move to Oxford in 1655 or 1656 to join the group of natural philosophers assembled there under the auspices of John Wilkins, warden of Wadham College, including such luminaries as Seth Ward, Thomas Willis, and Christopher Wren. Boyle now came into contact with a wider range of natural philosophical ideas, including the mechanical philosophy as adumbrated by Descartes and others, which profoundly affected his subsequent intellectual life. It was also now that Boyle discovered an extraordinary facility as an author, producing a torrent of writings which began to make their way into print over the following decade, establishing him as the international celebrity that he remained for the rest of his life.

The first work of natural philosophy that Boyle published was in many ways the most important, his *New experiments physico-mechanical, touching the spring of the air and its effects* (1660). This derived from his interest in the pneumatic experiments of Otto von Guericke, about which he heard in the late 1650s. With the help of Robert Hooke, his assistant and later a significant natural philosopher in his own right, Boyle devised a vacuum chamber that could be used to assess the characteristics and functions of air, notably by studying the effect of its withdrawal on flame, light, and living creatures. In his book, he presented a series of experiments of extraordinary ingenuity, together with reflections on them, in a format that was to prove as influential as it was novel.

Hardly less significant was a book published by Boyle in 1661, *Certain physiological essays*. In part, this was important for the sophisticated rationale that it offered for the practice of experiments and their presentation in the form of 'essays'. The work exemplified this particularly in the 'Essay on nitre', written early in Boyle's Oxford period, in which he showed how the changes that could be brought about on saltpetre by chemical means could be explained in 'corpuscular' terms (the name he coined for his version of the mechanical philosophy). A number of Boyle's later writings were presented as sequels to this epoch-making essay.

Also significant was a further programmatic work written in the late 1650s, the first 'tome' of Boyle's *Usefulness of natural philosophy* (1663), which comprised a series of essays justifying the study of natural philosophy partly on religious grounds and partly on practical ones. The section of this work published in 1663 dealt disproportionately with the medical applications of natural philosophy, but

Boyle's essays on more miscellaneous aspects of the utilitarian benefits of science came out in a sequel published in 1671.

The books that Boyle produced in the early to mid-1660s also included his famous, if rather diffuse, *The sceptical chymist* (1661), in which he criticised the principles of 'vulgar' chemists. In addition, he responded to critics of *Spring of the air*, thus enabling him to expound and vindicate his ideas more fully: he was to publish further work on pneumatics in the 1670s. The mid-1660s saw the publication of Boyle's massive experimental 'histories' of *Colours* (1664) and *Cold* (1665), which further exemplified his programme of using experimental and observational data to vindicate corpuscular explanations of nature. Equally important was his *Origin of forms and qualities* (1666), in which he attacked Aristotelian notions, arguing for the superior intelligibility of mechanical explanations.

The Royal Society had been founded in 1660, and Boyle was central to the society in its early years. His publications were widely seen as exemplifying its aims and objectives and they were heavily promoted in the journal *Philosophical Transactions*, inaugurated by the society's first secretary, Henry Oldenburg, himself a protégé of Boyle.

From the later 1660s, a further phase in Boyle's career opened; it may not be coincidental that this was juxtaposed with his move in 1668 from Oxford to London, where he was to live in the house of his sister, Katherine Jones, Lady Ranelagh, for the rest of his life. At this point Boyle ceased to publish substantial, continuous treatises, instead issuing a series of rather disparate volumes of 'tracts', often more essayistic in form and sometimes more speculative in nature, dealing with such themes as the 'cosmical qualities' or 'effluviums' of things, although this was not exclusive of the publication of case studies of the mechanical philosophy, as seen in his *Experiments, notes &c. about the mechanical origin of qualities* (1675). Boyle's unabated experimental acumen is revealed by his trials in the late 1670s of the qualities of phosphorescent substances, which came to the attention of English virtuosi at that time.

Although Boyle had earlier brought out devotional works alongside his scientific output, notably his *Seraphic love* (1659) and *Occasional reflections* (1665), the 1670s saw him publishing works concerned more overtly than hitherto with the mutual relations of science and religion. In such works as *The excellency of theology, compared with natural philosophy* (1674) and *Some considerations about the reconcileableness of reason and religion* (1675), Boyle dealt with issues to do with the religious significance of natural philosophy and with the role and limitations of reason, topics to which he was to revert repeatedly in publications of his later years.

Another topic on which he was to publish profusely in his later years concerned the medical spin-offs from natural philosophy, taking up one of the themes of *The usefulness of natural philosophy*, though he thought better of a direct assault on the medical profession. Among his works in this field was his *Medicina hydrostatica* (1690), which explored the value of the study of specific gravity in a medical context, while a volume published in 1685 comprised analytical tests of mineral waters.

Boyle also remained active throughout his life as a philanthropist and a promoter of missionary and other concerns. He was governor of the Corporation for the Propagation of the Gospel in New England, or New England Company, from 1662 to 1689, and he promoted various books aimed at the mission field, not least in the Near East, from 1660 to 1677. It is in this context that one should see his patronage in the early 1680s of the reprinting of the Irish translation of the New Testament and the publication of the William Bedell translation of the Old Testament. Subsequently, these translations were also distributed in the Scottish Highlands.

Boyle suffered a severe stroke in 1670, and he was increasingly infirm in his later years. He drew up an elaborate will in the summer of 1691, evidently feeling that the end was near, and he died on 30 December 1691 within eight days of his beloved sister, Katherine, whose house he had shared since 1668. A memorable funeral sermon was preached by his confidant, Gilbert Burnet, bishop of Salisbury, at St Martin-in-the-Fields, on 7 January 1692.

The Boyle letters and papers are housed at the Royal Society in London, where they were deposited in 1769. For a catalogue of the archive, see Michael Hunter et al., *The Boyle papers: understanding the manuscripts of Robert Boyle* (2007). The Royal Society also has portraits of Boyle by Johann Kerseboom and John Riley. Various other versions of the Kerseboom portrait exist. The three other principal images of him are (1) a sculpture of him as a boy on the tomb of the 1st earl of Cork in St Patrick's cathedral, Dublin; (2) an engraved portrait based on a drawing by William Faithorne now in the Ashmolean Museum, Oxford; and (3) a medal struck by C. R. Berch from a lost ivory medallion executed by Jean Cavalier. For a full account, see R. E. W. Maddison, 'The portraiture of the Honourable Robert Boyle', *Annals of Science*, xv (1959), 141–214. The standard editions of his writings are Michael Hunter and Edward B. Davis (ed.), *The works of Robert Boyle* (14 vols, 1999–2000), superseding the earlier edition by Thomas Birch (1744, reprinted 1772, 1965); Michael Hunter, Antonio Clericuzio, and Lawrence M. Principe (ed.), *The correspondence of Robert Boyle* (6 vols, 2001); 'The work-diaries of Robert Boyle' (revised 2004, available online at www.livesandletters.ac.uk/wd/

index.html); J. J. McIntosh (ed.), *Boyle on atheism* (2005); and John T. Harwood (ed.), *The early essays and ethics of Robert Boyle* (1991). Michael Hunter (ed.), *Robert Boyle by himself and his friends* (1994) is a collection of key early biographical sources.

Boyle left an important legacy. He was the leading exemplar of the new, experimental philosophy in late seventeenth-century England, his profuse books proving influential in exemplifying how experimental enquiries should be executed and reported, and in emphasising the significance of the 'matters of fact' obtained by such means. This was combined with a wariness of premature systematisation which was also highly influential – though Boyle's work was far from aimless, and his investigations were underlain by clear, if eclectic, explanatory goals.

Boyle was also a paradigm in terms of the broad affiliations of scientific inquiry. His aristocratic background gave him a patrician demeanour to which his contemporaries almost automatically deferred, and the pursuits to which he devoted himself undoubtedly gained kudos from this. Even more important was Boyle's role as 'the Christian virtuoso', to quote the title of one of his last books to be published in his lifetime. Quite apart from the extent to which he exemplified Christian principles in his own life, it now seems that Boyle's intense religiosity helps to explain his experimental activity, in that his laboratory practice can in many ways be seen as an extension of his indefatigable examination of his conscience. Equally significant was Boyle's conviction of the integrity of the study of nature to a proper understanding of religion, something which he not only exemplified in his own work but also promoted posthumously through the series of apologetic 'Boyle lectures' that were inaugurated under one of the provisions of his will. The early enlightenment synthesis of science and religion owed more to Boyle than to anyone else, and the same may arguably also be said for the experimental method of modern science.

Michael Hunter

Sources

R. E. W. Maddison, *The life of the Honourable Robert Boyle, F.R.S.* (1969); R. G. Frank, *Harvey and the Oxford physiologists: a study of scientific ideas and social interaction* (1980); Steven Shapin and Simon Schaffer, *Leviathan and the air-pump: Hobbes, Boyle and the experimental life* (1985); Antonio Clericuzio, 'A redefinition of Boyle's chemistry and corpuscular philosophy', *Annals of Science*, xlvii (1990), 561–89; Barbara Kaplan, '*Divulging of useful truths in physick*': *the medical agenda of Robert Boyle* (1993); Michael Hunter (ed.), *Robert Boyle reconsidered* (1994); Steven Shapin, *A social history of truth: civility and science in seventeenth-century England* (1994); Lawrence M. Principe, 'Virtuous romance and romantic virtuoso: the shaping of Robert Boyle's literary style', *Journal of the History of Ideas*, lvi (1995), 377–97; Rose-Mary Sargent, *The diffident naturalist: Robert Boyle and the philosophy of experiment* (1995); Jan W. Wojcik, *Robert Boyle and the limits of reason* (1997); Lawrence M. Principe, *The aspiring adept: Robert Boyle and his alchemical quest* (1998); Peter Anstey, *The philosophy of Robert Boyle* (2000); Michael Hunter, *Robert Boyle (1627–91): scrupulosity and science* (2000); William R. Newman and Lawrence M. Principe, *Alchemy tried in the fire: Starkey, Boyle and the fate of Helmontian chymistry* (2002); Michael Hunter, *Boyle: between God and science* (2009); Richard Yeo, 'Loose notes and capacious memory: Robert Boyle's note-taking and its rationale', *Intellectual History Review*, xx (2010), 335–54; Dmitri Levitin, 'The experimentalist as humanist: Robert Boyle on the history of philosophy', *Annals of science*, lxxi (2014), 149–82; Michael Hunter, '"Physia peregrinans, or the travelling naturalist": Boyle, his informants and the role of the exotic', Michael Hunter, *Boyle studies: aspects of the life and thought of Robert Boyle (1627–1691)* (2015), 185–232; Jan-Erik Jones (ed.), *The Bloomsbury companion to Robert Boyle* (2020)

Nicholas Callan
(1799–1864)

PIONEER IN ELECTRICAL SCIENCE AND PRIEST

Nicholas Joseph Callan was born on 22 December 1799 at Darver, between Drogheda and Dundalk, Co. Louth, third youngest among seven children of Denis Callan, farmer, and Margaret Callan (née Smith). His parents married in the last quarter of the eighteenth century and reared their family near Dromiskin village. The Callans were a well-to-do family who farmed extensively and were also bakers, maltsters and brewers. He received his early education at Dundalk Academy, went on to Navan seminary for initial preparation for the priesthood, and in 1816 entered the national seminary at Maynooth. During his third year there, he studied natural and experimental philosophy under Dr Cornelius Denvir, who introduced him to electricity and magnetism and exerted a strong influence on the young man. Callan completed his theological studies in 1822 and was ordained a priest on 24 May 1823.

He was sent to Rome (1824), where he attended the Sapienza University and was conferred with a doctorate in divinity (1826). During his time in Rome, he became acquainted with the work of the pioneers in electricity, Luigi Galvani (1737–93) and Allesandro Volta (1745–1827), who invented the first electrical cell (battery). When his former professor, Dr Denvir, resigned, Callan applied for the position and on 15 September 1826 he was appointed to the chair of natural and experimental philosophy at Maynooth.

He was a gifted and enthusiastic teacher. However, he showed his real inventive genius in his researches into electricity, and he made fundamental contributions in three areas – electromagnets and the induction coil; batteries; and electric motors. His main claim to fame is his invention of the induction coil, a device for producing high voltage currents and the forerunner of the step-up transformer, an essential device in the modern world of limitless electrical supply. In 1831 Michael Faraday (1791–1867) discovered electromagnetic induction, which basically means that a changing magnetic field can induce an electrical current to flow in a strip of wire. In 1825 William Sturgeon (1783–1850) invented the electromagnet in which wire is wrapped around a soft iron core and electrical current is passed through the wire, which strongly magnetises the iron core.

Callan combined these two ideas to produce his first induction coil in 1836. He wound two coils of wire, one connected to a low-voltage battery, around an iron core. He discovered that, when the current through the primary coil was interrupted, a high-voltage current was produced in the unconnected secondary coil. Sparks issued between the two ends of the secondary coil of wire. Callan noted that the faster he interrupted the current, the bigger the spark. In 1837 he produced a giant induction machine. He used a mechanism from a clock to interrupt the current twenty times a second. The machine generated 15-inch (38cm) sparks and an estimated 60,000 volts – the largest bolt of artificial electricity ever seen at the time. Callan published reports of his discovery in 1836 and 1837 ('On a new galvanic battery', *Philosophical Magazine*, 3rd ser., ix (1836), 472–8; 'A description of an electromagnetic repeater, or of a machine by which the connection between the voltaic battery and the helix of an electromagnet may be broken and renewed several thousand times in the space of one minute', *Sturgeon's Annals of Electricity*, i (1836–7), 229–30). At the 1857 meeting of the British Association for the Advancement of Science in Dublin, he vindicated his claim to priority of discovery of the induction coil. His claim ('On the electrodynamic induction machine', *British Association report, Dublin*, pt 2 (1857), 11–13) went unchallenged in his lifetime.

Needing reliable batteries, Callan carried out pioneering work on their development. Batteries contain positive and negative plates. Prior to Callan's improvements, batteries used expensive platinum or unsatisfactory carbon for one plate and zinc for the other. He showed that inexpensive cast iron could be used instead of platinum or carbon. Callan invented the 'Maynooth' battery in 1854 and the single fluid cell in 1855. In the Maynooth battery the outer casing was made of cast iron and the zinc plate was immersed in a porous pot in the centre. The Maynooth battery went into commercial production in London.

Callan would go on to connect large numbers of batteries and once connected 577 together to make the world's largest battery. There were no instruments available to measure voltage or current, so he measured the power of his batteries by the weight they could lift when powering an electromagnet. His best effort lifted two tons and was noted in *Encyclopaedia Britannica* (8th ed.). Callan's batteries produced very high voltages when connected to his experimental coils of wire. Those coils could give large electrical shocks, and Callan used this as another way of testing battery power. He persuaded his students to take shocks from the coils and gauged the power of the battery from their reactions. One student, William Walsh, who later became archbishop of Dublin, was rendered unconscious by a shock. The college authorities asked Callan to be more careful with his students, so he switched over to electrocuting turkeys.

In 1838 he stumbled on the principle of the self-exciting dynamo. He found that by moving an electromagnet in the earth's magnetic field he could produce electricity without the aid of a battery. The effect was feeble, and he did not pursue it. The discovery is usually attributed to Werner Siemens in 1866. Callan also discovered an early form of galvanisation to protect iron from rusting when he was experimenting on battery design, and he patented the idea in 1853. He also constructed electric motors, and in 1837 built a small motor to drive a trolley around his lab. He proposed using battery-powered locomotives on the new railways and, with considerable vision, predicted electric light.

William Parsons (1800–67), 3rd earl of Rosse, who built the giant telescope at Birr, was a member of the board of visitors to Maynooth College. The story is told that Callan visited Birr to view the telescope, but for some reason he was not admitted. When later the earl came to Maynooth to see the induction coil, Callan suggested that he should return to Birr and view the coil through his telescope.

Popular with both students and fellow-professors, Callan had a simple unaffected manner and displayed considerable charity towards the poor. He died of natural causes at Maynooth on 10 January 1864. The College Museum at NUI Maynooth holds a remarkable collection of old scientific instruments, including many items from Callan's laboratory.

After his death, Callan was largely forgotten by the wider world of science. Maynooth was a theological university, and science had a low priority on the curriculum. Callan's pioneering work was easily forgotten in such a setting. His invention of the induction coil was attributed to the German instrument-maker Heinrich Ruhmkorff (1803–77). However, it has been generally acknowledged by the world of science, since the 1953 edition of Sir R.

A. Gregory and H. E. Hadley, *A class book of physics*, that Nicholas Callan was the true inventor of the induction coil. A comprehensive bibliography of his publications may be found in M. T. Casey, 'Nicholas Callan', cited below.

William Reville

Sources

P. J. McLaughlin, *Nicholas Callan, priest-scientist 1799–1864* (1965); M. T. Casey, 'Nicholas Callan – priest, professor and scientist', *Institution of Electrical Engineers Proceedings*, cxxxii, pt A, no. 8 (1985), 491–7

George Boole

(1815–64)

Mathematician

George Boole was born on 2 November 1815 at Lincoln, the first of four children of John Boole (1777–1848), a cobbler, and Mary Boole (1780–1854).

Early life and first publications

Boole received only a simple education, but with the encouragement of his father, who was devoted to the study of science and the construction of optical instruments, and of Lincoln friends, he taught himself classical and modern languages, for which he had an unusual aptitude. From 1831, to assist his family's precarious finances, Boole taught at schools in Doncaster, Liverpool, and Waddington, near Lincoln. Then, from 1834 until 1849, he conducted a series of his own schools at Lincoln and in its environs, his entire family assisting in the running of the establishments. Boole's study of higher mathematics also began in 1831, when he embarked on reading books by Lacroix, Lagrange, Laplace, and Poisson. Following his return to Lincoln, Boole was active in the local mechanics' institute, whose president was Sir Edward Bromhead (1789–1855) of Thurlby Hall, near Lincoln.

Bromhead had studied mathematics at Cambridge University, where he had urged the foundation of the undergraduate Analytical Society, established in 1812 with the aim of reforming the Cambridge mathematical curriculum.

From the late 1830s Bromhead lent Boole books by leading French mathematicians and Boole corresponded with him in the course of his early mathematical researches.

Boole's first research paper appeared in 1841 in the *Cambridge Mathematical Journal*, whose co-founder and editor, Duncan Gregory (1813–44), advised Boole on mathematical subjects. Between 1841 and 1845 Boole published twelve papers in the journal, one of which, 'Exposition of a general theory of linear transformations' (1841), was proclaimed by George Salmon as the origin of modern algebra for its foundation of invariant theory, a subject linking the algebra of polynomial forms and geometry, which was much extended by Arthur Cayley, J. J. Sylvester, and Salmon himself in the next fifty years.

Gregory's development of the algebra of differential and difference operators, as presented in his important textbook *Examples of the processes of the differential and integral calculus* (1841), exerted a strong influence on Boole's subsequent work on differential equations, finite differences, and the algebra of logic. This influence is evident in Boole's paper 'On a general method in analysis' (1844), for which he received the Royal medal of the Royal Society of London; in this prize-winning paper Boole developed formal algebraic rules satisfied by differential operators and then employed the calculus of operations to solve differential equations and to sum series in closed form.

A controversy arose in 1846 between the Scottish philosopher Sir William Hamilton (1788–1856) and the English mathematician Augustus De Morgan (1806–71) concerning a minor refinement to the study of the syllogism, known as the 'quantification of the predicate'. Boole had been in correspondence with De Morgan since 1842 and, stimulated by the subject matter of the logical dispute, he wrote an eighty-two-page pamphlet entitled *The mathematical analysis of logic* (1847), in which he presented a calculus of deductive reasoning. Characteristic of Boole's analysis was the use of an algebra of so-called 'elective symbols', which obey the distributive and commutative rules and an additional idempotent rule, which distinguishes this algebraic system from the traditional algebra of quantities. Writing in 1851, Boole considered his treatise to be 'a hasty and (for this reason) regretted publication' (*Studies in logic and probability*, 252), written as it was only a few weeks after the initial conception of a logical calculus.

Academic appointment and the algebra of logic

The Colleges (Ireland) Bill of 1845 provided for public funding of new colleges in Ireland. Encouraged by support from William Thomson (later Lord Kelvin), Boole applied in 1846 for a professorship in mathematics or natural philosophy in one of the proposed colleges. He supported his application with testimonials from such accomplished mathematicians as Cayley, De Morgan, Charles Graves and Thomson, and was eventually appointed in August 1849 to the chair of mathematics at QCC, despite his lack of both formal secondary and university education. His salary was £250 per annum, augmented by yearly tuition fees of around £100. Boole retained the Cork position for the rest of his life, but he looked elsewhere for more congenial employment: in 1860, he submitted his name in candidacy for the Savilian professorship of geometry at Oxford University but as he did not send the necessary testimonials his application was not seriously considered.

In a lecture entitled 'The claims of science', given in Cork in 1851, Boole expressed his opinion that 'It is simply a fact that the ultimate laws of Logic, those alone on which it is possible to construct a Science of Logic, are mathematical in their form and expression, although not belonging to the mathematics of quantity' (*Studies in logic and probability*, 209). At this time, he was engaged in a new project on logic and probability, which he completed as his book *An investigation of the laws of thought on which are founded the mathematical theories of logic and probabilities* (1854). This was Boole's major contribution to the algebra of logic, but opinions varied as to its value and novelty.

Herbert Spencer considered that Boole's 'application to logic of methods like those of mathematics constituted another step far greater in originality and importance than any taken since Aristotle' (Spencer, *The study of sociology*, 223). The logician John Venn (1834–1923) wrote in 1876 (*Mind*, i (1876), 479) that, on first reading *The laws of thought*, it was as if the key of all knowledge had been placed into his hands, whereby the manipulation of symbols and the application of rules of interpretation led to results beyond those attainable by unassisted thought. Later reflection convinced him that this view was illusory, as by the ordinary deductive processes he could generally reach the same conclusions with less effort. In his *Symbolic logic* (1881) Venn opined that Boole's originality was not as complete as was sometimes claimed, given that Leibniz and Johann Heinrich Lambert had anticipated a symbolic calculus of reasoning; but he still held him to be 'the indisputable and sole originator of all the higher generalizations of the subject'. He also observed that Boole offered very little direct explanation of his system, especially in his use of the division operation in logic. The economist and logician W. Stanley Jevons (1835–82) believed Boole's logical system to be unnecessarily mathematical. In his *Principles of science* (1874), he articulates conflicting views: first that 'Boole produced a system which, though wonderful in its results, was not a system of Logic at all', and second that 'In spite of several serious errors into which he fell, it will probably be allowed that Boole discovered the true and general form of Logic, and put the science substantially into the form which it must hold for evermore.'

Probability theory and late mathematical treatises

Boole's work on logic encouraged his interest in probability theory, and he began a series of papers on the subject in 1851. In November of that year, he issued a challenge problem on probability that drew responses from the astronomer William Donkin, the German mathematician Richard Dedekind (1831–1916), and Arthur Cayley. Boole himself published his own solution to the problem in January 1854, using a method that was substantially developed in *The laws of thought*. He devoted over one third of the contents of his book to his idiosyncratic theory of probability, which drew much public criticism. The most serious attack on his solution to the probability problem and the whole theory expounded in his book was that of Henry Wilbraham (1825–83), whose objections appeared a few months after Boole's book was published. Wilbraham, though pursuing a career in the legal profession, was an accomplished mathematician: he had been seventh wrangler at Cambridge University in 1846 and had written a valuable contribution on the so-called 'Gibbs–Wilbraham phenomenon' in Fourier series.

Wilbraham's main contention was that most of the problems posed by Boole were indeterminate, and that in order to solve them, Boole made tacit assumptions about the data of the problems. Wilbraham argued that in determinate cases it was easier to proceed from first principles, whereas in the indeterminate cases, since Boole gave no explanation of his assumptions, it was not clear how the solution offered was distinguished from any number of similar, equally defensible, solutions. Boole published spirited replies to Wilbraham's strictures in August and September 1854 and challenged Wilbraham to provide an instance of a clearly erroneous deduction from his method.

The dispute on Boole's method resurfaced in 1862, when Cayley once more examined Boole's solution to the challenge problem and professed that he could neither explain nor understand the logical principles on which Boole based his solution. As part of a series of papers entitled 'The calculus of equivalent statements', Hugh McColl questioned Boole's method and showed by a simple numerical example how it must be wrong. Finally, in his *Treatise on probability theory* (1921), the economist John Maynard Keynes gave solutions to some of Boole's problems, commenting: 'Boole's method of solving them is constantly erroneous, and the difficulty of his method is so great that I do not know of anyone but himself who has ever attempted to use it.' Later writers have examined Boole's theory, but nobody has proposed a plausible interpretation of what Boole intended. After 1854, although he published further substantial papers on probability, in which he employed the notation and ideas of his logical method, Boole avoided the controversial aspects of his theory and developed an approach exploiting linear inequalities and properties of determinants. While he earned a substantial prize for a paper on probability in 1857, his work has had no impact on the subject and is rarely quoted in the historical literature.

In the later 1850s, Boole's attention turned to more traditional mathematical subjects, such as integration and differential equations, and in 1859 he published *A treatise on differential equations*. This was a pioneering work, giving numerous examples of special differential equations and modes of solution. It was based on an intimate knowledge of the research conducted on the subject and continued to be reprinted well into the twentieth century. In chapters XVI and XVII he gave an exposition of symbolical methods of solution, returning to the subject matter of some of his earliest papers. This work was followed in 1860 by *A treatise on the calculus of finite differences*, another successful production, in which, in addition to employing the symbolical methods, he also exhibited great facility in the theory of infinite series and applications of the integral calculus.

Marriage, family and personality

On 11 September 1855 Boole married Mary Everest (1832–1916), daughter of the Rev. Thomas Everest, and niece of both Sir George Everest, surveyor-general of India, and John Ryall, vice-president of QCC. Thomas Everest was a follower of Samuel Hahnemann, the founder of homeopathy, and his daughter inherited his views on medicine and the treatment of illness. When in November 1864 Boole developed a fever and infection of the lungs, after suffering a saturation in the rain of Cork, his wife supposedly treated him by wrapping him in wet sheets, a remedy suggested by homeopathy. The treatment failed and Boole died on 8 December 1864 in Cork.

The Booles had five daughters, several of whom were talented and achieved success in their careers. Alicia Boole (1860–1940), who married the actuary Walter Stott, was a self-taught mathematician and produced original work on the geometry and classification of polytopes. Lucy Boole (1862–1904) pursued research in chemistry and became a lecturer at the London School of Medicine for Women. Ethel Lilian Boole (1864–1960) was inspired by Russian culture and translated Russian literature; she married the Polish revolutionary Wilfrid Voynich and eventually settled with him in New York. Her suspense novel *The gadfly*

(1897), set at the time of the Risorgimento in Italy, became enormously popular in Soviet Russia. Margaret Boole (1858–1935) married the artist Edward Taylor; their son Sir Geoffrey Ingram Taylor (1886–1975) became a famous applied mathematician. Following Boole's death, after which she received a civil list pension of £100, Mary Boole returned to England and devoted herself to explaining the significance of her husband's ideas on logic. She developed eccentric views on education, medicine, philosophy, and religion, and moved in bohemian circles; she also published several books on educational psychology.

John Dowden was a pupil of Boole at QCC, and his brother Edward was also acquainted with Boole. In a letter of 1873 Edward Dowden wrote of Boole's strong intellectual simplicity and grave moral energy, as well as his love of cathedral music and hymn singing (he sang out of tune); Dowden also recalled Boole's arguing for the existence of a kind of aesthetics in mathematics – a quality some discerned in his books, by contrast with those of George Salmon. Of Boole's family life, Dowden wrote:

> His wife was a woman of intellect and attainment in mathematics, with a bright pure face, and they had two or three beautiful little girls. The Cork matrons had stories, partly mythical I am sure, concerning their novel experiments with the children; e.g. that one baby girl was found naked and tethered in a grass plot, chewing pebbles; which stories meant, I suppose, that they did not conform to all domestic conventions.

Reputation and influence

Boole received honorary degrees from Dublin University (1851) and Oxford University (1859). He was elected FRS in 1857; in filling out the certificate of candidature he completed the statement 'Distinguished for his acquaintance with the science of . . .' with the word 'psychology', not 'mathematics', suggesting that he considered his logical method as important for the study of the human mind as for deductive reasoning. Boole was not elected to membership of the Royal Irish Academy, a surprising omission given his eminence and wide acquaintance with scientific men of influence. He had little contact with the Irish mathematician William Rowan Hamilton, but in 1855 he sought a testimonial from Hamilton in support of his application for an examinership. Hamilton's lukewarm reply avoided any commitment to a proper assessment of the value of Boole's work or his originality; Boole had sent Hamilton a copy of *The laws of thought*, which was sold at auction with the rest of Hamilton's library in January 1866.

It is difficult to formulate a widely acceptable view of Boole's status in the history of mathematics and logic. He is generally regarded as the founder of mathematical or symbolic logic, but his theory of logic seemed too demanding in its mathematical requirements to be attractive to contemporary logicians, while offering few advantages as a working system for mathematicians. The philosopher A. N. Whitehead saw Boole's algebra of symbolic logic as part of the mid-nineteenth-century discovery of new algebraic systems, such as Hamilton's quaternions and Hermann Grassmann's extensive magnitudes, which broke free from the restrictions of interpretation of symbols in terms of arithmetic, but he doubted if Boole conceived of his achievement in this light (*A treatise on universal algebra* (1898), 115). At the end of the nineteenth century, Boolean algebra signified the study of the logic of propositions by Boole's method, but in the early twentieth century the related concept of an abstract Boolean algebra was developed. This has ensured Boole's continuing fame, as the 1937 master's thesis of Claude Shannon showed that Boolean algebra provides the best tool to study the digital circuits used in electronic computers. By a concatenation of ideas, Boole himself is sometimes held to be the forefather of modern high-speed computing.

The Boole Papers in the Boole Library, UCC, contain letters, lecture drafts, and material relating to Boole's wife and daughters, while Royal Society, London, MS 782 contains Boole's unpublished mathematical and logical papers. TCD MS 2398 is an incomplete, undated ten-page paper in Boole's hand, entitled 'Symbolical logic, being an essay towards a calculus of deductive reasoning'; parts of it are identical with pages 16–18 of *The mathematical analysis of logic*. Cambridge University Library holds correspondence between Boole and William Thomson and G. G. Stokes; Glasgow University Library holds letters from Thomson to Boole (1845–8); and University College London Library has correspondence between Boole and Augustus De Morgan.

Roderick Gow

Sources

H. Wilbraham, 'On the theory of chances developed in Professor Boole's *Laws of thought*', *Philosophical Magazine*, vii (1854), 465–76; G. Salmon, *Lessons introductory to the modern higher algebra* (2nd ed., 1866), 94; H. S. Spencer, *The study of sociology* (2nd ed., 1874); J. Venn, 'Boole's logical system', *Mind*, i (1876), 479–91; H. McColl, 'The calculus of equivalent statements', 4th paper, *Proceedings of the London Mathematical Society*, xi (1880), 113–21; J. Venn, *Symbolic logic* (1881); H. McColl, 'The calculus of equivalent statements', 6th paper, *Proceedings of the London Mathematical Society*, xxviii (1897), 555–79; E. D. Dowden, *Fragments from old letters, E. D. to E. D. W.* (1914); J. M. Keynes, *A treatise on probability theory* (1921); G. Boole, *Studies in logic and probability*, ed. R. Rhees (1952); G. C. Smith (ed.), *The Boole–De Morgan correspondence* (1982); *Irish Mathematical Society Newsletter*, x (1984), 9–11; D. MacHale, *George Boole: his life and work* (1985); I. Grattan-Guinness and G. Bornet (eds), *George Boole: selected manuscripts on logic and its philosophy* (1997); J. Gasser (ed.), *A Boole anthology* (2000)

William Rowan Hamilton

(1805–65)

MATHEMATICIAN

Sir William Rowan Hamilton was born on the night of 3–4 August 1805 (the time was recorded as midnight) at his father's house in Dominick Street, Dublin. He was the second of five children who survived infancy, and the only son, of Archibald Hamilton (1778–1819) and his wife, Sarah (1780–1817).

Background and education

William's father Archibald was the son of an apothecary; he had served his apprenticeship in an attorney's office and now conducted his own modest legal practice. Both Archibald and his father William before him were freemen of the city of Dublin and his great-uncle Francis Hamilton had been an alderman. William's mother, Sarah, came of a Dublin family called Hutton, who owned a coach-building firm. Queen Victoria, on a state visit to Ireland, was sufficiently impressed with the comfort of her ride from Kingstown to Dublin in a Hutton coach to command that the same coach-maker build her Irish state coach.

Archibald Hamilton had the misfortune to be the agent of Archibald Hamilton Rowan, a member of a landed family from Killyleagh in Co. Down, who had become actively involved with the United Irishmen. The two Hamilton families, though not apparently related, had a close association. Archibald Hamilton had been named after Archibald Rowan; his son was christened William Rowan, and Archibald Rowan was the boy's godfather. Rowan's involvement with the United Irishmen brought him into conflict with the law, and ultimately to prison. He escaped but was forced to live for many years in exile. During a period in the United States he was an active member of a group of United Irishmen based in Philadelphia, which included Wolfe Tone. Archibald Hamilton probably played a part in Rowan's escape from prison, and when, in 1805, Rowan inherited the family property in Killyleagh, Archibald Hamilton organised the successful petition that cleared the way for his return home. Unfortunately, all of this cost a great deal of money and Rowan's unwillingness to meet these costs led ultimately to his agent's bankruptcy.

Although Archibald Hamilton managed to re-establish himself in business, it was on a modest scale and the family lived in straitened financial circumstances. This must have been one of the factors in the decision to send William, at the age of three, to live under the tutelage of his uncle James, who ran the diocesan school at Trim in Co. Meath. He stayed there, apart from short vacation visits to his family, till he entered Trinity College some fifteen years later. William appears to have been quite happy at Trim. It was a quiet, pleasant town, historically interesting and relatively insulated from the poverty and hardship to be found in much of the country. The school was small but had some tradition: Arthur Wellesley, afterwards duke of Wellington, had attended it briefly some thirty years earlier, and the building in which it was housed had once belonged to Jonathan Swift. James Hamilton was a classicist with some knowledge of oriental languages; he recognised his nephew's precocious talent and fed him an extraordinary diet of the classics, Hebrew, and a wide range of oriental and modern languages. He was quite a taskmaster, albeit a kindly and supportive one, and his nephew responded positively.

James Hamilton observed William's remarkable computational skill but he was not competent, and probably not inclined, to encourage his mathematical bent. He did, however, produce for him a copy of *Analytical geometry* by Bartholomew Lloyd, which was to have a decisive effect. William was then sixteen, and his eyes were opened. 'Ill-omened gift!' he wrote, 'It was the commencement of my present course of mathematical reading, which has in so great a degree withdrawn my attention, I may say my affection, from the Classics' (letter to his cousin Arthur Hamilton, 1822, Graves, i, 112).

Hamilton entered TCD in 1823. He was particularly fortunate that in the decade immediately preceding his entry the teaching of mathematics within the college had been altered almost beyond recognition: new methods from France and Germany were brought into the curriculum, French texts were introduced, and new textbooks were written in English expounding recent continental work. The chief architect of this reform was Bartholomew Lloyd, who was professor of mathematics from 1813 to 1822, then professor of natural philosophy till he was elected provost in 1831. Although Lloyd was not himself a creative mathematician, he clearly appreciated the developments that had taken place within the subject and had the administrative ability to introduce the necessary radical changes.

There is no indication that the discipline of regular examinations was harmful to Hamilton, the revised syllabus was reasonably stimulating even to one of such prodigious abilities, and he had every opportunity and encouragement to read outside the course. His tutor, Charles Boyton, was a widely read and intelligent man, a competent mathematician, who, though he did not produce original work himself, could encourage and guide his brilliant student and appears generally to have been an excellent tutor.

Optics and astronomy

Hamilton's earliest attempts at original work were in geometry. His studies of the work of the French geometer Gaspard Monge on families of surfaces and their normals suggested a new approach to optics based on systems of rays treated mathematically as rectilinear congruences. Within a year of entering college Hamilton had submitted his first paper, describing this work, to the RIA. It was referred back with the recommendation that he should develop his ideas further before resubmitting. He did so, adding substantially to what he had already written, and in 1827 his first famous paper, 'Theory of systems of rays', was read before the academy. His achievement did not pass unrecognised: John Brinkley, the Andrews professor of astronomy, had lately been appointed to the bishopric of Cloyne and the youthful Hamilton, before he had even graduated, was elected to the Andrews chair. This appointment was remarkable, as the new incumbent had almost no practical experience in astronomical observation and the potential field for the job included some able men of established reputation. Hamilton's appointment to this post, which since 1792 had carried the title of 'royal astronomer of Ireland', was profoundly significant in the extent to which it shaped his subsequent career.

Fortunately, the new royal astronomer did not feel constrained to devote himself unduly to astronomy, though he continued for some time with his important and highly original work in optics. He was, nonetheless, conscious of his responsibility to carry out observations and measurements, and to process and analyse these. Immediately after his appointment he went to stay with Brinkley at Cloyne, receiving valuable advice and guidance; he then accepted the invitation of Thomas Romney Robinson to spend some time with him at the Armagh observatory to gain practical experience. This helped him to assume responsibility for the round of routine observations, which were made with the help of his assistant and his own two sisters who lived with him at the observatory. His position, with a house at Dunsink (a few miles out of Dublin) and a secure if not over-generous salary, was less demanding than a tutorial fellowship, which he would otherwise have held.

The field of optics, to which Hamilton still devoted his main efforts, had recently moved back into the centre of the scientific stage, following the discovery of the phenomenon of interference by Thomas Young, and subsequently the publication of two highly significant memoirs by Augustin Jean Fresnel in the early 1820s. For over a century the conflict between the wave and corpuscular theories of light had remained unresolved. Sir Isaac Newton had been led to reject the wave theory because the type of wave that would be required was transverse rather than longitudinal and he could not conceive of a mechanism whereby transverse light waves could propagate. He concluded that light must be corpuscular in nature. Young's demonstration of the phenomenon of interference for light pointed strongly towards a wave interpretation, as interference effects were already familiar features of wave systems – in sound, for example, or in water waves.

Among the various observed phenomena that any theory of light would have to encompass was that of double refraction, which had been discovered in 1669 by Bartholinus.

Certain crystals, in particular that known as 'Iceland spar', gave a double image: a single ray of light entering the crystal produced two refracted rays, and the phenomenon was thus described as 'double refraction'. Christiaan Huygens, as early as 1690, had invented an elegant and clever procedure for describing wave propagation, which could also allow for the simpler cases of double refraction, though the more complicated phenomenon in so-called 'biaxial crystals' could not be described by that method. Fresnel's remarkable achievement was to devise a model for the propagation of transverse light waves in crystals, which led to Huygens's construction where that was applicable but which could also describe the more complicated phenomena involving biaxial crystals. Fresnel's method was mathematically quite involved: it led to wave surfaces that were geometrically rather complicated and whose properties were by no means immediately obvious from their equations.

Hamilton knew and was deeply interested in Fresnel's results. By a stroke of luck or genius or a combination of the two, he noticed a remarkable feature of the wave surface: for a particular direction of the incident ray on a biaxial crystal, instead of double refraction each incident ray gave rise to a complete cone of refracted rays. Hamilton immediately described his discovery to his Trinity colleague, Humphrey Lloyd (son of Bartholomew Lloyd), the recently appointed professor of natural philosophy, and suggested that he should perform the experiment to see if this new and quite unexpected phenomenon did in fact occur. If it did it would strikingly corroborate the Fresnel theory and, by implication, the wave theory of light. Although Lloyd's background and training were in mathematics, he had become interested in experiment and it was as an experimental physicist working in optics and in geomagnetism that he was to achieve distinction. The experiment proposed by Hamilton was not an easy one – the effect was easily obscured and the quality of the crystals available to Lloyd was relatively poor – so the fact that his attempts had a positive outcome was a tribute to Lloyd's considerable skill, as well as to his patience and persistence.

The observation of conical refraction was generally seen as a powerful confirmation of the wave theory, the evidence for which was by now hard to reject, despite reservations about the hypotheses underlying Fresnel's theory and the problems posed by the newly observed absorption phenomena. It was a remarkable discovery, a triumph for Hamilton in particular, and one of the classic vindications of the scientific method. Fresnel's theory had been constructed to accommodate known experimental results; from it, following quite elaborate mathematical argument, a new prediction was extracted, which could not have been anticipated and in fact must have seemed rather improbable. Recognition followed swiftly. At the 1834 meeting of the British Association in Edinburgh, Lloyd was invited to give the main review talk on physical optics, and in 1836 he was elected to the Royal Society. In 1835, the year following the Edinburgh meeting at which Lloyd presented his report, the British Association met in Dublin and on this occasion Hamilton, who acted as local secretary and organiser of the meeting, now at the age of thirty a famous man, was knighted by the lord lieutenant.

Dynamics and algebra

Hamilton's interest now moved from optics to dynamics. In fact this did not represent a total change of direction, for his approach, described in his *Essays on a general method in dynamics*, closely paralleled his approach to optics. This parallelism between optics and dynamics, emphasised by

Hamilton, was to become particularly significant in the twentieth century with the introduction of wave mechanics; Hamilton's work on dynamics is now widely regarded as his most important contribution, though at the time the *Essays* did not attract a great deal of interest. Only in the twentieth century did the power and generality of the Hamiltonian methods come to be appreciated. Perhaps the most important influence was that on Erwin Schrödinger, who received a thorough grounding in Hamiltonian dynamics from his professor, Friedrich Hasenöhrl, who, in turn, was a student of Arnold Sommerfeld. Schrödinger gave the Hamiltonian formulation a central role in his construction of quantum mechanics.

From the mid-1830s until his death in 1865, Hamilton's preoccupation was with algebraic questions; his culminating achievement, which in his own view outweighed all his other work, was the discovery of quaternions in 1843. Hamilton believed that quaternions would provide a valuable key for the understanding of the physical world. This belief has not been vindicated: quaternions have made little direct contribution to the development of physics, though they have found extremely useful applications in the control of spacecraft and in three-dimensional computer modelling (as, for example, in video games). The profound and lasting influence of Hamilton's work in algebra, which began with his description of complex numbers as number pairs, and was followed by the discovery of quaternions and the recognition of their non-commutativity, was the stimulus it gave to the development of algebra as an abstract axiomatic discipline.

There is some irony in this. Hamilton was led towards quaternions by a deep metaphysical motivation, based particularly on his reading of Kant, to whose work his friend Coleridge directed him. Hamilton grappled with the

German original of the *Critique of pure reason*, and like his literary friends discovered a natural sympathy for Kant's idealism. But he also found in the *Critique* technical answers to the questions which he regarded as fundamental to his mathematics. Wanting an intuitive interpretation for the objects of mathematics, he could not accept a mathematics in which the basic elements were merely symbols. Following Kant, he gave meaning to the number system through the intuition of pure time. From this starting point, which he regarded as fundamental, he constructed the real numbers, then the complex numbers as pairs of real numbers, and then quaternions. Hamilton's outlook parallels exactly that of L. E. J. Brouwer and the intuitionists of the twentieth century, whose constructive approach to mathematics contrasts with the emphasis on consistency alone which marks the more widely held formalist viewpoint. From a historical perspective it is interesting that it was Hamilton's intuitionist approach that led to the radical idea of a non-commutative algebra. The formalist outlook of his Cambridge contemporaries could in principle permit non-commutativity without any difficulty, but until Hamilton constructed the algebra of quaternions the old laws, derived from the real number system, were held to be sacrosanct.

Hamilton's own account of his discovery of quaternions, the resolution of the problem that had thwarted and frustrated him for over a decade, is well known. It is an authentic and compelling description of the moment of discovery. It was 16 October 1843 and he was walking from Dunsink into Dublin to attend a meeting at the academy. 'I then and there felt the galvanic circuit of thought close; and the sparks which fell from it were the fundamental equations between i, j, k; ... I felt a problem to have been at that moment solved – an intellectual want relieved – which had haunted me for at least fifteen years before' (letter to P.

G. Tait, 1858, Graves, ii, 435–6). Hamilton straightaway recorded the equations that give the multiplication law for his so-called quaternions in his pocket book: 'nor could I resist', he wrote, 'the impulse – unphilosophical as it may have been – to cut with a knife on a stone of Brougham Bridge, as we passed it, the fundamental formula' (letter to his son Archibald, 1865, Graves, ii, 435).

Marriage, friends and character

Hamilton's personal life did not match the brilliant success of his academic and professional career. He suffered unrequited love for Catherine Disney, the sister of student friends, which was thwarted by her enforced and unhappy marriage to the Rev. William Barlow; as she lay dying, Hamilton, on his knees, offered her his book *Lectures on quaternions*. In 1833 he married Helen Maria Bayly (1804–69), to whom he seems to have been devoted, though the marriage was difficult and Helen, who was subject to frequent illnesses and was often absent from their home, was unable to provide an orderly domestic regime for her husband. They were plagued by periodic financial anxieties and Hamilton was troubled by excessive drinking during some periods of his life.

But he had many close friends in whom he could confide and with whom he maintained a lively correspondence. Apart from his academic colleagues these included the Dunravens, whose son Lord Adare had been his pupil and lived for a time with him in Dunsink, and the de Veres who lived in remote and romantic Curragh Chase; Hamilton was the friend of Aubrey de Vere – as was Tennyson, who was a visitor to Curragh Chase – and as a young man he intended to propose marriage to Ellen de Vere, though the declaration came to nothing. The novelist Maria Edgeworth and her family were also Hamilton's close friends. Another friend was Lady Wilde, or Speranza as she was known, who invited him to be godfather to her son Oscar, describing him as her 'little pagan', which may have been what prompted Hamilton, for whom the responsibility of a godparent would not have been taken lightly, to decline.

Hamilton was strongly influenced by the Romantic movement, which accorded with his natural temperament. Wordsworth, whom he visited on several occasions and who came to stay at Dunsink, was a much-admired friend, as was Coleridge, who introduced him to the philosophy of Kant. As this influence suggests, Hamilton's science was much affected by his philosophical views and literary connections; at first strongly Berkeleian – not surprising in one connected with Trinity College at that time – his ideas and motives were later influenced by the Kantian perception of algebra as the science of pure time. Poetry was a continuing passion for him, and although Wordsworth gently persuaded him that his vocation was mathematics and not poetry he still wrote verse prolifically, finding an outlet for his deeper sentiments particularly in sonnet form. He saw mathematics as poetic in nature and judged the work of his contemporaries in terms of poetical quality. Among the French mathematicians Fourier commanded his particular respect: He wrote: 'Fourier was a true poet in mathematics, and in the applications of mathematical science to nature (especially to the theory of heat). So was (though not Laplace) Lagrange, to whose memory I consider as having inscribed those essays on a general method in dynamics' (letter to John Nichol, 1855, Graves, iii, 48).

Politically, Hamilton might be described as a moderate conservative. He was a committed member of the anglican Church of Ireland and a firm supporter of the established order. He certainly did not espouse the radical views that, to some extent, his father shared with his godfather, Archibald Rowan. In 1852 he wrote to the English mathematician Augustus De Morgan: 'my uncle, the Rev. James Hamilton, was a Tory to the backbone, and doubtless taught me Toryism along with Church of Englandism, Hebrew and Sanskrit. My father used to enjoy provoking me into some political or other argument, in which I always took my uncle's side' (letter to Augustus de Morgan, 1852, Graves, iii, 392). But although Hamilton did not share his godfather's political outlook, and although he firmly supported the union, he was nonetheless a patriotic Irishman who loved his country and was loyal to, and took pride in, its institutions.

Hamilton was president of the RIA (1837–46). He was deeply committed to the academy, attached considerable significance to his responsibilities as president, and worked assiduously to promote its interests. He received many honours. His knighthood was conferred in 1835. The year before, he was awarded the Cunningham medal of the academy and the Royal medal of the Royal Society, both of these in recognition of his work in optics and in particular the discovery of conical refraction. He was an honorary member of many learned societies though (extraordinarily and for some reason not fully understood), he was not a fellow of the Royal Society. Perhaps the best indication of his international standing is the decision of the newly founded National Academy of Sciences in the USA to place his name first on the list of distinguished scientists to be elected foreign associates.

Death and reputation

Hamilton died on 2 September 1865 at his home at Dunsink, aged sixty, and was buried at Mount Jerome cemetery. His wife died four years later. There were two sons of their marriage, William Edwin and Archibald, and one daughter, Helen, who married Archdeacon John O'Regan (d. 1898) and whose son, John, was Hamilton's only grandchild. At the time of his death Hamilton's reputation was strongly linked with quaternions. Despite the importance of his contributions to algebra and to optics, posterity accords him greatest fame for his dynamics. The formulation that he devised for classical mechanics proved to be equally suited to quantum theory, whose development it facilitated. The Hamiltonian formalism shows no signs of obsolescence; new ideas continue to find this the most natural medium for their description and development, and the function that is now universally known as the Hamiltonian, is the starting point for calculation in almost any area of physics.

Hamilton's manuscript notebooks and miscellaneous papers are in Trinity College Library. A portrait by Sarah Purser hangs in the RIA and there is a portrait bust by J. H. Foley in the Long Room, Trinity College Library.

David Spearman

Sources

Robert Perceval Graves, *Life of Sir William Rowan Hamilton* (3 vols, 1882–9); Thomas L. Hankins, *Sir William Rowan Hamilton* (1980); Sean O'Donnell, *William Rowan Hamilton: portrait of a prodigy* (1983); David R. Wilkins (ed.), *Perplexingly easy: selected correspondence between William Rowan Hamilton and Peter Guthrie Tait* (2005); William Rowan Hamilton, *The mathematical papers* (4 vols, 1931–2000); *ODNB*

William Dargan
(1799–1867)

ENGINEER

William Dargan was born on 28 February 1799 in Co. Carlow. His parents were Patrick and Elizabeth Dargan, his father being a well-to-do farmer who was a tenant of Lord Portarlington. Much of William's early life is obscure. Likewise, the exact place of birth is uncertain but may have been Ardristan near Tullow. When William was a boy the family moved to an area west of Carlow town in Queen's County (Laois), although he always referred to himself as a Carlowman and in later years bought a family homestead of 101 acres near Ballyhide. He had about eight siblings, four of whom died in infancy, while his brother James also became an engineer, and a sister, Selina, is named as a beneficiary in Dargan's will.

Dargan's education is slightly less obscure. It is believed he went to school in Graiguecullen, a suburb of Carlow town where he excelled at maths and accounting. After leaving school he worked on his father's land before starting work in a surveyor's office but failed to get a position with the Carlow grand jury, which was responsible for public buildings such as jails, courthouses, asylums and fever hospitals. Soon after this, two influential patrons took a hand in Dargan's career: John Alexander of the milling family based at Milford, Co. Carlow, and Sir Henry Parnell, MP for Queen's County.

Roadbuilder 1819–33

Parnell chaired a parliamentary commission to improve the London–Holyhead road, then the main communication artery between Ireland and Britain. The road was dangerously neglected in parts, especially through north Wales, and the great Scottish engineer Thomas Telford was engaged to rebuild it. Parnell secured a position for Dargan with Telford during the years 1819–24, when he learned many of his building skills. In 1836 Dargan told a commons committee he had been an inspector of works and later a resident engineer under Telford, and it is believed the 1,000-yard (914m) embankment carrying the road (and later the railway) across the Stanley Sands sea inlet to Holy Island is Dargan's work.

Telford then asked Dargan to survey the road from Dublin to the packet station at Howth (the Irish end of the London–Dublin route), which was also in poor condition and subject to frequent flooding. Dargan rebuilt the entire road with a stone wall to restrain the sea from Clontarf to Sutton. Parnell described it as 'a model for other roads in the vicinity of Dublin' and the treasury awarded Dargan a special premium of £300 for this work, a substantial sum. In 1824 Dargan became superintendent of the Barrow navigation and resigned from Telford's firm. His mentor was sorry to lose him and said his conduct was always 'perfectly satisfactory'. But Dargan maintained his connection with Telford for a while, surveying the Birmingham and Liverpool Junction Canal and then acting as superintendent and contractor on the Middlewich Canal. While working on these projects Dargan met his wife-to-be, Jane Arkinstall, and the couple married in her hometown at the anglican parish of St Michael and All Angels, Adbaston, Staffordshire, on 13 October 1828. Back in Ireland Dargan then took on a number of turnpike road contracts: these were with the Malahide, Carlow and Dunleer turnpikes, followed by improvement works on the Shannon at Limerick and excavation of a large cut through the centre of Banbridge, Co. Down.

Railway engineer, 1833–1850s

Ireland's first railway line, the Dublin & Kingstown, opened in 1834 and Dargan was fortunate to win the contract to build it against six competitors. Working under another Telford pupil, Charles Vignoles, as engineer, Dargan began work near Salthill in April 1833, and although he was six months late finishing the line (which opened on 17 December 1834) the penalty clauses in his detailed contract were not enforced. The successful completion of this line gave Dargan a springboard to winning a substantial share of Irish railway construction contracts on offer in the 1840s and 1850s.

Moving to Caledon, Co. Tyrone, Dargan built the Ulster Canal, connecting Lough Erne to Lough Neagh, and then ran canal steamers, as well as cross-channel vessels from Newry to Liverpool. From his Belfast office he completed major improvements to the harbour there (1839–49), followed by works at Solitude and the Bann reservoirs and a complex land reclamation project at Lough Foyle which brought him to the verge of ruin. Moving on to safer ground, he built all but a few miles of the line from Belfast to Armagh for the Ulster Railway and substantial parts of the Dublin & Drogheda Railway. The Dublin & Belfast Junction Railway, largely his, includes the magnificent Craigmore viaduct near Newry, his finest piece of work. He was lucky not to have got the contract to build the Boyne viaduct at Drogheda, which was so troublesome it bankrupted the contractor, William Evans from Cambridge.

Less well known is Dargan's involvement in building railways in the north of England. In 1846 he and his partner William McCormick won the contract for the Liverpool & Bury Railway (opened 1848) and for parts of the difficult line of the Manchester & Leeds Railway.

Back in Ireland, Dargan came to dominate railway construction in the 1850s. After successfully completing small sections for the Great Southern & Western Railway he then swept his competitors aside by winning the eighty-mile (128km) section from Thurles to Cork for the astonishing sum of £600,000. At this time a labourer did well to earn 1*s.* 6*d.* (£0.075) a day and a good-quality loaf cost 8*d.* (£0.033). After this came the line from Mullingar to Galway, Longford, and Cavan for the Midland Great Western Railway (MGWR), the precarious Waterford & Limerick Railway, the Belfast & Ballymena, the Belfast & Co. Down to Bangor, and the Banbridge Junction Railway. There were few railway projects in which he was not involved as contractor and/or financier. At one time Dargan said he had 50,000 men working for him; even allowing for subcontractors, this makes him a key influence in the economy of nineteenth-century Ireland.

Cultural pursuits

Dargan funded and put up the building for the Art Industry Exhibition held in Dublin in 1853 and is linked to the subsequent foundation of the National Gallery of Ireland. He approached the Royal Dublin Society (RDS) to say he would like to develop its usual exhibition, all at his own expense and guaranteeing against any loss, making it a national event along the lines of the highly successful one held in London's Hyde Park in 1851. Dargan built the glass and iron-framed building on Leinster Lawn, facing Merrion

Square, which opened from May to October 1853. The exhibition was primarily a celebration of art, there being few examples of Irish industry, but it was a major personal achievement for Dargan and a much-needed expression of national self-confidence. It attracted over a million visitors including 'Mr Punch', who praised Dargan's generosity and named the exhibition 'the Darganeum'. Another prominent visitor was Queen Victoria (August 1853). One of her first outings was to visit Dargan at Mount Anville, his house outside the city. It was rare for a monarch to visit a commoner, and her diary notes that she wanted to make Dargan a baronet but he declined the honour, as he did many other attempts to gentrify him. In fact the only honour he ever accepted was the nominal one of deputy lieutenant of Dublin.

Dargan lost almost £21,000 on the exhibition, a serious blow even for such a wealthy man. A testimonial subscription followed and there was a plan to establish an art gallery to be known as the Dargan Institute, but it was eventually named the National Gallery of Ireland. At its opening (30 January 1864) the lord lieutenant unveiled a statue of Dargan by Thomas Farrell, standing 3.3m high at the front of the building. Erecting a statue while the subject is still alive is a rare occurrence, and a plaque on the front of the Gallery records Dargan's generosity. One section was later renamed the Dargan Wing and has a portrait by Catterson Smith painted in 1862. A magnificent portrait by George Mulvany hangs in the boardroom at Heuston station.

Later railway and business projects

Continuing his railway contract activities, Dargan went on to build a number of other railways: the lines between Mallow and Tralee, from Limerick to Foynes and Ennis, the Athenry

& Tuam Junction Railway, and the Waterford & Tramore Railway are all his. He also completed improvements to Glenstal Castle, Co. Limerick, and built the troublesome graving dock in Dublin, which proved so acrimonious an undertaking that William Cubitt became involved in a lengthy arbitration, eventually finding in Dargan's favour.

The railway most associated with Dargan was the Dublin & Wicklow (D&WR); he built most of its routeing from Harcourt Street to Wicklow and was successively contractor, investor, board member, and finally (1864) chairman. The demands this company made on his time and resources were enormous, putting some strain on both, as evidenced by the number of loans he took out from several banks, mainly the Bank of Ireland. Dargan negotiated the lease of the pioneer Dublin & Kingstown to the D&WR, accepting debentures and bonds by way of payment for construction; thereafter his fortunes were inextricably linked with the D&WR, which almost single-handed he kept afloat. In February 1856, Dargan joined the board and thus no longer took construction contracts but closely supervised the works on the extension towards Wexford.

Dargan is credited with the development of Bray, which before the arrival of the railway (1853) was a small fishing village. He built the seafront esplanade as well as a group of six houses on Quinsboro Road, known as Dargan Terrace, and the famed Turkish baths. He laid out a common, a fairgreen, and a market place, and helped install gas lights in the town. He was a major investor in the four-storey, 130-room International Hotel near the seafront, as well as the Royal Marine Hotel in Kingstown (Dún Laoghaire) and the Grand Hotel, Malahide.

In the west, the MGWR promoted transatlantic steamers from Galway to the US and Canada, and for a time Dargan also invested in these. His other business interests included a flax mill at Kildinan, Co. Cork, a distillery at Belturbet, Co. Cavan, a sugar factory at Mountmellick, and substantial slobland reclamation around Wexford harbour. At Chapelizod, Co. Dublin, Dargan ran a large thread mill which at one time employed 900 people and was known as Dargan & Haughton mills. In the summer of 1860 Dargan took 700 of his employees on a pleasure trip to Bray, where they dined and danced before taking the train back to Harcourt Street.

Later years 1865–7

On 1 May 1865 Dargan had a serious accident when his horse was startled near Booterstown and he was thrown to the ground. Suffering from concussion, he was brought unconscious to Mount Anville. He recovered sufficiently to attend a royal commission on railways in London a few weeks later and made a significant and lengthy presentation on the current state and future prospects of Irish railways. However, the accident took its toll and Dargan was by this time in some business difficulties. A few months later he sold Mount Anville to the Sisters of the Sacred Heart and moved permanently to 2 Fitzwilliam Square, Dublin, a four-storey-over-basement house with courtyard and coach house. The financial crisis in Britain and the collapse of bankers Overend Gurney in May 1866 caused the value of railway shares to plummet, a serious blow for Dargan. At the end of the year he appointed two trustees to run his businesses, Valentine O'Brien O'Connor (1811–73) and Richard Martin (1831–1901). The move caused some alarm among his creditors and in particular among his fellow directors of the Dublin, Wicklow & Wexford Railway (as the D&WR had become), who decided the only way to save the company was to offer their personal security against the loans Dargan had negotiated.

In January 1867, Dargan made his will, with Alexander Boyle as executor, leaving his wife, Jane, a legacy of £3,000 and an annuity of £600. Other beneficiaries were Boyle, who received £2,000; Louisa Haslam (Jane's niece), £1,000; and his sister, Selina Dargan, £500. Although there was some question as to Dargan's religious affiliations he received the last rites of the catholic church from Fr John Boland and died, three weeks short of his sixty-eighth birthday, on 7 February 1867, the cause of death being malignant liver disease. Lengthy tributes appeared in the press all over Ireland and Britain and the funeral took place on 11 February. Estimates of the number of carriages varied from 150 to 250, but all agreed it was one of the largest funerals in Dublin for many years. Several hundred Dublin, Wicklow and Wexford Railway (DW&WR) men led the procession from Fitzwilliam Square to Glasnevin cemetery, and after a funeral service in the mortuary chapel Dargan was buried close to the O'Connell circle, a position of some status in the mortality league. The plot was a gift from the cemetery authorities and the elegant tomb is almost certainly the work of the talented architect John Skipton Mulvany. Some months later an unpleasant sectarian dispute broke out over whether to use the King James version of John 3:36 for an inscription on the grave as Jane Dargan wanted, or the Douai version as the cemetery committee insisted. The argument rumbled on for some weeks, involving Cardinal Cullen, till finally Jane Dargan decided to omit the biblical text altogether. The inscription on the grave thus appears as 'William Dargan, died 7 February 1867, aged 68 years'.

Jane Dargan wrote to a number of distinguished people asking for financial help after her husband's death, and two years later Dargan's property, mainly reclaimed sloblands in Wexford and a number of houses in Bray, was sold.

His trustees did an excellent job and far from his dying bankrupt, as has been suggested, Dargan's solicitor, Croker Barrington, told Jane in 1875 that when all debts had been met there was a healthy surplus of £30,000. Soon after, Jane Dargan left Ireland and moved to Glenmore, 21 Anerley Park, Penge, south London. It is quite a large house with a tall cypress tree in the front garden, like those in Mount Anville. She died there on 22 June 1894, aged ninety-one, of diabetes asthenia. The couple had no children.

Assessment

Many aspects of Dargan's personal life are tantalisingly obscure. He had a phenomenal capacity for work, managing several major projects simultaneously at opposite ends of the country. Some suggested he enjoyed hunting, and the couple entertained quite often at Mount Anville. It is clear Dargan drank quite a lot but what interests and pastimes he had are unknown. The RDS and Royal St George Yacht Club both elected him a member, but he was not active in either.

William Le Fanu, an engineering colleague of Dargan, knew him well, and the personal description in his whimsical memoirs has the ring of authenticity rather than Victorian hyperbole: 'I have settled as engineer for different companies many of his accounts, involving many hundred thousand pounds. His thorough honesty, his willingness to concede a disputed point, and his wonderful rapidity of decision, rendered it a pleasure, instead of a trouble, as it generally is, to settle these accounts; indeed in my life I have never met a man more quick in intelligence, more clear sighted and more thoroughly honourable' (Le Fanu, 208).

Fergus Mulligan

Sources

Jane Dargan papers, private collection; Ena Dargan papers, private collection; index to railway inspectors' reports 1842–59, Public Record Office; diaries of W. R. Le Fanu 1846–67, Trinity College Dublin; council minutes and letter books, 1851–4, RDS archives, Dublin; diaries of James Dargan, 1863–70, private collection; Dublin & Kingstown Railway, plans, estimates, correspondence and papers, House of Lords Record Office; railway company minute, committee and letter books, CIE archives, Heuston station, Dublin; Reilly, Caledon, and Dargan papers, Public Records Office of Northern Ireland; W. R. Le Fanu, *Seventy years of Irish life* (1893); Kevin Murray, 'William Dargan', *Irish Railway Record Society Journal*, ii (1950–51), 94–102; Fergus Mulligan, 'William Dargan 1799–1867: a business life' (Ph.D. thesis, Trinity College Dublin, 2002); Fergus Mulligan, *William Dargan: an honourable life 1799–1867* (2013)

Mary Ward
(1827–69)

MICROSCOPIST, ASTRONOMER, ARTIST AND AUTHOR

Mary Ward (née King) was born on 27 April 1827 to the Rev. Henry King, landowner, and Harriette (née Lloyd) at Ballylin, Ferbane, Co. Offaly. She was the youngest of their four children, alongside John Gilbert (1822–1901), Jane (1823/6–95) and Harriett (1823/6–96). Ward was first cousin to William Parsons, 3rd earl of Rosse (son of Harriette's sister Alice), a notable astronomer and president of the Royal Society (1848–54). These familial relationships proved formative as Mary developed her scientific interests from a young age.

Mary and her two sisters were educated at home, in accordance with nineteenth-century gender norms. However, in addition to providing a stereotypically feminine curriculum via a governess, their parents encouraged an interest in astronomy and natural history. Mary, in particular, demonstrated an aptitude for these scientific disciplines. Consequently, when she turned eighteen her father bought her a microscope from Andrew Ross, one of the leading microscope-makers of London. Mary used this instrument to make drawings and paintings of specimens, and she frequently presented these as microscopical shows to family, friends and estate workers. The visual representations were evidently skilled and accurate, and she received much encouragement from distinguished scientific professionals who visited the family home at Ballylin and Lord Rosse at his nearby home of Birr Castle.

Among the notable visitors to Ballylin was Scottish scientist and author, Sir David Brewster (1781–1868). He recognised Mary's talents and sent her specimens to mount for microscopical examination; he later used her illustrations to accompany some of his published articles in *Transactions of the Royal Society of Edinburgh*. He also obtained books for her to study and sent her copies of his own works.

During her teenage years, Ward spent a lot of time with her cousin William and his wife, also Mary (née Field, 1813–85). This close friendship meant that Ward was often at Birr during the construction of Lord Rosse's enormous telescope, nicknamed the 'Leviathan'. Completed in 1845, the instrument was fifty-eight feet long with a six-foot diameter mirror; when completed it was the largest telescope in the world. Mary was therefore privileged to be one of the first to make observations from it and illustrations of it; the latter appear, along with a drawing of Newton's telescope, in Brewster's *Memoirs of the life, writings and discoveries of Sir Isaac Newton* (1855). This inclusion was a significant validation of Mary's technical abilities at a time when it was difficult for women to obtain expertise and recognition beyond the domestic sphere.

In 1854 Ward married Henry William Crosbie Ward (1828–1911), second son of Edward Ward, viscount Bangor, of Castle Ward, Co. Down. Henry's elder brother Edward had inherited the title and the estates, yet Henry resigned from his army commission soon after the marriage and never again assumed regular employment. This caused increasing financial difficulties for their growing family. The couple had eight children, from eleven pregnancies, between 1855 and 1867.

Remarkably, however, in addition to her duties as wife and mother, Ward wrote several books and a scientific article on natterjack toads in Ireland. Her first book-length study,

A windfall for the microscope (1856), was privately printed and distributed to family and friends. This was followed by *Sketches with the microscope* (1857), a collection of letters about and illustrations of common objects suitable for microscopic examination. Ward initially commissioned a local printer in Parsonstown to produce 250 copies of the manuscript. When these proved popular, a relative took a copy of the text to the London publisher Groombridge and Sons, who reissued it under the title *A world of wonders revealed by the microscope* (1858). In 1864 this was extensively revised and expanded into *Microscope teachings*, a companion volume to *Telescope teachings* (1859), later published as *The microscope* and *The telescope* (both 1869). Mary also produced, in collaboration with her sister, Lady Jane Mahon, *Entomology in sport; and entomology in earnest* (1859), a playful and instructive volume that was dedicated to their mother. These various publications were favourably received due to their relaxed yet informative style, conversational tone, and the quality of Mary's illustrations.

Mary aimed her writing at amateur scientists, young readers and other women. She also positioned her work within traditional Christian values, using religious rhetoric to balance academic knowledge; she frequently reiterated that her scientific studies of the natural world ultimately revealed the wonders of God's work. As such, she took care not to encroach upon the male-dominated domain of professional science. Mary was only too aware of nineteenth-century gender constraints: as a woman she could not gain membership of professional scientific bodies. Yet, notably, Sir William Rowan Hamilton requested that the Royal Astronomical Society include her on its list of eminent people and institutions entitled to receive its monthly notices. Ward was one of only three women to achieve this honour, holding rather esteemed company with Queen Victoria (1819–1901) and Mary Somerville (1780–1872). In further recognition of her work, she was allowed entry to Greenwich Observatory, despite their strict rule against admitting women.

Ward's life and work ended prematurely when, while visiting Birr Castle on 31 August 1869, she was killed in an accident, falling from a steam-powered road locomotive designed by Lord Rosse. She is thought to have been the first person killed in an automobile accident in Ireland. Ward is commemorated by plaques mounted in her name at Birr Castle and at the Mary Ward Centre, Ferbane. At Castle Ward there is also a room dedicated to Ward's memory, with many of her books and her microscope on display. Along with Mary Rosse, she is the subject of a documentary and a play, both of which focus on the ways in which she negotiated the difficult role of women in nineteenth-century science and contributed to the popularisation of natural history.

Éadaoin Agnew

Sources

David Brewster, *Memoirs of the life, writings and discoveries of Sir Isaac Newton* (1855); Mary Ward, *A world of wonders revealed by the microscope. A book for young students. With coloured illustrations* (1858); Mary Ward and Jane Mahon, *Entomology in sport; and entomology in earnest* (1859); Mary Ward, *Telescope teachings* (1859); eadem, *Microscope teachings: descriptions of various objects of especial interest and beauty adapted for microscopic observation* (1864); eadem, 'The natterjack toad in Ireland', *Intellectual Observer*, 5 (May 1864), 227–33; eadem, *The microscope* (1869); eadem, *The telescope* (1869); Owen Harry, 'The Hon. Mrs Ward (1827–1869): a wife, mother, microscopist and astronomer in Ireland, 1854–1869' in John Nudds, Norman McMillan, Denis Weaire and Susan McKenna-Lawlor (eds), *Science in Ireland, 1800–1930: tradition and reform* (1988); Éadaoin Agnew, 'A microscopic look at Mary Ward: gender, science, and religion in nineteenth-century Ireland' in Juliana Adelman and Éadaoin Agnew (eds), *Science and technology in nineteenth-century Ireland* (2011), 83–93; Aintzane Mentxaka, 'A pair of new eyes' (2014); Mary Ward, *Sketches with a microscope* (2019 repr.); *Ladies of science: the extraordinary story of Mary Rosse and Mary Ward* (documentary, 2015; dir. Alessandra Usai)

Robert Mallet
(1810–81)

Engineer and seismologist

Robert Mallet was born on 3 June 1810 in Ryder's Row, Dublin, eldest child and only son among three children of John Mallet (1780–1868), plumber, hydraulic-engine maker, and iron founder, and his wife and first cousin Thomasina Mallet (d. 1861). The Mallet family originated in Devon, and Robert's maternal grandfather, Robert Mallet sen. (1761–1804), came to Dublin and set up as a cabinet maker at 62 Capel Street. He married Anne, daughter of William Pike, who had a plumbing business in Dublin since the 1750s. On Pike's death Robert sen. appeared to take over some of his father-in-law's business. After an invitation to his nephew in Devon, John Mallet came to join him and married his daughter Thomasina. John also persuaded his father Richard Mallet to come to Dublin with his mother, brother, and sister. Richard Mallet set up business as an ironmonger at 90–91 Marlborough Street, along with his other son, William. John took over the business on his uncle's death (1804), moving to premises at 7–9 Ryder's Row. He expanded the business and became involved in municipal affairs, acting as high sheriff of Dublin for a period.

Robert jun. showed an early interest in physical science and, as a youth, had a chemical laboratory fitted out for himself in his father's foundry. Educated at Bective House Seminary at 2 Denmark Street, he entered Dublin University in December 1826. On graduating (1830) he joined his father's works at Ryder's Row, while receiving instruction in surveying and levelling from Joseph Byrne at 23 Lower Mount Street. In 1831 he went on an extended tour of the Continent and visited the Mer de Glace at Chamonix, where he developed an interest in glacial flow. He later published a number of papers on the subject. The following year he became a full partner at his father's firm and developed it into one of the most important and successful engineering works in Ireland. At one stage his father built an extensive building on the banks of the Royal Canal near Phibsborough. Intended as a flour mill to be driven by a water wheel, it remained unused for several years because of problems in acquiring the water rights. The building was nicknamed 'Mallet's folly'. The advent of the railway era led to large contracts for engineering and other works, and Robert converted the mill into a large factory with over forty smiths-fires, and planing and screwing machines. The firm built cast-iron bridges over the River Shannon, railway works for the Dublin–Kingstown and Great Southern & Western Railways, fire engines for Dublin city, castings for the first Fastnet lighthouse (1848–9) and the Nore viaduct, and contract work for Guinness & Co., TCD, Dublin Castle, the Records Office, and the Four Courts, among others. Developing his experimental skills further, Mallet researched extensively into the properties and strengths of various materials including alloys and the problems associated with the cooling of large iron castings and was one of the first to carry out research on the corrosion of iron. He was one of the few iron founders of the period to attempt a scientific explanation of fracture in terms of the 'molecular strength' of the metal. In 1834 he made his reputation as an engineer of exceptional skill by raising, by means of screw-jacks, the roof of St George's church in Dublin, for which he was later awarded the Walter premium from the

Institution of Civil Engineers (1842). He invented and patented buckled plates (1852), which combined maximum strength with minimum depth and weight and were used to floor the Westminster and London bridges. During the Crimean war (1853–5) he began developing huge mortars for the war department, in the hope they would break the Russian hold on Sevastopol. The work was discontinued in 1858 after inconclusive tests and the cessation of hostilities.

Interest in scientific phenomena, particularly geological, was popular at the time, and Mallet took a keen interest in new developments. Using his knowledge of engineering and physics and applying his skills of observation along with experimental measurement of natural phenomenon, he made several advances. He presented papers on magnetism and geology to the annual meetings of the British Association for the Advancement of Science in 1835 and 1837. In 1841 he surveyed the River Dodder, in an attempt to provide a steady water supply for the city and for a paper mill on its banks. During the same year he unsuccessfully applied for the chair of engineering at Dublin University. In February 1846, he read his classic paper 'On the dynamics of earthquakes' to the RIA, in which he proposed that the structural damage effected by earthquakes was caused by the action of 'waves of elastic compression' through the ground. He stressed the need for a quantified, experimental approach to the study of earthquakes. In October 1849, he conducted what were some of the first active seismic experiments – on the rate of shock waves in wet sand at Killiney beach. He buried gunpowder charges in the sand and measured the transit time of the resultant shock wave with a 'seismoscope', an instrument co-invented by Mallet and Thomas Romney Robinson. He carried out similar experiments in the granite of Dalkey Island in October 1850. The Royal Society and the British Association commissioned more experiments at the government quarries in Holyhead between 1856 and 1861. Between 1852 and 1854 Mallet, with the cooperation of his son John William, compiled a bibliography of seismological literature and a chronological catalogue of all the earth's known earthquakes, and published a seismographic map of the world, which noted the coincidence of seismic areas with volcanic activity. Through this published work he proposed and established the word 'seismology' for the study of earthquakes, and from this several new terms with the prefix 'seism-' were coined. He has been considered as the father of instrumental seismology.

In 1858 he was commissioned by the Royal Society to spend three months in Italy studying the after-effects of the great Neapolitan earthquake of December 1857. He examined the structural damage to buildings and crustal fixtures to determine the epicentre of the earthquake. His report was published as *The great Neapolitan earthquake of 1857: the first principles of observational seismology* (1862). During his stay in Italy, he developed an interest in volcanoes, and he visited Vesuvius, Etna and Stromboli in 1864, which formed the basis of his important paper 'Volcanic energy', which he read to the Royal Society (1873).

In 1860, owing to a shortage of contracts, he closed his business and relocated to London, where he set up offices at 11 Bride Street and later at 7 Westminster Chambers, and worked as a consultant engineer and writer. He edited (1861–7) the *Practical Mechanic's Journal*, contributed articles to the *Engineer*, and reported on the collieries of Westphalia. He was a prominent member of the scientific communities of Dublin and London and a member of the RIA (1832), Irish Society of Civil Engineers (1836), Institution of Civil Engineers (1842) (president 1866), Geological Society of Ireland (1838), the Geological Society of London (1859), an FRS (1864), and a member of the

Institution of Mechanical Engineers (1867). He was the recipient of various honours and distinctions: an honorary degree from Dublin University (1864), the Cunningham medal from the RIA (1862), the Walker premium (1842), the Telford medal from the Institution of Civil Engineers (1859), and the Wollaston medal from the Geological Society of London (1877). He served as president of the Geological Society of Dublin (1846–8) and of the Institution of Civil Engineers of Ireland (1866).

A strongly independent spirit, Mallet stood apart from the fossil-loving geologists of his era. His inventive mind sought to find novel solutions to fresh problems in physical geology, and he always embraced the bigger picture. Somewhat overbearing, he frequently deprecated the efforts of others and seemed to view himself as above a general sea of mediocrity. On a personal basis he was a good friend and charming companion, which contradicted the supercilious tone he adopted in his writings. This may have been a defence against being seen as an outsider by the scientific community. He was, after all, an engineer and an amateur scientist among a community of professional scientists, academics, and gentlemen of science! He was proud of his native country and never neglected an opportunity to offer solutions to its problems, including the importation of technology to make it less dependent on agriculture. Left blind for the last seven years of his life, he became bedridden after an attack of diffuse cystitis in October 1880. He died on 5 November 1881 at his home in Enmore, The Grove, Clapham Road, Surrey, and was buried in Norwood cemetery.

He married (November 1831) Cordelia Watson (d. 1854), daughter of a Dublin bookseller. In 1836 they moved from their home at Ryder's Row to Delville House in Glasnevin; they had three sons and three daughters. He later moved to 1 Grosvenor Terrace, Monkstown (1858). After moving to London in 1860 he married (1861) Mary Daniel, the daughter of the landlady of the house where he initially lodged on his arrival to London. They had no children. She and five of his children survived him. His three sons all engaged in careers in science or engineering: Dr John William Mallet, chemist, of the University of Virginia, USA; Robert Trefusis Mallet, chief engineer of the Indian State Railways; and Frederick Richard Mallet (1840–1921) of the Geological Survey of India. A complete list of papers published by Robert Mallet between 1835 and 1880 can be found in R. C. Cox (ed.), *Robert Mallet FRS 1810–1881* (1982), 135–9. The Mallet–Milne lectures, a series of public biennial lectures, have been established by the Society of Earthquake and Civil Engineering Dynamics at the Institute of Civil Engineers, London, in his honour.

Enda Leaney and Patricia M. Byrne

Sources

Ir. Builder, xxiii, no. 528 (1881), 360; *Proceedings of the Royal Society*, xxxiii (1881–2), xix–xx; Michael J. Tutty, 'John and Robert Mallet 1780–1881', *Dublin Hist. Rec.*, no. 2 (Mar. 1976), 42–58; R. C. Cox (ed.), *Robert Mallet FRS 1810–1881* (1982); T. Ó Raifeartaigh, *The Royal Irish Academy* (1985), 266; Dennis R. Dean, 'Robert Mallet and the founding of seismology', *Annals of Science*, xlviii (1991), 39–67; Charles Mollan, William Davis, and Brendan Finucane, *Irish innovators in science and technology* (2002), 106 (portr.); www.seced.org.uk (accessed 13 Mar. 2006)

John Tyndall
(1820–93)

Scientist and mountaineer

John Tyndall was born on 2 August 1820 in Leighlinbridge, Co. Carlow, only son among two children of John Tyndall (1792–1847) and Sarah Tyndall (née McAssey; d. 1867). His father came from a family of small landowners in Co. Kilkenny, acted as land agent for the Steuart estate, and supplemented his income by mending boots. His mother came from the Malone family, which owned considerable landed property near Fenagh, Co. Carlow; however, his maternal grandmother, having married against her father's wishes, had been disinherited. At some stage the family moved to Castlebellingham, Co. Louth, where Tyndall nearly drowned in the River Clyde during one of the first of his life-threatening adventures. His main school education was in Ballinabranagh, Co. Carlow, under the tutelage of John Conwill. This former hedge-school teacher ended his career in what was, for him, the luxury of a one-room 'non-denominational' national school in the grounds of the catholic church. John left at nineteen years, with an education that included English, logic, bookkeeping, drawing, and, most importantly, surveying and associated mathematics.

Early career; Queenwood Hall and Marburg
He joined the Ordnance Survey office in Carlow from school, moving from there to Youghal, Co. Cork. Tyndall felt fortunate to be chosen (1842) to transfer to the English

survey, where he was posted to Preston, Lancashire. Despite working long hours, Tyndall began attending classes in the local mechanics' institute. As leader of the malcontents over the working conditions in the Ordnance Survey, he was summarily dismissed (November 1843) and entered into a public dispute with Robert Peel in the *Liverpool Mercury*. He was unemployed for a period but eventually found work as a surveyor with Manchester partners Nevin & Lawton, and then on the West Yorkshire line as a railway surveyor. During this time he developed his prodigious walking capacity and the stamina that was to serve him so well later as a mountaineer.

Tyndall's interest in physics and engineering education began in 1847 when he met George Edmondson, who at the time was endeavouring to introduce the elements of experimental science into his quaker school, Tulketh Hall, Preston. Edmondson shortly thereafter entered into negotiations with representatives of the communalist Robert Owen to take over 'Harmony Hall' near Stockbridge, Hampshire, the unsuccessful school which was Owen's last great social experiment. The Hall stood on its own 500-acre self-sufficient farm, boasting palatial buildings with the latest educational facilities, including an agricultural school with a purpose-built science laboratory, printing office, and carpenter's and blacksmith's shops. The name was changed to Queenwood College. Edward Frankland, another passionate self-improver, became superintendent of the chemistry laboratory, and the younger Tyndall superintendent of the engineering laboratory. The two established the first programme of practical science and engineering ever established in Great Britain and Ireland, in what were almost certainly the earliest science and engineering school laboratory facilities. The importance of this pioneering work was, a decade later, amplified into the national arena with the appointment (1853) of both men as examiners in the Department of Arts and Science. Frankland was the first government examiner in chemistry and Tyndall in physics. Indeed, physics – which as a subject Tyndall did so much to define in Britain – was a new school subject that came from revolutionary France via Germany. Tyndall was also appointed (1857) as the first chief examiner for military examinations for the Royal Engineers and Royal Artillery.

In October 1848 Frankland and Tyndall left Queenwood to attend – at their own expense – Marburg University, the centre of the radical scientific materialist movement. Tyndall wrote his Ph.D. thesis in 1849, after intense study, on 'Die Schraubenfläche mit geneigter Erzeugungslinie und Bedingungen des Gleichgewichts für solche Schrauben' ('Screw surfaces with inclined generatrix, and the conditions of equilibrium for such screws'). He studied chemistry under the illustrious Robert Bunsen, whose own research interests in spectroscopy were to fire and shape much of Tyndall's own later research ambition. On completing these studies, he moved decisively towards physics, collaborating with Heinrich Knoblauch, who had arrived in Marburg from Berlin, to produce his first published paper on the topic of diamagnetism. He extended his stay in Germany long enough to produce a second memoir with Knoblauch, and then to spend several months in Gustav Magnus's laboratory in Berlin. His research fame by now was such that in his first memoir he felt able to dispute with Michael Faraday and Julius Plücker, both senior eminent Victorian scientists. In Berlin he cemented what were to be lifelong ties to the elite of Germany's scientific community, working alongside Magnus, Poggendorff, Heinrich Dove, Emil du Bois-Reymond, and Rudolf Clausius.

In June 1851 Tyndall returned to Queenwood and continued his work on diamagnetism with small equipment grants from the Royal Society. His considerable work on this topic was only much later consolidated and published as *Researches on diamagnetism and magne-crystallic action* (1870). During a second spell at Queenwood, he also undertook a considerable amount of translation work for William Francis. These translations in the Royal Society's *Philosophical Magazine* cemented his German research links and brought to the British audience the latest and most important papers emanating from Germany.

Professor of natural philosophy; conflict with the scientific establishment

Tyndall gave the discourse at the Royal Institution of Great Britain (RI) on 11 February 1853 on the topic of diamagnetism, opposing his own theory to that of Michael Faraday. He was invited to give a second discourse and a course of lectures, and in May 1853 was elected to the chair of natural philosophy at the RI. Tyndall, indeed, abandoned his earlier German mathematical methodology and became an open disciple and advocate of Faraday's pure experimental method. He repaid his debt to Faraday with his excellent scientific-biographical study *Faraday as a discoverer* (1868). He began his first series of independent researches on slatey cleavage as an extension of Faraday's work on the effects of pressure on magnetism. His subsequent work on glacial motion brought him into conflict with James D. Forbes of Edinburgh and thereby much of the Scottish scientific establishment, including William Thomson (Lord Kelvin) and his brother James Thomson.

After the publication of Darwin's *On the origin of species* (1859), this enmity with the Scottish establishment deepened. Initially, eight London-based evolutionists were organised from 1864 by Tyndall and Frankland from their base on Albemarle Street for the defence of the 'great hypothesis'. The ninth member, William Spottiswoode, was admitted at the second meeting, and the club eventually became known as the 'X-Club' – so named because of the nine members plus their acknowledged, but always absent, 'Xth' member and leader Charles Darwin, who was too retiring to attend X-Club meetings, or indeed even to defend publicly his own theory. The members all adopted epithets – Xcentric (Tyndall), Xalted (T. H. Huxley), Xpert (Frankland), Xperienced (J. D. Hooker), Xquisite (John Lubbock), Xemplary (George Busk), Xhaustive (Herbert Spencer), Xtravagant (T. A. Hirst), and Xcellent (Spottiswoode). Each member took on the role of defending and deepening aspects of the theory. Tyndall's was to provide the physics that underpinned life on earth, namely atmospheric physics.

Meteorology

Tyndall's own research on radiation through gases and vapours from 1860 had provided the essential experimental basis for the science of meteorology, which was obviously central to the scientific arguments concerning life on earth. His book *Contributions to molecular physics in the domain of radiant heat* (1872) marshalled an array of new observations supporting the theory of evolution. He had come on this virgin field in 1860 through an invention. By improving the Melloni differential thermopile, he devised a new system of measurement to compare thermal radiation from two different sources. He systematically proceeded to measure the absorptions and emissions of all known gases and vapours. In his initial work Tyndall helped to disprove Melloni's contention that infrared radiation was a different form of energy to visible rays but importantly demonstrated that the Italian's experimental results were otherwise valid. Tyndall and Melloni can be considered the founders of optoelectronics, and fathers of both infrared analysis and spectroscopy, based on Tyndall's subsequent exhaustive heat studies over the next decade.

This long series of meteorological studies formed the basis of three Royal Society Baconian lectures on the subject (1861, 1864, 1881), in which Tyndall formulated a quantitative understanding of atmospheric physics and dealt with related issues such as nephelometry and floating matter in the air. Tyndall opened up the debate on the 'greenhouse effect' and used his experimental knowledge on the large absorptive capacity of water vapour to explain, for instance, meteorological conditions in deserts and other climates to great effect.

In the latter part of these studies, he turned to shorter wavelengths and found that these rays of 'high refrangibility' (ultra-violet) caused photochemical reactions. The resulting clouds of small particles scattered visible light to produce colours and in particular the vivid blue of the sky, known frequently as 'Tyndall blue'. His investigations into scattering have led him to be honoured by the term 'Tyndall scattering' deriving from particulate matter. Tyndall made an impressive and comprehensive experimental study of the phenomenon, including polarisation studies. He pointed out with amazing prescience that space would be black and produced (1869) 'A cometary theory' to explain the tail of a comet. His paper 'A new series of chemical reactions produced by light' (1869) was groundbreaking work in photochemistry, following the earlier efforts of Draper in 1843. These two men, together with Scheele in his pioneering work in 1775, founded photochemistry.

Nature; conflict between science and religion

Tyndall played a central role in setting up the appropriately named evolutionist journal *Nature*, which would have again been deeply resented and seen as threatening by the scientific establishment with its own journals providing control of published science. In Britain Tyndall popularised Kant's work and, with Huxley, established a fundamentally dualist philosophical basis to underpin the evolutionists' position. He formally broke with religion in aiding Huxley formulate a new world-view of sceptical, materialistic 'humanism'. Tyndall joked that he had been an agnostic long before his friend invented the word. For Huxley and Tyndall, this creed was directed at purging metaphysical remnants from the province of science. Tyndall famously tackled religion head-on with his criticism of religious revelation and the efficacy of prayer in the long debate from 1861 to the mid-1870s; he suggested a 'prayer gauge or test' and openly stated his conviction that theological speculations were harmful. His strong anti-catholic tendencies saw miracles, the power of prayer, and observance of the Sabbath as violations of natural law. In the last analysis the evolutionists, like their German counterparts, were inspired to demand a new scientific and progressive ideology for the nation in a new imperial age.

Importantly, in philosophy Tyndall made an enormous leap in developing the position of the German reductionists in his famous Belfast address (1874) but thereby deepened the gulf between religion and science. However, this position was perhaps more fully expounded in his 1870 British Association for the Advancement of Science lecture, 'On the scientific use of imagination', where notably he presaged du Bois-Reymond's 1872 lecture, which is seen (probably wrongly) as 'the' philosophical milestone on this issue. He included human volition in an atomicist-evolutionary philosophical description of matter. Tyndall's position was one of so-called 'transcendental materialism' in which matter having creative power does not lead to atheism, but rather agnosticism. Divorced from matter, Tyndall asks, where is life? He took a fundamental Feuerbachian position and, in his 1877 lecture before the Birmingham and Midland Institute, sought to demolish the 'hypothesis of a human soul'. In his essay 'Science and man', the soul was 'a poetic rendering of a phenomenon which refuses the yoke of ordinary physical laws'. In the Belfast address he already 'had rejected the notion of a creative power' and referred the 'choicest material of the teleologists' to natural causes.

Publication, education and invention

From 1859, Tyndall joined Huxley in preparing a regular science column for the *Saturday Review* and contributed to the middle-class publications *Reader*, the *Fortnightly Review*, the *Contemporary Review*, and the *Nineteenth Century*. His essays were collected into books still widely read, *Fragments of science for unscientific people* (1871) and *New fragments of science* (1892). Tyndall also held a chair of physics in the Royal School of Mines (later Imperial College), where he lectured regularly from 1859. His lectures to children were especially well received, and for many years he delivered the RI's famous Christmas lecture series that grew into the series of school textbooks for the physics examination programmes of the Department of Science and Arts. He published a series of popular textbooks based on his lectures – *Sound: a course of eight lectures* (1867), *Notes on a course of six lectures on the motion and sensation of sound* (1873); *On sound: a course of nine lectures* (1878); *Notes of a course of nine lectures on light* (1869) which was followed by his *Six lectures on light. Delivered in America 1872–3*, reprinted usually simply under the title *On light* (1873); *Notes on a course of seven lectures on electrical phenomenon and theories* (1870); *Lessons in electricity* (1876); *Notes on electricity* (1881); *Heat considered a mode of motion* (1863); *Notes of a course of juvenile lectures on heat visible and invisible* (1877); and *Notes of a course of six lectures (adapted to juvenile auditory) on ice, water, vapour and air* (1871).

An important educator through his lecturing and writing, Tyndall was also a prolific inventor of experimental, demonstrational and other equipment, including in 1854 the 'light-pipe', which led to modern fibre optics, and in 1871 the forerunner of all modern respirators. His researches in sound were important in the improvement of fog signals. A leader in developing the profession of physics, he refused to patent any of his inventions.

Pasteur and the debate on spontaneous generation

The biochemist Louis Pasteur experienced great difficulty in defending his germ theory against attacks by the hostile French medical establishment. Tyndall was induced in 1871 by Pasteur himself to begin work on disproving the theory of 'spontaneous generation' and hence settling the fierce ongoing dispute in favour of the germ theory. Tyndall entered the field of disease and infection with a paper, 'Dust and disease' (1871), based on studies using his nephelometric technique. Abiogenesis (spontaneous generation) held that living organisms could arise from inorganic matter. Tyndall, after incredible commitments of time over nearly a full decade, succeeded in devising methods of rigorous sterilisation and was thus able to prove the germ theory by reproducible bacteriological experiments. Pasteur had been unable to do so, because his process of sterilisation (later known as pasteurisation) had just a single heat stage, and consequently does not kill the spores of bacteria. Tyndall showed (1877) that the only reliable method of sterilisation (known as tyndallisation) is a process of intermittent heating. His monumental researches were published as *Essay on floating matter of the air in relation to putrefaction and disease* (1881). This work establishes Tyndall's claim to be the founder of the experimental science of bacteriology, with Pasteur the theoretical founder of bacteriology/microbiology.

Tyndall worked very closely with Huxley and Lister, who all conducted painstaking microscopic examinations of their respective infusions and media. All three independently reported the attenuating effect of *Penicillium* some fifty years before the same observation by Alexander Fleming. Tyndall did not take the work further, probably because he did not want to be deflected from his and Pasteur's agreed research objective, the destruction of Henry Charlton Bastian's spontaneous-generation theory. Both Tyndall and Huxley saw victory in the late 1870s, in the Xs' final defence of the theory of evolution. Tyndall demonstrated that life came from life in extended evolutionary processes that ruled out any possibility of spontaneous generation.

Mountaineering

It is worth commenting briefly on Tyndall's role in founding the sport of mountaineering, as it is impossible to understand his great contributions to science without seeing them in this context. His work on glaciers, geology, meteorology and the germ theory was closely linked to his mountain experience, and some of his experimental results could only have been obtained by a great climber. The British played the central role in the development of mountaineering, perhaps because their national eccentricities matched the needs of this sport. Any ambivalence Tyndall had over sport and science was, however, decisively swept away in his competition with Edward Whymper over the Matterhorn, the greatest prize of the Alps. Tyndall, despite an advanced age of forty-eight, completed the first traverse of the Matterhorn from the Italian side on 29 July 1868 and descended to Zermatt.

This was the culmination of his climbing career, which had seen him make notable ascents, including three ascents of Mount Blanc (1856, 1858, 1859), the first solo ascent of Monte Rosa (twice in 1858), the first ascent of the Weisshorn (1861), the Finsteraarhorn (1858), traverses of Ganli, Théodule (again in 1862) and first of Old Weissthor (1861), Jungfrau (1863), Titlis (1866), Monte Confinale and Monteratch (both 1864), Sparrenhorn (1866), and Eiger (1867). He made failed attempts on the Matterhorn (1860, 1862), Todi (1865), Aletschhorn (1866), and Wetterhorn (1869). He added immeasurably to the sport by his pioneering ascents, but also by his development of climbing techniques, with his strong preference for rocks over snow. His high proportion of successful climbs (or, to put it colloquially, his 'hit rate') was outstanding. Tyndall's mountain books, beginning with *The glaciers of the Alps* (1860) and *Mountaineering in 1861* (1861), were all bestsellers, going into several reprints and into translation. *Hours of exercise in the Alps* (1871) gave a reflective view of his career in the mountains after his retirement from climbing, and *Forms of water in clouds, rivers and glaciers* (1872) concentrated on his Alpine researches and related topics.

Tyndall and Ireland

From the evidence of his journal, Tyndall as a young man was anxious to leave Ireland and showed no sympathy for the declining Irish language around Youghal. His Belfast address (1874) and subsequent *Apology* (a forthright defence) evoked from the catholic church in Ireland a pastoral letter (1875) denouncing him for blasphemy. This is believed to have been written for Cardinal Paul Cullen by P. F. Moran. Moran, like Tyndall, came from Leighlinbridge, where both have commemorative monuments. Tyndall in later life became an active opponent of home rule for Ireland, and his unionism was a means of reconciliation between himself and G. G. Stokes, who opposed him in the politics of science. Otherwise, one of his most enduring links with Ireland was as scientific advisor to the Board of Trade and Trinity House; in this capacity he supported from 1869 a gas illumination system for lighthouses, developed in Dublin by John Wigham. In 1883 he resigned as scientific advisor in protest against Trinity House's treatment of Wigham, who was eventually compensated. Tyndall was proposed for honorary membership of the RIA in 1866; but Darwin was elected instead, and Tyndall never subsequently became an MRIA.

He married (29 February 1876) Louisa Charlotte (1845–1940), eldest daughter of Lord Claud Hamilton, the brother of James Hamilton, 1st duke of Abercorn; the marriage, though happy, was childless. After repeated illness, aggravated by the medical treatments of the time, Tyndall died on 4 December 1893 from an accidental overdose of chloral, and was buried in Haslemere, Surrey, near his Hindhead home.

Correspondence and other papers survive in the BL, Cambridge University Library, and other archives. Many likenesses are in the National Portrait Gallery and the Royal Institution of Great Britain, both in London. Tyndall is commemorated by the names of towns, mountains, and other geographical features in North America, New Zealand, and the Alps (notably Pic Tyndall on the Matterhorn), and by monuments erected by his widow (who also wrote the *DNB* article on him) at Bel Alp, Switzerland, and at Leighlinbridge.

Norman McMillan

Sources

J. Tyndall, *Discourses given by John Tyndall at the Royal Institution of Great Britain*, i: *1853–71*; ii: *1872–86*; A. S. Eve and C. H. Creasey, *Life and work of John Tyndall* (1945); D. Thompson, 'George Edmondson (1798–1863)', *The Friends' Quarterly*, x (1956), 24–9; J. R. Friday, R. M. MacCleod and P. Shepherd, *John Tyndall, natural philosopher, 1820–1893: catalogue of correspondence, journals and collected papers* (1974); S. Brush, 'The prayer test', *American Scientist*, lxi (1974), 561–3; R. Barton, 'The X-club: science, religion and social change in Victorian England' (Ph.D. thesis, Pennsylvania, 1976); idem, *The scientific clerisy: examples of influence through journalism and education* (1976); W. H. Brock, N. D. McMillan and C. Mollan (eds), *John Tyndall: essays on a natural philosopher* (1981); N. D. McMillan and J. Meehan, *John Tyndall: 'X'emplar of scientific and technological education* (1981); J. Morrell and A. Thackray (eds), *Gentlemen of science: early correspondence of the British Association for the Advancement of Science* (1985); B. V. Lightman, *The origins of agnosticism: Victorian unbelief and the limits of knowledge* (1987); N. D. McMillan, 'British physics – the Irish role in the origin, differentiation and organisation of a profession', *Physics Education*, xxiii (1988), 272–8; idem, 'Tyndall studies: Part 1, biography'; 'Part 2, Tyndall in the mountains', *Tyndall Mountaineering Club commemorative book* (1991), 4–8, 44–5; idem, 'John Tyndall', *Dictionnaire des philosophes de France* (1982; enlarged entry in 2nd ed., 1993); N. D. McMillan, D. D. G. McMillan and J. Cooke (eds), *Prometheus's fire: a history of scientific and technological education in Ireland* (2000) (analysis of the G. G. Stokes–Tyndall correspondence); J. D. Burchfield, 'John Tyndall and the Royal Institution', F. A. J. L. James (ed.), *The common purposes of life* (2002), 147–68; J. S. Wilkins, 'Spontaneous generation and the origin of life' (2004; www.talkorigins.org/faqs/abioprob/spontaneous-generation.html); B. Lightman, 'Scientists and materialists' in G. Cantor and S. Shuttleworth (eds), *Science serialised: representations of the sciences in nineteenth-century periodicals* (2004), 199–237

George Francis Fitzgerald

(1851–1901)

PHYSICIST

George Francis Fitzgerald was born on 3 August 1851 at Kill o' the Grange rectory, Monkstown, Co. Dublin, the son of William Fitzgerald (1814–83), who went on to become bishop of Cork and later of Killaloe, and his wife Anne Frances, a niece of George Johnstone Stoney. In later life Fitzgerald lived at 7 Ely Place, Dublin. After an education at home, in which he was tutored by Mary Boole, the sister of George Boole, he entered TCD and took first place in mathematics and experimental science in 1871. Having secured a college fellowship in 1877, he became Erasmus Smith professor of natural and experimental philosophy in 1881, and the rest of his life centred on that role. In 1883 he was elected FRS, and he was awarded the Society's Royal medal in 1899. He served as president of the Physical Society of London in 1892–3 and was an active editor of the *Philosophical Magazine* in the 1890s. He married (21 December 1883) Harriette May (1861–1919), daughter of John Hewitt Jellett, in a further intertwining of notable Trinity lineages; they had eight children.

Fitzgerald was the outstanding physicist of his generation working in Ireland and an acknowledged international leader of his subject. Among physicists his main claim to fame is the Lorentz–Fitzgerald contraction, which has an enduring place in the theory of relativity. In 1889 the idea occurred to him, while visiting Oliver Lodge in Liverpool, that the length of a moving body should be reduced in its direction of motion, as an explanation of the puzzling null result of the Michelson–Morley experiment. This he published in a short note in the American journal *Science*, forgetting about it until Hendrik Lorentz published something similar several years later. The brevity of Fitzgerald's paper invited later misunderstanding, it being assumed to have depended largely on guesswork; rather it arose out of his deep understanding of the electromagnetic theory formulated by James Clerk Maxwell. Indeed, he was the doyen of an international 'invisible college' devoted to the subject. These so-called Maxwellians included many of the greatest physicists of that period: J. J. Thomson, Oliver Lodge, Joseph Larmor, Heinrich Hertz and Oliver Heaviside. Out of their debates arose another remarkable inspiration for Fitzgerald, to the effect that electromagnetic waves might be generated by oscillating electrical circuits. This was vindicated by Hertz in 1887, in an experiment that was the birth of the age of radio transmission. Nevertheless, Fitzgerald seems to have played little part in the practical development of radio by Guglielmo Marconi and others.

Many other fertile ideas (and a few wrong ones) were promulgated by him in correspondence or short publications, and at the meetings of the British Association for the Advancement of Science. For example, he speculated that the speed of a moving body could not exceed that of light, and that gravity might have to do with a distortion of space by matter. On a more practical level, he participated with W. H. S. Monck in the first photoelectric measurements in astronomy. He recognised his own tendency to 'rush out with all sorts of crude notions in hope that they may set others thinking and lead to some advance' (*Scientific writings*). His collected works would do little justice to his contemporary stature and influence (even if supplemented by dozens of items not included), were they not prefaced by extended tributes in obituaries.

Closer to home, Fitzgerald cut an imposing figure in TCD and Dublin society as 'the idol of the undergraduates and the hope of the senior men' (ibid.), campaigning for science and decrying the more traditional subjects. He promoted sports, and in 1895 put his own athletic ability to use in flying a Lilienthal glider (the first in the British Isles) in the College Park. He was active in the Dublin University Experimental Science Association, where the latest inventions were regularly displayed and discussed. His students and assistants included E. E. Fournier D'Albe, John Joly, Thomas Preston, J. S. E. Townsend, Frederick Trouton and T. R. Lyle. He also served as a commissioner of national education and intermediate education, seeking to promote a practical approach and the foundation of technical schools. His impassioned speeches on this theme, to which he intended to devote his later years, retain much of their force. His name has been memorialised in the renaming of the Physical Laboratory (1906) at TCD, latterly the Fitzgerald Building. He had just begun to plan for its construction at the time of his death of a stomach ulcer on 22 February 1901. John Joly saw the project through to completion with the support of Lord Iveagh. The building houses portraits of Fitzgerald and a bronze plaque, on which the undergraduate Fitzgerald medal is based.

Of the many anguished obituaries (including one in the new American journal *Physical Review*), Oliver Lodge's (reprinted in *Scientific writings*) goes to the heart of his nature: 'impulsive, hot-tempered and totally unselfconscious; he alternated between abstract meditation, highly individual experimentation, and passionate advocacy for his favourite causes'. In one intemperate episode provoked by the home rule movement, he proposed to transfer Trinity College to England. But he was kind and generous as well and was personally responsible for saving the eccentric English genius Oliver Heaviside from poverty, by framing a strategy that would obtain for him a government pension and induce him to accept it. Others of similar gifts and steadier temperament (such as William Thomson, Lord Kelvin) registered more explicit achievements, but Fitzgerald's hidden influence is increasingly recognised. A substantial collection of Fitzgerald's letters is available in the RDS Library and Archives.

Denis Weaire

Sources

The scientific writings of George Francis FitzGerald, ed. J. Larmor (1902); B. Hunt, *The Maxwellians* (1991)

George Gabriel Stokes
(1819–1903)

MATHEMATICIAN, PHYSICIST
AND SCIENTIFIC ADMINISTRATOR

George Gabriel Stokes, 1st baronet, was born on 13 August 1819 in Skreen, Co. Sligo, youngest child among five sons and three daughters of Gabriel Stokes (1761–1834), rector of Skreen, and his wife Elizabeth, daughter of John Haughton, rector of Kilrea, Co. Londonderry. A brother and sister died in infancy. His three surviving elder brothers all became clergymen; one was archdeacon of Armagh. George Gabriel Stokes was a great-grandson of Gabriel Stokes (d. 1768), and was thus related to many distinguished clergymen, doctors and scholars, including William Stokes (d. 1878), who was his second cousin. His early education was at home; he was taught by his father and by the parish clerk. From 1831 he attended Dr R. H. Wall's school in Hume Street, Dublin, proceeding in 1835 to Bristol College in England. Teachers who greatly influenced him there included the Irish-born headmaster Joseph Henry Jerrard (d. 1853) and Francis Newman (brother of John Henry Newman), both able mathematicians.

Academic career and scientific work

Stokes entered Pembroke College, Cambridge, in 1837, graduating as senior wrangler and first Smith's prizeman (1841). After graduation, he was elected a fellow of Pembroke, a position he held until 1857 when, under college statutes, his marriage rendered him ineligible for fellowship. When a new statute permitted fellows to marry, he was re-elected in 1869 and held the position until his death. In 1849 he was appointed Lucasian professor of mathematics at Cambridge and supplemented his rather limited income from the post by contributing scientific articles to encyclopaedias and by holding a lectureship in physics at the Government School of Mines, London (1854–60). Unlike his predecessor in the Lucasian chair, Stokes lectured regularly. For several decades, Britain's ablest students of mathematics and physics profited from Stokes's rigorous lectures and experiment demonstrations. He was convinced that physical experiments and observations were of primary importance in science, and throughout his career retained an interest in the practical applications of physics, acting as scientific consultant to the optical-instrument maker Howard Grubb. He was also a consultant on lighthouse illuminants for Trinity House and was advisor to the Trigonometrical Survey of India.

His early work was in hydrodynamics, and he gained recognition in 1845 for his paper on the internal friction, or viscosity, of an incompressible fluid, 'On the theories of the internal friction of fluids in motion, and of the equilibrium and motion of elastic solids', deducing the equations of motion for elastic solids. Arguing from the law of continuity, he held that the equations of motion he obtained for an elastic solid were the same for viscous fluids; he was later to extend this insight in his work on the luminiferous ether. His report on recent developments in hydrodynamics for the British Association for the Advancement of Science in 1846 confirmed his reputation as a promising young talent. In one of his most important papers on hydrodynamics, 'On the effect of the internal friction of fluids on the motion of pendulums', presented in 1850, he applied his theory of the internal friction of fluids to the behaviour of pendulums in liquids and also in air, indicated how the friction of the air would affect measurements of the pendulum's motion, and derived an expression for the drag force on a sphere or spheres moving relative to a fluid of known viscosity.

This expression now forms part of the set of Navier–Stokes equations, which bear the name of Claude-Louis Navier, a French scientist, as well as that of Stokes; Navier had been engaged in earlier studies of the physics of flow and viscosity, but Stokes's formulations improved on his work. The Navier–Stokes equations are a set of differential equations that are of fundamental importance in many applications of hydrodynamics. They are used in meteorology, for instance, to explain how clouds, composed of tiny water droplets, are able to form in the atmosphere, because the drops are so small that the friction of the air operates against gravity to keep them in suspension. Stokes dealt with the formation of clouds in his original paper, but many other economically important applications have been discovered since. The flow of liquids in pipes, clouds of dust, and pollutants, airflow over aircraft wings, and even blood flow, are all phenomena that can be analysed and predicted using Navier–Stokes equations.

An 1849 paper by Stokes on the variation of gravity was also based on a further development of his work with pendulums. In it he discussed the changes in the value of the force of gravity over the earth's surface and pointed out that these could be measured without needing to make any assumptions about the conditions pertaining in the earth's interior. This suggested methodology was the major impetus to the modern science of geodesy. Stokes also worked on the physics of water waves, and on summer holidays in Ireland in the early 1880s he waded into the sea at Portstewart Strand to take measurements. These enabled him to validate a hypothesis about the greatest possible angle of a wave crest.

Stokes devoted a great deal of attention to the wave theory of light, and to investigation of the properties of the ether. Physicists of the day accepted the concept of the ether (or aether) as a basis for understanding fundamental aspects of the laws of nature; the ether was a medium of unascertained composition, within which light waves could propagate and through which heavenly bodies were able to move. Stokes's knowledge of the properties of fluids led him to regard the ether as an incompressible elastic medium, perhaps jelly-like, partaking of the properties of both liquid and solid states. This description accounted for much of what was then known about the behaviour of light, and contemporaries were impressed by Stokes's theory. The conceptualisation enabled him to make important additions to the mathematical formulations of the theory of the diffraction and polarisation of light, which have survived the almost complete rejection by the scientific community of the concept of the ether.

In 1851 he became interested in the blue shimmer elicited from near the surface of an otherwise colourless and transparent solution of sulphate of quinine when it was illuminated (a phenomenon that had been reported by Sir William Herschel in 1845). He carried out experiments which showed that this phenomenon contradicted the hitherto unchallenged Newtonian principles of the prismatic analysis of light, as the blue colour appeared even when it was not a constituent of the exciting incident light. He realised that the blue shimmer was caused by the quinine solution absorbing invisible ultraviolet rays, which were then emitted at longer wavelengths, visible as blue light. He named this emission of light 'fluorescence'. He later discovered that quartz, rather than glass, prisms could be used to study the ultraviolet segment of the spectrum (glass absorbs the UV wavelengths); and suggested that fluorescence would be useful in chemical analyses. For this fundamentally important research, published (1852) in the *Philosophical Transactions of the Royal Society* as 'On the change of the refrangibility of light', he was awarded the Rumford medal by the Royal Society in the same year.

In discussions around 1854 with his close friend William Thomson, Stokes speculated on the possibility that the Fraunhofer lines in the spectrum of sunlight could be used to elucidate the chemical composition of the sun. Since he did not publish on this topic, he was unwilling to claim that he had anticipated the discovery of the principles of spectrum analysis in 1859 in the work of Gustav Robert Kirchhoff and Robert Wilhelm Bunsen. However, Stokes is associated with, and his name perpetuated in, an important device for measuring sunshine hours; the Campbell–Stokes recorder was invented by John Francis Campbell, but greatly improved by Stokes in 1879; it is a simple device that focuses the sun's rays to burn a trace on a card, and it was for at least 100 years the most widely used sunshine recorder in the world. His final mathematical study of light – an important paper on the dynamical theory of double refraction – was presented to the British Association in 1862.

Although only a few of his papers are purely mathematical, they are of great importance. His insights into the asymptotic forms of functions were highly original and very relevant to applications such as the explanation of diffraction effects in the rainbow. Their importance is recognised in the use of the term 'Stokes phenomena' for such manifestations. However, the 'Stokes theorem' or 'Stokes formula' used in vector calculus, and of great importance in mechanics, was first formulated by William Thomson in a letter to Stokes; it came to be associated with Stokes because he set it in the Cambridge tripos examinations.

Stokes is remembered, rather unusually for a mathematical physicist, for an important discovery in physiology. This came about as a result of his work in spectroscopy. A German biochemist, Ernst Hoppe-Seyler, in 1862 had described the absorption spectrum of the red pigment in blood, which in 1864 he named 'haemoglobin'; when he repeated Hoppe-Seyler's experiment, Stokes was intrigued by the resulting spectrum. It occurred to him that it would be interesting to try to produce the change of colour from arterial to venous blood, by adding a reducing agent to a dilute solution of blood. When he added alkaline ferrous tartrate to blood, the blood darkened in colour, but when the resulting solution was shaken in air, it appeared again to have the scarlet colour of oxygenated blood. Crucially, the absorption spectra at different stages of the experiment clearly indicated the role of haemoglobin in carrying oxygen in the blood. Stokes's 1864 publication was thus a breakthrough in physiology and ultimately in biochemistry and medicine.

Science administration and public life

In 1851 Stokes was elected a fellow of the Royal Society and served as secretary (1854–85) and president (1885–90). Thirty years as secretary, dealing with all aspects of the Society's work at a time when it was becoming an increasingly professional and complex institution, with a developing public and international role, left little time for Stokes's own research and publishing. Among many other tasks, he undertook the responsibility for the Society's *Philosophical Transactions* and personally reviewed and corrected over 100 papers between 1852 and 1900, as well as engaging in a far-flung and voluminous correspondence with authors and other referees. When he retired after serving on the council of the Royal Society from 1853 to 1892, he was awarded the Copley medal (1893), honouring his service to the Society as well as his scientific achievements. In 1887 he was elected unopposed as Conservative MP for Cambridge University – the first scientific man to represent the university in parliament since Sir Isaac Newton – and sat in the house of commons until 1891. In 1859 he was secretary to the Cambridge University commission, and in 1888–9 he sat on the royal commission on the University of London. For many years he was involved with the work of the Solar Physics Laboratory in London.

From childhood on, Stokes was a profoundly religious man, though his beliefs were not founded on an unexamined childhood faith; he was very much influenced by the thought of the day and by his own scientific training, and he became a leading advocate of natural theology. Stokes and fellow thinkers hoped that it would be possible to develop a theology derived from the operation of reason and supported by science, rather than deriving from a system of belief relying on revelation or appeal to the miraculous. He served (1886–1903) as president of the Victoria Institute in London, founded to examine the relationship between Christianity and contemporary thought. He was the first Burnett lecturer at Aberdeen (1883–5); the lectureship was founded with the intention of providing evidences of divine goodness. Stokes's Burnett lectures on the nature of light were published in 1887 (second ed. 1892); he did not otherwise publish a full-scale consideration of optical topics. He was Gifford lecturer at Edinburgh (1891–3); the prestigious Gifford lectureships were also founded to promote the knowledge of God. Stokes's theological essays were collected and published as *Natural theology* in two volumes

(1891, 1893). In his *Conditional immortality: a help to sceptics* (1897), Stokes tried to deal with what he saw as the horrifying prospect of eternal punishment; he believed that an eternity in torment was not part of the Bible's message, and that immortality would only be granted to those who merited eternity in God's presence.

Public reputation

On the occasion of the jubilee of his professorship in Cambridge in 1899, fifty years after taking up the post, Stokes was celebrated by the contemporary scientific world as one of the outstanding thinkers of the age; the university marked the occasion with two days of academic festivities, attended by distinguished guests from all over the world, and he received the Arago medal from the Institute of France, as well as a gold medal from his own university. In October 1902, he was elected master of Pembroke. He was an honorary member of scientific societies in Edinburgh, Uppsala, Göttingen, France, Vienna, Washington, Glasgow, Rome, Berlin, Moscow, Belgium and Turin, and received honorary doctorates from the universities of Oxford, Cambridge, Edinburgh, Glasgow, Aberdeen, Dublin, Victoria and Christiania (Oslo). He was awarded the Helmholtz medal by the Prussian Academy of Science. He was a knight of the Prussian order Pour la Mérite (an honour accorded also to his kinsman William Stokes) and was president of the British Association for the Advancement of Science at its Exeter meeting of 1869.

In the early twenty-first century, more than 100 years after his death, he was commemorated in the naming of a research institute in the University of Limerick, in an important annual summer school held in his honour in Skreen, Co. Sligo, and in the name of a large-scale science investment programme funded by the Irish government (2007). His name is also perpetuated in a number of scientific terms familiar to scientists in a variety of disciplines worldwide. The 'Stokes line' is a spectrum line observed in fluorescence; its wavelength is longer than that of the exciting radiation and thus is in agreement with 'Stokes's law', formulated in 1852, which holds that the wavelength of emitted fluorescent light is always greater than the wavelength of the exciting light. This effect is measured in Stokes and anti-Stokes Raman scattering in spectroscopy; the associated 'Stokes shift' is the name given to the conversion in fluorescence of shorter wavelengths of light into longer visible wavelengths. 'Stokes parameters' are used in the description of the state of polarisation of an electromagnetic wave, such as a beam of light. 'Stokes's solution' (or 'Stokes's reagent') is ferrous tartrate, a reducing agent used in the biochemical study of blood; a 'stokes' is the unit of kinematic velocity, and there are craters on Mars and on the moon bearing his name.

Private life

Stokes met Mary Susanna Robinson (d. 1899), daughter of Thomas Romney Robinson, at a meeting of the British Association; like several of her relatives, including Arthur A. Rambaut, Mary Robinson was interested in science. However, the apparently cold-hearted emphasis on his commitment to mathematical studies in Stokes's letters to her during their courtship, and presumably also when they met, was almost too much for her, and at one stage she thought of calling off their wedding. His legendary shyness and intellectual intensity and his lack of emotional experience were probably to blame. However, plans went ahead and they were married in Armagh on 4 July 1857, when Stokes was 38. They were to have two sons and three daughters in what turned out to be a very happy marriage, though there were great sadnesses when two of their daughters died in infancy, and the younger son, a doctor, died before his father, in 1893, of an accidental overdose of morphine. George Gabriel Stokes was created a baronet by Queen Victoria in July 1889; his eldest son, Arthur Romney Stokes, succeeded as 2nd baronet when George Gabriel Stokes died in his daughter's home in Cambridge on 1 February 1903. He was accorded the traditional funeral dignities of a master of Pembroke and was buried at Mill Road cemetery in the town.

His collected scientific papers were published between 1880 and 1905 in five volumes, the first three edited by himself, and two posthumous volumes edited by Joseph Larmor. His unpublished papers are in the library of Cambridge University. The voluminous correspondence between Stokes and his friend William Thomson, Lord Kelvin, edited (2 vols, 1990) by David B. Wilson, is a very valuable source of information on the history of science. Kelvin was very fond of Stokes, and like other recipients, gratefully acknowledged the intellectual stimulus and mathematical and scientific assistance provided in untold numbers of letters which Stokes somehow found time to write to scientific friends. He knew almost all of the great nineteenth-century scientists of the UK and corresponded and collaborated fruitfully with many of them. The importance of Stokes's influence on the science of his day as administrator, arbiter, consultant, experimentalist, facilitator, teacher, theologian, and theorist can scarcely be overstated.

Linde Lunney and Enda Leaney

Sources

G. G. Stokes, 'On the reduction and oxidation of the colouring matter of the blood', *Philosophical Transactions of the Royal Society*, xiii (1864), 355–64; *Nature*, lxvii (1903), 337–8; *Proceedings of the Royal Society of London*, lxxv: *containing obituaries ... for the period 1898–1904 ...* (1905), 199–216; Joseph Larmor, *Memoir and scientific correspondence of the late Sir George Gabriel Stokes – including personal and biographical recollections* (1907) (portr.); *WWW*; *DNB*; Burke, *Peerage* (1912), 1793; Burke, *IFR* (1976), 1050–56; David B. Wilson, *Kelvin and Stokes: a comparative study in Victorian physics* (1987); John C. McTernan, *Worthies of Sligo: profiles of eminent Sligonians of other days* (1994), 62–5; Norman McMillan, 'Ireland and the reform of the politics and government of British science and education', *Prometheus's fire: a history of scientific and technological education in Ireland* (2000), 501–24 (portr.); Alastair Wood, 'George Gabriel Stokes 1819–1903' in Ken Houston (ed.), *Creators of mathematics: the Irish connection* (2000), 33–8 (portr.); Alistair Wood, 'George Gabriel Stokes 1819–1903' in Mark McCartney and Andrew Whitaker (eds), *Physicists of Ireland: passion and precision* (2003), 85–94; assistance and information from Prof. Denis Weaire, FRS, MRIA, and from Prof. James Lunney; Hal White, 'CHEM-342 Introduction to biochemistry', Department of Chemistry and Biochemistry, University of Delaware, www.udel.edu; Science Foundation Ireland, 'Grants and awards: SFI Stokes professorship and lectureship programme (2007)', www.sfi.ie; 'George Stokes biography', Stokes Research Institute, www.stokes.ie; 'The Fourth Stokes Summer School. Skreen, County Sligo, Ireland 18–22 June 2004', www.cmde.dcu.ie/Stokes/announce.htm; 'George Gabriel Stokes 1819–1903', http://www.giffordlectures.org; Michael W. Davidson, 'George Gabriel Stokes', 'Molecular Expressions: science optics and you', http://www.micro.magnet.fsu.edu/optics/timeline/people/stokes.html (many of these websites include photos; internet material accessed June 2007)

Agnes Clerke
(1842–1907)

HISTORIAN OF ASTRONOMY
AND SCIENTIFIC WRITER

Agnes Mary Clerke was born on 10 February 1842 in Skibbereen, Co. Cork, second child and younger daughter of John William Clerke, manager of the Provincial Bank, Bridge Street, and his wife Catherine Mary, youngest sister of the politician and lawyer Rickard Deasy. Agnes and her sister Ellen were educated entirely at home by their intellectual parents. Their father, a graduate of TCD, was well versed in the sciences, and maintained a telescope with which he provided a time-service for the town of Skibbereen. Instructed by him, Agnes covered a substantial course of basic astronomy while still a young girl. Later, her brother Aubrey, who excelled in mathematics at university, coached her in more advanced topics.

In 1861 the Clerkes moved to Dublin when the father became court registrar to his brother-in-law. After some years' residence there, the sisters spent ten years in Italy, principally in Florence, where they continued their studies privately, becoming fluent linguists. Agnes's particular interest at that time was the science of the renaissance. In 1877 the entire family settled in London, where Agnes, at the age of thirty-five, commenced her career as a professional writer with twice-yearly contributions, mainly with an astronomical flavour, to the erudite *Edinburgh Review*. Her excellent scientific biographies in the *Encyclopaedia*

Britannica, begun in 1879, including those on Galileo and Laplace, brought her name to the notice of the educated public.

She now set about studying the 'new astronomy' or astrophysics, a relatively new branch of astronomy, working alone in the library of the British Museum. This resulted in the work for which she is best known and which remains a classic of the history of science, *A popular history of astronomy during the nineteenth century* (1885). The *History*, labelled 'popular' to denote that it was a non-mathematical treatment, was an immediate success for its usefulness to the professional astronomer and its appeal to the general reader. It went into three editions in its author's lifetime.

The book brought her a wide circle of admirers, including the astronomer and writer Joseph Norman (later Sir Norman) Lockyer, founder of the journal *Nature*, and William (later Sir William) Huggins and his Irish wife and collaborator Margaret, who became a close personal friend. Among her correspondents were Edward Holden, first director of Lick Observatory in California, E. C. Pickering of Harvard, and leading astronomers in the United States and Europe whose work she reported in British and American journals, principally *Nature*, *The Observatory*, *Knowledge*, and *Astronomy and Astro-Physics*. So reliable, thoughtful, and wide-reaching were her analyses that she became a revered authority and an influential propagandist, especially in the rapidly expanding field of astronomical spectroscopy. Her practical experience, however, was limited to three months in 1888 spent at the Royal Observatory, Cape of Good Hope, as the guest of its director David (later Sir David) Gill, where she made actual astronomical observations of stellar spectra which were published. She declined an opportunity of employment at the Royal Observatory at Greenwich, preferring to devote her life to writing. Her second important book, *The system of the stars* (1890), championed the one-system universe, the favoured model at that time. In this system all objects are held to belong to one finite agglomeration, as opposed to the rival model of multiple island universes filling infinite space. The one-system model as defined by Clerke was widely accepted till the discovery of the expanding universe in the 1920s.

Clerke had close associations with the Royal Institution, where she was an assiduous attendant at its scientific lectures. In 1893 she received the Institution's distinguished Actonian prize, awarded septennially for work demonstrating the 'beneficence of the Almighty' in science. She was commissioned to write an account of Sir James Dewar's experiments in the liquefaction of gases for the Hodgkins Trust (*Low temperature research at the Royal Institution 1893–1900* (1901)). She was elected a Member of the Royal Institution in 1902.

In 1903 Clerke published her third major book, *Problems in astrophysics*, which attempted to identify unresolved questions and to suggest projects that might solve them. This book was deemed her most impressive by her contemporaries, though, as the problems of the day gave way to later quite different ones, it has not proved as enduring as her *History*. Shortly after it appeared, Clerke was made an honorary member of the all-male Royal Astronomical Society. *Problems in astrophysics* was followed by *Modern cosmogonies* (1905), a popular historical account of the various models of the world leading to contemporary ideas in physics and biology. It was noteworthy for its philosophical tone, and for its revelation of the author's antipathy to the agnostic view of science.

Clerke was a core contributor to the original volumes of the *Dictionary of national biography*, providing 150 entries, to which may be added some thirty biographies of astronomers in *Encyclopaedia Britannica* (eleventh ed., 1911). Among her subjects were the Herschels – William, Caroline and John – whose lives she also published in book form (*The Herschels and modern astronomy* (1895)). Her writings on non-scientific subjects include some charming essays on references to everyday life in Homer's poetry, *Familiar studies in Homer* (1892). Clerke's sister, Ellen Mary (1841–1906), pursued her own career as a poet, writer and journalist, principally in the London catholic press.

Agnes Clerke died at her home in Redcliffe Square on 20 January 1907. A plaque commemorating her and her sister marks their birthplace in Skibbereen. Agnes has also been commemorated by the naming of a crater on the moon.

M. T. Brück

Sources

Lady [Margaret] Huggins, *Agnes Mary Clerke and Ellen Mary Clerke, an appreciation* (1907); M. T. Brück, *Agnes Mary Clerke and the rise of astrophysics* (2002) (bibliog., portr.); eadem, 'Agnes Clerke's work as a scientific biographer', *Irish Astronomical Journal*, vol. xxiv, no. 2 (1997), 193–8

William Thomson
(1824–1907)

PHYSICIST

William Thomson, 1st Baron Kelvin of Largs, was born on 26 June 1824 at College Square East, Belfast, son of James Thomson, who taught in the RBAI, and Margaret Thomson (née Gardner). Together with his brother James Thomson he was tutored from an early age by his dedicated father, who was widowed in 1830. The Thomsons were of Scottish Covenanter stock and had a farm in Co. Down until 1847. In 1831 James was appointed to the chair of mathematics at Glasgow University. By 1834 William had already matriculated in the university, where he and his brother excelled in a variety of subjects. Having reached the relative maturity of sixteen years, he left for Cambridge in 1841 without taking a degree. Already a devoted student of the French school of mathematics, and the author of several papers, he was clearly bound for great success in the mathematical tripos yet somehow was placed only as second wrangler in 1845. He was consoled by first place in the Smith's prize competition.

After a brief period as a fellow of Peterhouse and a sojourn in France, he returned to Glasgow as professor of natural philosophy in 1846. He remained in that position to the end, resisting temptations to move. These included the Cavendish chair at Cambridge, offered and declined three times. Despite his model career in Cambridge, which included athletic pursuits (single sculls, appropriately), he saw positive advantages in remaining remote from the energy-sapping centres of power and bureaucracy that lay to the south. He did not refuse responsibility (for example, as editor of *Philosophical Magazine*, and president of the Royal Society), but he preferred it at arm's length.

Thomson was elected FRS (1851), was awarded the Copley medal (1883), was knighted (1866), became Lord Kelvin (1892), and was one of the founding recipients of the Order of Merit (1902). To these honours were added a very long list of foreign academic awards and recognition by a splendid professorial jubilee celebration in 1896. At the end of this life of extraordinary fulfilment, he was still active, although bypassed by the new currents in physics. He died on 17 December 1907 at home at Netherhall, Largs, and was buried near Isaac Newton in Westminster abbey.

Kelvin applied his prodigious energy and talents to a wide range of physical research, from fundamental speculation (vortex model of the atom, speculation on the ether) to the commercialisation of many inventions. His mind was constantly on the move, as evidenced by his notebooks, now kept in the Cambridge University Library, and he was tenacious in working out fresh ideas in numerical calculations and mechanical models. In this he was self-reliant, but he collaborated with P. G. Tait on an important textbook, *Treatise on natural philosophy* (1867).

Optics, elasticity, electricity, magnetism, thermodynamics, hydrodynamics, navigation, geophysics, crystallography, metrology and telegraphy by no means exhaust the contents of his more than 650 papers. On the fundamental side, his name is enshrined in the Kelvin unit of temperature, effectively introduced by him in 1848 as the absolute thermometric scale. He contributed (together with Clausius and Carnot) to the confused but ultimately fruitful debate on the emerging theory of thermodynamics, and shares credit for its key concept of entropy. Characteristically, his deep understanding of this subject led him to inventions such as air cooling by refrigeration, which was to be found among his many patents.

In commercial terms, Thomson's most successful work was in submarine telegraphy. Following the failure of the first transatlantic cable he successfully persuaded the promoters of a further attempt to adopt his ideas for improvement, which included the use of a sensitive mirror galvanometer of his own design. In approaching difficult technical problems such as this one, he was able to call on mathematical theory, practical skill, and a wide appreciation of the properties of materials. While less prominent in the conventional histories of science, his many investigations of materials formed one of the foundation stones of today's solid-state physics. It retains much of his terminology ('permeability', 'susceptibility', 'bulk modulus').

One of the few weaknesses of his authoritative view of physical science was a reluctance to accept fully Maxwell's electromagnetic theory of light (see G. F. Fitzgerald above). He stubbornly refused to abandon the notion that light was a vibration of a material ether, which was 'a real thing'. Maxwell's abstract fields did not appeal to his realistic view of the physical world, in which the mechanics of matter took pride of place. This was a more serious shortcoming than his oft-cited mistaken estimate of the age of the Earth.

From his time in Cambridge, Kelvin maintained a close correspondence with G. G. Stokes. Another Cambridge Irishman, Joseph Larmor, edited his collected works. He readily acknowledged his Irish identity and was a staunch supporter of the unionist cause.

Following the death (1870) of his first wife, Margaret Crum (m. 1852), he married (1874) Frances Anna, of the Blandy family of Madeira wine producers. There was no issue of either marriage. In his later years he lived at Netherhall, a substantial mansion that he had built on the Ayrshire coast, and cruised on his 126-ton yacht, the *Lalla Rookh*.

Lord Kelvin was a towering presence in the world of physics for more than half a century. He played a defining role in its emergence as a distinct subject and has often been called the last of the great classical physicists. There is a museum in Glasgow to house a selection of his many instruments and other memorabilia. Numerous biographies and a fascinating published collection of the Kelvin–Stokes correspondence document his long career. Various portraits exist in Cambridge and Glasgow, and a splendid statue looks out towards his birthplace from the botanic gardens of Belfast.

Denis Weaire

Sources

C. Smith and M. N. Wise, *Energy and empire: a biographical study of Lord Kelvin* (1989)

Bindon Blood Stoney
(1828–1909)

CIVIL ENGINEER

Bindon Blood Stoney was born on 13 June 1828 at Oakley Park, King's County (Offaly), younger son of George Stoney and his wife Anne, second daughter of Bindon Blood of Cranagher and Rockforest, Co. Clare. He had one elder brother, the renowned mathematical physicist George Johnstone Stoney, and one sister, who married a cousin, William Fitzgerald, later bishop of Cork (1857–62) and of Killaloe (1862–83). Stoney was privately educated at home while his father's properties lost value in the post-Napoleonic depression and were sold during the famine of 1845–52. After attending TCD, where in 1850 he obtained his BA and a diploma in civil engineering with distinction, he immediately joined his elder brother at the observatory of William Parsons, 3rd earl of Rosse, at Parsonstown (Birr) to assist with astronomical observations using what was then the world's largest telescope. Stoney improved the known delineation of nebulae and determined the spiral nature of the great nebula in Andromeda.

In 1852–3 he worked on surveys for a railway in Spain. Having returned to Ireland, he was appointed in 1854 as resident engineer (under James Barton) on the construction of the railway viaduct designed by Sir John Macneill spanning the River Boyne near Drogheda, Co. Louth, till its completion in 1855. His pioneering work with Barton in building a metal bridge with a span of such dimensions using shock-absorbent wrought-iron latticed bars rather than a continuity of plate was possibly the earliest such example. It was the basis for his later two-volume publication *The theory of strains in girders and similar structures, with observations on the strength and other properties of materials* (1866), dubbed 'Stoney on strains' and reproduced in two further editions (1873, 1886).

Meanwhile, in 1856, he became assistant engineer to George Halpin jr, chief engineer (and inspector of works) of the Dublin Port Authority (Ballast Board) at the Ballast Office on Westmoreland Street and remained at Dublin port throughout his impressive subsequent career. He became an associate of the Institution of Civil Engineers (ICE) in January 1858 and a full member in November 1863. Similarly, he became a member of the Institution of Civil Engineers of Ireland (ICEI) in 1857, joint honorary secretary 1862–70, and president 1871–2. During and after this time, from 1858 to 1905, he presented a series of papers to the ICEI, one of which, *Strength and proportions of riveted joints*, was published as a book in 1885. He also presented papers to the ICE.

Stoney's practical achievements had a significant effect on the development of central Dublin. Appointed executive engineer in 1859 owing to the illness of Halpin, he became chief engineer when Halpin retired in 1862. On becoming first chief engineer of the Dublin Port and Docks Board, when it replaced the Ballast Board in 1867, he moved to new offices at Alexandra Road. His main works between Dublin Bay and the city lay within the channel extending from the North Bull and Poolbeg lighthouses westwards to Essex (Grattan) Bridge on the River Liffey. He rebuilt and upgraded berthing facilities on the North Wall quays east of the Custom House in 1864–9. He took his MA at TCD (1870), and in 1871 began to build further eastwards the 700-metre North Wall extension. The installation of his massive 350-ton precast concrete blocks, using a purpose-built diving bell and floating crane, became a world-renowned feat of engineering, and he was awarded the Telford medal and premium of the ICE in 1874 for a paper on this work. He also began forming the Alexandra basin directly behind the Extension, completing its first phase in 1885.

Within the city centre, Stoney rebuilt a number of bridges at key crossings of the Liffey. In 1872–5 he largely rebuilt Essex Bridge, designed in the 1750s by George Semple to his own flamboyant design; it was renamed Grattan Bridge after Henry Grattan the elder. In 1877–80 he redesigned the 1790s Carlisle Bridge of James Gandon, renamed O'Connell Bridge after Daniel O'Connell, to provide a crossing linking Sackville (later O'Connell) Street with the converging streets to the south. He built a new iron swivel bridge in 1877–9, just west of the Custom House. Named Beresford Bridge, it was later renamed Butt Bridge after Isaac Butt and replaced by a wider concrete bridge in 1932.

He erected the North Bull lighthouse (1877–80) to replace the inadequate light on the Bull Wall marking the northern side of the port channel entrance opposite Poolbeg lighthouse. He surrounded the bases of both lighthouses with his trademark concrete monolithic blocks. Elected FRS (1881), he received an honorary LLD (1881) from the University of Dublin, was a member of the RDS, the Institution of Naval Architects, and the RIA (1857), to the *Proceedings* and *Transactions* of which he contributed four papers on the theory of structures. He retired in 1898, was succeeded by his pupil and long-serving assistant, John Purser Griffith, and lived at 14 Elgin Road, Dublin, where his chief recreation was reading the *Times*. He died on 5 May 1909 and was buried in Mount Jerome cemetery.

Stoney married (1879) Susannah Frances, daughter of John Francis Walker, QC, of Grangemore, Co. Dublin; they had one son and two daughters. The *Irish Builder* (15 May 1909) published a glowing obituary of a man of great personal and professional integrity. An excellent portrait photograph is held by the ICEI. Panels on Grattan and O'Connell Bridges bear his name.

Patrick Long

Sources

Ir. Builder, 15 May 1909; *Annual Reg., 1909*; Howard Grubb, 'Memoir of B. B. Stoney', *Proc. Roy. Soc.*, ser. A (1909); *WWW*; *DNB*; Crone (1937 and 1970 eds); Ronald C. Cox, *Bindon Blood Stoney: biography of a port engineer* (1990); J. W. de Courcy, *The Liffey in Dublin* (1996); Ronald C. Cox, *John Purser Griffith 1848–1938, 'grand old man of Irish engineering'* (1998); R. C. Cox and M. H. Gould, *Civil engineering heritage, Ireland* (1998); Douglas Bennett, *The encyclopaedia of Dublin* (revised and expanded ed., 2005), 26, 205; information from Prof. Ronald C. Cox, TCD, and from John Callanan, librarian, ICEI

Osborne Reynolds
(1842–1912)

ENGINEER

Osborne Reynolds was born on 23 August 1842 in Belfast, son of the Rev. Osborne Reynolds and Jane Reynolds (née Hickman). He came from a clerical family: his father, grandfather, and great-grandfather were rectors of Debach, Suffolk. His father was thirteenth wrangler (ranking in the mathematical tripos at Cambridge University) in 1837 and subsequently fellow of Queens' College, Cambridge, principal of Belfast Collegiate School, headmaster of Dedham Grammar School, Essex, and finally, in his turn, rector of Debach.

Reynolds's early education was by his father, first at Dedham and afterwards privately. In 1861, at the age of nineteen, he entered the workshop of Edward Hayes, mechanical engineer, of Stony Stratford, in order (as Hayes expressed it) 'to learn in the shortest time possible how work should be done, and, as far as time would permit, to be made a working mechanic before going to Cambridge to work for honours'. In October 1863, he was admitted to Queens' College, Cambridge, to study for the mathematical tripos. The entry requirements included a pass in Greek achieved by Reynolds through 'the obstinate labour of a few weeks' to reach the standard of the 'previous' examination. He graduated in 1867 as seventh wrangler and was immediately elected to a fellowship of Queens' College.

Reynolds left Cambridge to enter the offices of Lawson & Mansergh, civil engineers in London, but just one year later, in 1868, at the age of twenty-six, he was appointed to the newly established chair of engineering at Owens College, which later became the Victoria University of Manchester. He occupied this chair for thirty-seven years, retiring in 1905. This was almost the first chair of engineering in England. That distinction probably lies with King's College, London, where William Hosking was appointed in 1840 at the same time as Lewis Gordon became regius professor of civil engineering and mechanics at the University of Glasgow. In Ireland the first chair of civil engineering was established at TCD in 1842, while chairs of civil engineering were established at the Queen's Colleges in Belfast, Cork, and Galway in 1849. The selectors for the Owens College chair were highly successful men, distinguished in the practice of business and engineering in the Manchester area, and their selection of such a young and relatively inexperienced engineer seems remarkable. Reynolds's subsequent career proved their choice to be inspired.

Reynolds was of the view that engineering students required a strong scientific training. The course of instruction which he arranged for his students was noteworthy for the thoroughness and completeness of the theoretical groundwork. He was of the opinion that engineering, from the student viewpoint, was a unified whole, requiring the same fundamental training irrespective of the nature of the specialisation to come afterwards in practice. He was equally concerned with the practical aspects of engineering and established and developed the famous Whitworth engineering laboratories. Several of the more important appliances in these laboratories, such as the triple-expansion engines and the hydraulic brakes, were specially designed by Reynolds for study by students and for research and contained many novel features.

There are two aspects to Reynolds's scientific work. As an engineering professor he addressed some major practical issues of his time. These included ship propulsion, pumps, turbines, models of rivers and estuaries, cavitation, condensation of steam, thermodynamics of gas flow, rolling friction and lubrication. But he was also concerned with understanding the fundamental scientific principles underlying engineering processes, and hence he developed fundamental theory in a number of areas of the mechanical sciences. Two examples are presented here as illustrations. Many others might have been similarly selected.

Reynolds conducted experiments of fluid flow in long glass tubes. He was able to demonstrate (in terms of modern notation, not used by Reynolds) that the transition to turbulence of flow in a pipe occurs at a critical value of what is now called 'the Reynolds number'. The critical value of the Reynolds number (for transition to turbulence of pipe flow) is approximately 2,000. Turbulence is an extremely important theoretical and technological problem, since the presence of turbulence increases resistance to motion; it augments heat transfer rates and general diffusion properties of fluids and gases; it creates noise both directly and through forced vibrations of adjacent structures. Reynolds provided insight into turbulent behaviour in a simple experimental situation; research on turbulent behaviour continues unabated to the present, since turbulence normally occurs in complicated geometries and in a variety of environments.

From the middle of the nineteenth century, industrial advance saw the development and operation of a vast range of machines such as lathes, drills, mechanical harvesters, threshing machines, sewing machines, typewriters, road carriages, railway engines and carriages, which depended for their efficient operation on the lubrication of their moving parts. This technology of lubrication, friction and wear is called tribology. There was concern in industry at the weakness in design of bearings, evidenced by failure in operation. This exposed the lack of understanding of the physical basis of effective lubrication. Reynolds sought to establish a hydrodynamic model for the thin film of lubricant in journal bearings which would yield pressure distributions in agreement with experiments. In this he was successful. From his model he identified an equation (now called the 'Reynolds equation') which offers understanding of the underlying scientific basis for the effective operation of gas and fluid bearings. Research on and development of thin film lubrication devices continued to be vigorously active at the start of the twenty-first century.

Osborne Reynolds married first (1868) Charlotte, daughter of Dr Chadwick of Leeds, but unfortunately she died a year later; there was one son from this marriage, who died in 1879. He married secondly (1881) Annie Charlotte, daughter of the Rev. H. Wilkinson, rector of Otley, Suffolk; they had three sons and a daughter. One of the sons graduated in engineering at Manchester in 1908 and later held the Vulcan and Osborne Reynolds fellowships. Failing health caused Reynolds to retire in 1905. His retirement years were spent in Watchet, Somerset, where he died on 21 February 1912. A portrait (1904) by the Hon. John Collier is at Manchester University.

Frank Hodnett

Sources

D. M. McDowell and J. D. Jackson (eds), *Osborne Reynolds and engineering science today* (1970); D. Dowson, 'Osborne Reynolds centenary (1886–1986)', *Proceedings of the Institution of Mechanical Engineers*, cci (1987), C2, 75–96; F. Hodnett, 'Osborne Reynolds 1842–1912' in K. Houston (ed.), *Creators of mathematics: the Irish connection* (2000), 71–7

John Holland
(1841–1914)

INVENTOR OF THE SUBMARINE

John Philip Holland was born on 24 February 1841 at Castle Street, Liscannor, Co. Clare, son of John Holland, a coastguard officer, and his second wife, Mary (née Scanlon). He was educated at St Macreehy's national school, Liscannor, and by the Christian Brothers in Limerick, where his family moved in 1853 after his father's death. During his childhood, a younger brother and two uncles also died.

In June 1858 he entered the Christian Brothers and trained to be a schoolteacher. For many years he taught at schools in Cork, Maryborough (Portlaoise), Enniscorthy and Drogheda, becoming known as a maths teacher. Because of ill health, on 26 May 1873 he received a dispensation from the order releasing him from his initial vows. Sailing for America, he lived first in Boston with his younger brother Michael, a member of the American Fenian Brotherhood who had left for America a few years earlier along with his mother, an elder brother and a sister. In November 1873 he suffered a broken leg after a fall. Moving to New Jersey, he became a teacher in a catholic school in Paterson and continued the experiments that he had begun in Drogheda on the concept of a submarine; a term apparently first coined by Holland himself. His initial interest in the idea stemmed from reading about a pioneering battle between ironclad ships during the US civil war. In February 1875, he offered his patent to the US navy, but the navy secretary at first rejected it as 'a fantastic scheme of a civilian landsman'.

Through his brother Michael's association with Jeremiah O'Donovan Rossa, Holland met John J. Breslin and John Devoy in 1876. Considering that Britain's mastery of the seas was a great obstacle to Irish independence, Devoy convinced Clan na Gael to use their 'skirmishing fund' to finance Holland's experiments, although there is no evidence that Holland ever joined the revolutionary organisation. With the assistance of Breslin, he gave up teaching in 1876 and worked steadily on the project, mostly at Delamater Iron Works, West 14th Street, New York. He produced his first model, the *Holland I*, in 1878. It was a one-man, fourteen-foot craft, powered by a two-cylinder engine. In summer 1881 he produced a more advanced model, which was thirty-one feet long and could hold a crew of three. A journalist for the *New York Sun* nicknamed this model 'the Fenian ram' and described it as a 'wrecking boat'. It was successfully launched but defective riveting made it unseaworthy when submerged for long periods. Refining his plan, Holland launched a third vessel the following year that weighed nineteen tons. This was capable of prolonged submersion but developed engine problems, and further testing was prevented by its failure to comply with the New York Harbour Board's shipping laws. During 1883 this model was brought to New Haven, Connecticut, where it was kept in storage after its use was forbidden. Later, it was exhibited by Clan na Gael at a bazaar at Madison Square Gardens to raise funds for the families of the 1916 rebels and then donated to the naval school at Fordham University, New York, before its ultimate relocation to the Paterson Museum in New Jersey.

The total cost of Holland's experiments had been nearly $60,000 and legal issues had also arisen. Therefore, the Clan tried to assume exclusive ownership of the models, much to the annoyance of Holland who parted their company and began to conduct his experiments privately.

Supported by Edmund L. G. Zalinski, an American military engineer and inventor, Holland developed a fourth vessel, the *Zalinski*, which proved seaworthy but unattractive to investors. Thereafter Holland was forced to work as an engineer to earn a living until financial assistance from E. B. Frost, a wealthy lawyer, allowed him to set up the John P. Holland Torpedo Boat Company in 1893. Two years later, it was contracted by the US navy to build a submarine, the *Plunger*. This project, however, was dominated by the navy's own engineers who largely ignored Holland's advice. The *Plunger*'s poor manoeuvrability led to it being scrapped by the navy. Holland returned to working on his own design and in 1897 launched the *Holland VI*. This model, which was fifty-three foot long and could hold a crew of six, performed well in tests. It proved capable of reaching speeds of up to 9 knots, diving to a depth of 60ft, and remaining submerged for forty hours. Utilising compressed air technology, it was armed with a torpedo launcher and an underwater cannon. In April 1900 the US navy agreed to purchase it for $150,000 and commissioned him to build several more. It was named the *USS Holland* and became the prototype for the US navy's submarine fleet as well as for other forces throughout the world. In 1901, despite Holland's personal reservations, the navy's Electric Boat Company sold the plans to the British admiralty, leading to its creation of the Holland-class submarine. Holland continued to work on improvements to his basic model. In 1910, shortly after his retirement from the submarine business, he was decorated by the emperor of Japan for his work on behalf of the Japanese navy.

A man of considerable versatility and ingenuity, he also worked on developing a viable motor truck and was an amateur astronomer and musician. He married (January 1887) Margaret Foley, daughter of an Irish immigrant; they had five children. In late 1911, the death of his daughter Julia in her nineteenth year affected him badly. His own death on 12 August 1914 at 38 Newton Street, Newark, New Jersey, coincided with the start of the first world war, during which the devastating military potential of the submarine was amply demonstrated. He was buried at the Holy Sepulchre cemetery, Paterson, New Jersey.

To mark the centenary of his death, with the support of the Irish Maritime Institute, a monument was erected on the site of the school in which he taught in Drogheda during a ceremony that was attended by representatives of the American, British and Japanese navies. A limited-edition commemorative coin was also issued by the Central Bank of Ireland while the school in which he taught in New Jersey was renamed in his honour and a centre dedicated to his life was created in his birthplace of Liscannor.

Owen McGee and Aidan Breen

Sources

Gaelic American, 9, 16 July 1927; D. J. Doyle, 'The Holland submarine', *An Cosantóir*, vii (June 1947), 297–302; William O'Brien and Desmond Ryan (eds), *Devoy's post bag* (2 vols, 1948, 1953), i, 470–1, ii, 514–6, 189, 234, 306–7; Richard K. Morris, *John P. Holland, inventor of the modern submarine: 1841–1914* (1966); idem, 'John P. Holland and the Fenians', *Journal of the Galway Archaeological and Historical Society*, xxxi, nos 1–2 (1964–5), 25–38 (further bibliog., 37–8); J. de Courcy Ireland, 'John Philip Holland: pioneer in submarine navigation', *North Munster Antiquarian Journal*, x, no. 2 (1967), 206–12; K. R. M. Short, *The dynamite war* (1979), 36–7, 168–70; J. A. Garraty and M. C. Carnes (eds), *American national biography* (1999); *Drogheda Independent*, 28 Aug. 2014

Margaret Huggins
(1848–1915)

PIONEER ASTROPHYSICIST

Margaret Lindsay Huggins was born on 14 August 1848 at 62 Lower Gardiner Street, Dublin, the first child of John Majoribanks Murray (1822–93), a Dublin solicitor who had been born in Scotland, and Helen Murray (née Lindsay) from Taree, Arbroath. A brother, Robert Murray (1851–1934), probably born in Inverness, later became a barrister, and as an old man was 'father of the Free State bar'. Margaret's paternal grandfather, Robert Murray, had brought his family to Ireland from Scotland in the mid-1820s; he became chief officer of the Provincial Bank. Margaret was educated at home, and apparently at a private school in Brighton, perhaps after the early death (1857) of her mother. With his second wife, John Murray had two sons and a daughter. Margaret's precocious interest in astronomy was fostered by her grandfather Murray, who taught her to recognise the constellations. As a teenager she read popular works by Dionysius Lardner and John Herschel, carried out observations with a small terrestrial telescope (which she may have made herself), and was interested in photography and apparently also in the developing science of spectroscopy. She seems to have met William Huggins (1824–1910), an amateur astronomer of her father's age, and of independent means, in London, possibly at musical evenings at the house of the Montefiore family. He pioneered stellar spectroscopy in his private observatory at Tulse Hill, south-west London. He achieved fame through his study of the spectra of nebulae, which led to his discovery in 1864 that planetary nebulae were composed of gases. In recognition of his achievements he received from the Royal Society the long-term loan of a set of new instruments designed and built for him by Howard Grubb in Dublin. Apparently Howard Grubb reintroduced Murray to Huggins while he was in Dublin between 1870 and 1871, arranging the acquisition and transfer of this astronomical equipment. They married (8 September 1875) at the parish church in Monkstown.

Margaret Huggins worked along with Huggins in the observatory and seems to have been largely responsible for the introduction of photography to assist their recording of data. The Hugginses pioneered photographic spectroscopy of celestial bodies, and Margaret Huggins was particularly adept at modifying apparatus for the work. They used the recently introduced gelatine photographic plates in association with a telescope and spectrograph to observe and identify a series of hydrogen lines (the 'Balmer lines') in the spectrum of the star Vega (α Lyrae); and, using the dry photographic plate process (1881), photographed the spectrum of Tebbutt's comet. In 1889 Margaret Huggins was listed as 'co-author' with her husband, rather than as his 'assistant', when they jointly published *On the spectrum, visible and photographed, of the great nebula in Orion*. This paper mentioned two mysterious lines in the nebula spectrum, which did not coincide with spectral lines produced by known terrestrial elements, suggesting that they emanated from an element unknown on earth, but the Hugginses did not put forward any hypothesis to explain the occurrence.

In her influential writings on astrophysics Agnes Mary Clerke, a close friend, discussed the supposed new element, backing the use of 'nebulium' as its name. It was not till 1927, after the development of the quantum atomic theory, that the American astronomer Ira S. Bowen realised that the 'nebulium' emission lines were actually produced by forbidden transitions in singly and doubly ionised oxygen, and singly ionised nitrogen atoms. The Hugginses investigated the spectra of the recently discovered Wolf–Rayet stars, without coming to firm conclusions, and, in 1892, they studied the spectrum of the nova T Aurigae. In 1897 they published a *Photographic atlas of representative stellar spectra*; it was well received by the scientific community, and they were awarded the Royal Institution's Actonian prize for an important scientific work, which according to the citation, was 'illustrative of the beneficence of the Almighty'.

While William was president of the Royal Society (1900–05), the Davy prize was awarded to Pierre and Marie Curie. William and Margaret Huggins became interested in radioactivity and tried to develop ways of observing radioactive radiation spectroscopically. Their work on the spectra of certain radioactive substances between 1903 and 1905 constituted their last published research. Between 1889 and 1905 they published twelve research papers in the *Proceedings of the Royal Society* and two papers in the *Astrophysical Journal*. Margaret and William Huggins jointly edited and published the *Collected scientific papers of Sir William Huggins* (1909). Margaret Huggins also contributed obituaries of the astronomers William Lassell and Warren de la Rue to the *Observatory* magazine in 1880 and 1889. She was a competent artist and a keen musician and published a monograph on the sixteenth-century violin maker Gio Paulo Maggini (1892). She contributed articles on the history of astrolabes and armillary spheres to the eleventh edition of the *Encyclopaedia Britannica*.

In 1890 she was one of the four women elected to the council of the recently established British Astronomical Association. Although barred (as a woman) from becoming a fellow of the Royal Astronomical Society, she was admitted as an honorary member in 1903. In 1897, Queen Victoria's diamond jubilee year, William Huggins was knighted; Margaret was mentioned in his citation, the only woman (other than Victoria) whose name appeared in the honours list. After William's death (12 May 1910) she worked on a biography of her husband. This was not completed but formed the basis of a memoir published in 1936 as *A sketch of the life of Sir William Huggins*. She was awarded a £100 annual pension from the Royal Society and in 1913 she moved to a flat in More's Garden, London. Throughout her life she had a keen interest in the education of women and donated observing notebooks and scientific equipment to a women's college, Wellesley College, Mass., USA; Huggins was friendly with the founding director of its observatory.

She died after a long and difficult illness at her home in London on 24 March 1915, and was cremated at Golders Green. She had no children. In March 1917, a memorial to the couple was unveiled in the crypt of St Paul's cathedral, London. The plaque, describing her as her husband's 'fellow worker', records her significance in their joint achievements in astrophysics. The concomitant status, not always accorded in her earlier years, was undoubtedly deserved.

Linde Lunney and Enda Leaney

Sources

IBL, vi, no. 9 (Apr. 1915), 153–4; 'Margaret Huggins – obituary', *Observatory*, no. 488 (June 1915), 254–6; Richard F. Hirsh, 'The riddle of the gaseous nebulae', *Isis*, lxx (1979), 196–212; Mary T. Brück, 'Companions in astronomy: Margaret Lindsay Huggins and Agnes Mary Clerke', *Irish Astronomical Journal*, vol. xx, no. 2 (Sept.

1991), 70–77; Mary T. Brück and Ian Elliott, 'The family background of Lady Huggins (Margaret Lindsay Murray)', *Irish Astronomical Journal*, xxi (1992); Ian Elliott, 'An Irish galaxy', *Irish Studies Review*, no. 4 (autumn 1993), 19–23; Barbara J. Becker, 'Eclecticism, opportunism and the evolution of a new research agenda: William and Margaret Huggins and the origins of astrophysics' (Ph.D. thesis, Johns Hopkins University, 1993), http://www.uci.edu/clients/bjbecker/huggins; Susan McKenna-Lawlor, *Whatever shines should be observed* (1998), 75–123 (bibliog. of the Hugginses' joint papers, 126–7); I. Elliott, 'The Huggins' sesquicentenary', *Irish Astronomical Journal*, vol. xxvi, no. 1 (1999), 65–8

Percy Ludgate

(1883–1922)

PIONEER IN DIGITAL COMPUTING

Percy Edwin Ludgate was born on 2 August 1883 at the house of his parents, Michael Ludgate and Mary (née McMahon), in Townsend Street, Skibbereen, Co. Cork, the youngest of at least eight children. His father taught shorthand, later joined by some of Ludgate's elder siblings, and from 1890 the family lived in Foster Terrace, Ballybough, Dublin.

Ludgate attended St George's school in Dublin's north inner city from 1890–92; where he undertook the remainder of his schooling, then required until aged fourteen, is not known. In 1898 Ludgate became a 'boy copyist' in the Irish civil service. He and his elder brother Alfred were living with their mother, Mary, at 30 Dargle Road, Drumcondra, in 1901; Michael Ludgate was living in Balbriggan, suggestive of marital breakdown.

Ludgate was working in the National Education Office when, in March 1903, he came first in Ireland in the civil service exams for 'abstractors' (assistant clerks). Although he passed the medical examination he was not recruited, while the next six ranked candidates were; the reason for this remains unknown. His 'boy copyist' post expired when he reached the age of twenty in August 1903. In October 1904, he passed the civil service exams for second-division clerkships, but on this occasion failed the medical exam. T. C. Harrington, MP for Dublin Harbour, raised the issue in the house of commons in February 1905, petitioning for a new medical examination for Ludgate, but to no avail.

By 1911 Ludgate was working as a commercial clerk to a corn merchant and later that decade began working with the accounting firm of Kevans & Son, 31 Dame Street, Dublin. He studied accountancy at the Rathmines College of Commerce and qualified in 1917, being awarded a gold medal. He remained with Kevans & Son until his death.

Ludgate is best known for his work in the field of computational mathematics and is the earliest known successor to Charles Babbage, the Victorian scientist and mathematician who invented, in 1834, most of the fundamental concepts involved in the modern digital computer, well over a century before the first such computers saw the light of day. In 1903 Ludgate had commenced work on a computational device, as described in his paper 'On a proposed analytical machine', published in the *Scientific Proceedings of the Royal Dublin Society* in April 1909. Sir Charles Vernon Boys, fellow of the Royal Society (FRS) and eminent British physicist and an expert in calculating machines, reviewed Ludgate's paper in the 1 July 1909 issue of the prestigious journal *Nature*.

Though Ludgate asserted that he was unaware of Babbage's 'analytical engine' when completing the first iteration of his own 'machine', he stated that 'I have since been greatly assisted in the more advanced stages of the problem by … the writings of that accomplished scholar' (Ludgate, 78). Ludgate's machine incorporated fully automatic mechanisms for storing and accessing nearly 200 twenty-digit decimal numbers, and for executing a sequence of the arithmetical operations (addition, subtraction, multiplication and division) on these numbers under the control of a punched perforated paper. His design comprised four main parts: the arithmetic unit, storage, input and output, and a sequencing mechanism. The arithmetic unit performed calculations using a device called a 'mill', as had Babbage's.

However, Ludgate introduced an 'index' to undertake multiplication, employing novel discrete logarithms which Boys described in *Nature* as 'Irish logarithms' (Boys, 14).

Apart from the mill, these mechanisms were both novel and ingenious – and significantly different from any devised previously. For example, Ludgate's index could undertake multiply–accumulation calculations (MAC), comprising multiplication followed by addition to any previous result in the mill. This makes Ludgate's analytical machine the first computer arithmetic unit to undertake such calculations, later widely utilised in digital signal processing (deployed in radar, radio astronomy and elsewhere), and also in deep artificial intelligence research. For storage, he used the lateral position of a sliding rod to represent a decimal digit, holding numbers in shuttles within rotatable cylinders, an entirely novel approach. Indeed, his techniques of what would later be termed 'programme control' and 'storage addressing' were significant advances on Babbage's work. Ludgate understood the fundamental importance of being able to change the sequence of calculations based on previous results (later known as 'conditional branching').

There is no evidence that Ludgate ever made any attempt to build his machine, essentially the world's second ever design for a computer, and beyond his paper and Boys' report his work largely passed without mention. He contributed a second paper, 'Automatic calculating machines', to the *Handbook of the Napier tercentenary celebration* (1914). This focused on Babbage's 'analytical engine' and modestly only briefly mentioned his own 1909 design for such a machine.

Percy Ludgate died on 16 October 1922 at 30 Dargle Road, where he had been nursed while sick by his late brother Frederick's wife, Alice, who then died six days later. His death certificate lists the cause of death as catarrhal pneumonia, which mostly accompanies diseases like influenza. He was buried in the family grave at Mount Jerome cemetery, Harold's Cross, Dublin, which for a long time was unmarked before a grave marker was erected in 2019. Little is known of Ludgate's personal life. However, a colleague in accountancy later recounted that Ludgate 'possessed characteristics one usually associates with genius', while his niece recalled that he 'took long solitary walks ... [and] always appeared to be thinking deeply' (Randell, 1971, 319). New research into Ludgate's life and career since 2016 has drawn together a variety of sources and interested experts, generating new genealogical and biographical data. A summation of this research asserts Ludgate 'designed a potentially disruptive mechanical technology; his storage scheme was extremely compact; his index would have dramatically reduced average multiplication times relative to repeated addition; these and his approach to division were novel' (Coghlan et al., 26). Archival material unearthed during this renewed interest in Ludgate's life is housed in the John Gabriel Byrne Computer Science Collection at Trinity College Dublin, while a collection of essays published in 2022 addresses various facets of his life and career. A blue plaque in honour of Percy Ludgate was unveiled at 30 Dargle Road in October 2022, to mark the centenary of his death.

Research undertaken in 2022 and 2023 established that Ludgate's 'On a proposed analytical machine' (1909), previously assumed to have had no impact on the emergence of modern computing, was in fact utilised in a successful 1960 bid, supported by International Business Machines (IBM), to block Konrad Zuse's attempt (in Germany) to obtain what would have been the first patent on a programmable computer.

Brian Randell and Turlough O'Riordan

Sources

General Register Office, birth and death certs; Percy E. Ludgate, 'On a proposed analytical machine', *Scientific Proceedings of the Royal Dublin Society*, vol. 12, no. 9 (28 Apr. 1909), 77–91; Charles Vernon Boys, 'A new analytical engine', *Nature*, 81 (1 July 1909), 14–15; Percy E. Ludgate, 'Automatic calculating machines' in E. M. Horsburgh (ed.), *Napier tercentenary celebration: handbook of the exhibition* (1914), 124–7; B. Randell, 'Ludgate's analytical machine of 1909', *Computer Journal*, xiv (1971), 317–26; B. Randell, 'From analytical engine to electronic digital computer: the contributions of Ludgate, Torres, and Bush', *Annals of the History of Computing*, vol. iv, no. 4 (1982), 327–41; Brian Coghlan et al., 'Percy Ludgate (1883–1922), Ireland's first computer designer', *Proceedings of the Royal Irish Academy: Archaeology, Culture, History, Literature*, 121C (2021), 303–32, https://doi.org/10.1353/ria.2021.0007; Brian Coghlan and Brian Randell (eds), *Percy Ludgate (1883–1922): Ireland's first computer designer* (2022); Brian Coghlan, Brian Randell and Ralf Buelow, 'How Percy Ludgate's 1909 paper (and IBM) helped thwart Konrad Zuse's computer patent in 1960', *IEEE Annals of the History of Computing*, vol. 46, no. 3 (2024), 20–35, https://doi.org/10.1109/MAHC.2024.3369024 (internet material accessed Dec. 2024)

William Parsons
(1800–67)

ASTRONOMER

and

Charles Algernon Parsons
(1854–1931)

ENGINEER AND SCIENTIST

William Parsons, 3rd earl of Rosse, was born on 17 June 1800 at York, England. Raised at the family estate at Birr Castle, near Parsonstown (Birr), King's County (Offaly), he was educated at home, and then briefly at Trinity College Dublin (TCD). He transferred to Magdalen College, Oxford University, from where he graduated first class in mathematics. An MP for King's County (1822–35), he was drawn to astronomy, inspired by William Herschel. Parsons joined the Astronomical Society (1824) and commenced a major programme of telescope design, manufacture and construction at Birr Castle.

Parsons designed and fabricated apparatus to shape the surfaces of mirror lenses, powered by a small steam engine which he also assembled. This he used to systematically grind and polish lenses of increasing size and weight, publishing an account of this work in 1830, which contributed to his being made a fellow of the Royal Society in 1831. Drawing on his wife's wealth (he married Mary Field, form Yorkshire, on 14 April 1836) he continued to refine methods of casting, fabricating and shaping mirrors. His 1840 account of this work detailed his novel method of constructing casting moulds from slatted steel strips, which enabled gasses to dissipate. This culminated in his casting of a 6ft (1.8m) mirror, weighing 3.5 tons, with a 45ft (16.45m) long telescope tube, housed on enormous, reinforced stone walls. Known as the 'Leviathan' of Birr and constructed by local craftsmen trained by Parsons, it enabled nebulae to be studied at dramatically improved resolutions, revealing their fabulous structures. These he reported to the British Association meeting at Cambridge in 1845. Succeeding his father, that year he became 3rd earl of Rosse, and was elected as an Irish representative peer in the house of lords.

The Leviathan was the largest telescope in the world for a time. However, its unwieldy nature rendered it unsuited to the emerging field of astronomical photography. Interested in engineering and manufacturing, as president of the Royal Society (1848–54) Parsons urged continued support for Charles Babbage's mechanical 'difference engine'. Awarded many honours, in later life he enjoyed sailing with his family on their yacht. He died on 31 October 1867. He was very close to his children, who were educated by the able astronomical assistants he employed at Birr, but of eleven children only four boys survived to adulthood. The eldest, Laurence was an astronomer, while Clere graduated as an engineer from TCD.

The youngest surviving son, **Charles Algernon Parsons**, was born on 13 June 1854 in London. Strongly influenced by his father, who encouraged him to use the workshops at the Birr Castle observatory, along with his brothers he was tutored at home by some of his father's assistant astronomers before entering TCD (1871). He transferred to St John's College, Cambridge, and on graduation (1877) as eleventh wrangler in a class of thirty-six studying mathematics, he took the unusual step, for the son of an earl, of becoming a premium apprentice at the Elswick Engine and Ordnance Works (more usually, the 'Elswick Works') of Sir W. G. Armstrong at Newcastle upon Tyne. In the period following this he developed a unique high-speed steam engine, and a torpedo which was powered by a gas turbine. He joined Clarke Chapman at Gateshead as a partner in 1884. In a matter of months, he filed patents for the world's first effective steam turbine. These embodied many novelties, but the key feature was an electricity generator rated at 6kW and designed to run, directly coupled, at the astonishing speed of 18,000rpm.

Unsatisfied that his partners' efforts to promote turbine development were sufficiently aggressive, in 1889 Charles left to establish his own company at Heaton near Newcastle upon Tyne. The price of this impetuous action was the loss of access to his original patents. He quickly established alternative designs, however, and by 1892 he had built a turbo-alternator with an output of 100kW for the Cambridge Electricity Company; exhausting to a condenser, it had a steam consumption comparable with the best steam engines. Even his 1884 patents envisaged applying turbines to marine propulsion, but it was 1893 before he could embark on the design of a suitable demonstration boat of 40 tons. By using careful tests on models, he perfected the hull shape and predicted the power requirements. At this time, he recovered his 1884 patents and even won the very rare prize of an extension for five years, which was a measure of the perceived national importance of his invention.

A syndicate was formed to raise the capital necessary to build his turbine-powered vessel *Turbinia*. At the Spithead naval review in 1897 it sped among the ships of the world's navies at 34.5 knots. In 1905 the Royal Navy decided to adopt turbines for its future warships. This example was followed by navies worldwide, from the USA to Japan. Builders of mercantile vessels followed quickly and the turbines of the Cunard liner *Mauretania* (1907), each developing 26,000kW, were the largest in existence at the time. The *Mauretania* held the Blue Riband for the speediest Atlantic crossing until 1929, a fact that kept Parsons's name before the public.

The firm of C. A. Parsons (1889), which built turbines for use on land, was privately owned, but the Parsons Marine Steam Turbine Co. (1897) was a public company. Parsons also earned income from over 300 patents through the Parsons Foreign Patents Company (1899). He readily licensed others to use his patents but he avoided costly litigation, the ruin of many inventors. He inherited an interest in optical instruments from his father and in 1890 developed a cost-effective method for manufacturing searchlight mirrors, using sheets of plate glass and an iron mould heated in a gas furnace. During the first world war he supplied most of the national requirements. In 1921 he acquired the optical instrument manufacturers Ross Ltd and the Derby Crown Glass Company, makers of optical quality glass. In 1925 the firm of Howard Grubb, which made large astronomical telescopes, was rescued from insolvency by Parsons. He believed that it was of national importance to maintain the industrial capacity to make optical equipment. Not all of his projects were commercially profitable, as for example his acoustic amplifier, dubbed the 'Auxetophone', or his attempts at synthesising diamonds, which absorbed much time and effort. In the development of his many inventions, he displayed great tenacity in the face of reverses and always employed a meticulously scientific approach.

The supply of power on a large scale was revolutionised by the steam turbine. During the twenty years following the building of his first turbo-generator, Parsons remained at the forefront of promoting, building, and selling ever larger and more efficient turbines. He was not only a scientific engineer and inventor, but also a successful manufacturer and businessperson. Modest and retiring in manner, his chief weakness lay in a lack of skill in managing interpersonal relationships, though this was compensated to a large extent by his integrity and loyalty. He sought out the ablest men to run his businesses, among them several fellows of the Royal Society; he was elected a fellow himself in 1898 and was knighted in 1911. For his outstanding contributions to society, in 1927 he became the first engineer to be awarded the Order of Merit. He was honoured by many universities and institutions in Europe and America.

Charles Parsons married (1883) Katharine Bethell, a Yorkshire woman, and had one daughter and a son who died on active service in 1918. He kept a residence in London and in Northumbria. He died on 11 February 1931 while on a cruise to the Caribbean and was buried at Kirkwhelpington near his Northumbrian home. His estate was valued at £1,214,355 gross. A portrait painted by Maurice Codner hangs in the Institution of Mechanical Engineers, London; there is also a portrait by Sir William Orpen in the Laing Art Gallery, Newcastle upon Tyne, and a portrait by Walter Stoneman in the National Portrait Gallery, London.

W. Garrett Scaife

Sources

Tyne and Wear Archives Service, Newcastle upon Tyne, Parsons archive; Science Museum, London, Parsons archive; C. A. Parsons (ed.), *The scientific papers of William Parsons* (1926); Rollo Appleyard, *Charles Parsons: his life and work* (1933); *Scientific papers and addresses of the Hon. Sir Charles A. Parsons*, ed. G. L. Parsons (1934); Patrick Moore, *The astronomy of Birr Castle* (1971); A. P. W. Malcolmson, *Introduction to calendar of the Rosse papers held at Birr Castle* (1982); D. H. Davison, *Impressions of an Irish countess: the photography of Mary, countess of Rosse* (1989); W. G. Scaife, *From galaxies to turbines: science, technology and the Parsons family* (2000)

Thomas Grubb
(1800–78)

and

Howard Grubb
(1844–1931)

Engineers and makers of telescopes and optical instruments

Thomas Grubb was born into a quaker family on 4 August 1800 near Portlaw, Co. Waterford, the youngest child among two sons and one daughter of William Grubb (d. 1831), farmer, and Eleanor Grubb (née Fayle), his second wife; there were also three children from his father's first marriage. Probably self-educated, he was employed as a clerk in Dublin and may have worked in the Waterford shipyards or in a British machine-tool factory. About 1830 he established a foundry and engineering works near Charlemont Bridge, Dublin, which began by making metal billiard tables, but later earned an international reputation for the sound manufacture and original design of machine tools and high-precision optical and mechanical instruments, which included the construction of some of the world's finest telescopes.

As a hobby he built a small observatory equipped with a 9-inch (22.9cm) reflecting telescope. His telescope came to the attention of Thomas Romney Robinson, director of Armagh observatory, who befriended and promoted Grubb in his professional pursuits. Grubb's first big telescope commission (1834) was for the construction of an equatorial mounting for the 13.3-inch (33.8cm) lens (by R. A. Cauchoix (1776–1845) of Paris) for Edward Joshua Cooper's observatory at Markree, Co. Sligo. This was at the time the world's largest aperture, and according to Robinson it was a 'great leap forward' (Glass, 13), representing a significant improvement in stability. In 1835 he produced for the Armagh observatory a 15-inch (38cm) reflecting telescope, equatorially mounted, in which for the first time a triangular system of balanced levers shared the weight of the primary speculum – a system which, on Grubb's suggestion, was adopted by William Parsons (later 3rd earl of Rosse), for his 36-inch (91.5cm) and later his 72-inch (183cm) reflector, the 'Leviathan' of Parsonstown (Birr), in King's County (Offaly), the largest telescope in the world in 1845.

Other major commissions included those for the Royal Greenwich Observatory, London (1838), and for the US military academy at West Point, New York (1840). In 1853 he exhibited a 12-inch (30.5cm) refractor telescope at the Dublin Industrial Exhibition, which was later purchased for the Dunsink Observatory, Dublin, fitted with a lens donated by Sir James South (1785–1867) and installed in a revolving dome designed by Grubb in 1868; overhauled in 1987, it remains in use. His last design and greatest achievement was the 48-inch (122cm) equatorially mounted reflector for Melbourne, Australia; new workshops were built in Rathmines and his son Howard Grubb (see below) curtailed his engineering studies at Trinity College Dublin (TCD) and entered the business in 1865 to aid his father. Completed in 1867, it was hailed as a masterpiece of engineering; however, the speculum mirror required sophisticated maintenance which was lacking in Melbourne, and it was eventually regarded as a relative failure. Grubb published privately *The great Melbourne telescope* (1870) in which he described its construction and replied to his critics.

Though Grubb was famous for his telescopes, only a minor part of his time was spent constructing them. An inventor of great originality, he was appointed to what became his main source of income, the post of engineer to the Bank of Ireland (*c.* 1840–78), where he designed and built ingenious machinery (which remained in use till 1921) for engraving, printing, and numbering banknotes; every banknote was identical, making the detection of forgeries much easier. In 1847 he devised for the government an early pantographic machine for engraving registration numbers on gun barrels. A pioneer in scientific lens design, he was probably the first to use the technique of ray-tracing, which is the standard technique for computer graphics, and contributed significantly to the development of microscopes; one of his microscopes is held in the Museum of the History of Science, Oxford, England. Other work undertaken included the supply of instruments for Humphrey Lloyd, director of the Magnetic Observatory, TCD, for a network of forty magnetic observatories, which were built throughout the British colonies. An early practitioner of photography, he was a founding committee member (1854), secretary for many years and honorary treasurer (1857) of the Dublin Photographic Society (from 1858 the Photographic Society of Ireland) and lectured on photographic optics; he contributed articles to photographic journals and patented an improved camera lens (1858).

He published papers in a variety of learned journals (including the RIA *Proceedings* and the RDS *Journal*), recorded in I. S. Glass, *Victorian telescope makers*. He became a member of the British Association for the Advancement of Science (1835), and was elected MRIA (1839), FRS (1864) and fellow of the Royal Astronomical Society (1870). He retired *c.* 1870 and died on 19 September 1878 at his home, 141 Leinster Road, Rathmines, Dublin, and was buried in Mount Jerome, Dublin.

When Thomas married Sarah Palmer on 12 September 1826, he was disowned by the Society of Friends as Sarah was not a quaker. Of their five sons and four daughters, three sons and two daughters died young. Their eldest son, Henry Thomas Grubb (1833–1902), studied engineering at TCD and succeeded his father as engineer to the Bank of Ireland.

His youngest son, **Sir Howard Grubb**, took over and expanded the family firm. An engineer and manufacturer of optical and astronomical instruments, Howard was born on 28 July 1844 in Dublin. He studied engineering at TCD, though left (1865) before completing his degree, when his father tasked him with supervising the 48-inch (1.22m) Cassegrain reflecting telescope, with a metal speculum, for the Melbourne Observatory, Australia.

From the early 1870s Grubb took over the business as Thomas entered retirement. The most technologically advanced enterprise in nineteenth-century Ireland, the firm served the expanding worldwide market for telescopes as astronomical advances spurred the proliferation of observatories globally. Grubb, often in consultation with Sir George Gabriel Stokes, produced innovative telescopes in response to the emerging needs of astronomers. These comprised high-quality objective lenses and often included clock drives and equatorial mountings to enable precise astronomical photography, which spurred astronomical advances. The firm supplied telescopes to the Royal Society in London and to leading observatories in Aberdeen (Scotland), Cape Town (South Africa) and Vienna (Austria).

Grubb opened a specialist factory in 1875 on Observatory Lane, Rathmines, Dublin, to manufacture these increasingly sophisticated telescopes; by 1888 it was employing over thirty-five men. The company supplied astrographic (photographic) telescopes to major international survey projects. However, it was best known for its large refracting telescopes, which ranged from 24 to 40 inches in diameter, and were installed in Santiago (Chile), California (USA), Johannesburg (South Africa) and Simeiz (Crimea). Also specialising in small equipment, the firm manufactured heliostats, spectroscopes and micrometers, amongst a range of devices utilised across the scientific and technological research communities. After developing a lucrative trade in producing submarine periscopes (used on almost the entire fleet of Royal Navy submarines) and gun sights, the firm moved – for security reasons – to St Albans, England, from 1916. Unable to adapt to post-war economic conditions, the firm went into liquidation in 1925 and was purchased by Charles Parsons. Grubb returned to Dublin.

Prominent in photographic and astronomical circles, Grubb was knighted in 1887 and elected FRS in 1883. He was a member of the Royal Dublin Society, the Royal Irish Academy (awarded its Cunningham gold medal in 1881 and the Boyle medal in 1912) and made a fellow of the Royal Astronomical Society in 1911. A leading figure in Irish science and technology at the turn of the twentieth century, Grubb was active in a range of engineering and artistic institutions. Modest, courteous and hospitable, he died on 16 September 1931 at his home 13 Longford Terrace, Monkstown, Co. Dublin. He married (1871) Mary Hester Walker (d. 12 April 1931), daughter of Irish parents living in Louisiana, USA; they had four sons, two of whom died young, and two daughters. Observatory Lane remains the only reminder of the famous Grubb works.

Helen Andrews

Sources

Friends Historical Library, Dublin, disownment, no. 312, 12 Sept. 1826; *List of fellows of the Royal Astronomical Society* (1911), 15; *Who was who ... 1897–1916* [etc.], (1920–); S. S. C., 'Sir Howard Grubb 1844–1931', *Proceedings of the Royal Society of London, ser. A*, vol. cxxxv, no. 828 (Apr. 1932), iv–ix (photo); O. S. Merne, *The story of the Photographic Society of Ireland, 1854–1954* (1954) (photo); James Meenan and Desmond Clarke, *The Royal Dublin Society* (1981), 281; P. A. Wayman, 'Dublin's Grubb telescope', *Technology Ireland*, vol. xx, no. 5 (Sept. 1988), 53–7; J. E. Burnett and A. D. Morrison-Low, *'Vulgar and mechanick': the scientific instrument trade in Ireland, 1650–1921* (1989); C. C. Gillispie (ed.), *Dictionary of scientific biography* (1972); Richard McKim, *The history of the British Astronomical Association* (1989), 8; I. S. Glass, *Victorian telescope makers: the lives and letters of Thomas and Howard Grubb* (1997) (photo); Edward Chandler, *Photography in Ireland – the nineteenth century* (2001); Bill Irish, *Shipbuilding in Waterford, 1820–1882* (2001); Mary Mulvihill, *Ingenious Ireland* (2002); information from Ian Elliott

William 'Student' Gosset
(1876–1937)

SCIENTIST, GUINNESS BREWER
AND APPLIED STATISTICIAN

William Sealy ('Student') Gosset was born on 13 June 1876 in Canterbury, Kent, eldest of five children of Agnes Sealy Gosset (née Vidal) and Frederic Gosset, colonel in the Royal Engineers, who were married in 1875. Gosset was a scholar of Winchester College 1889–95. Due to poor eyesight, he was unable to follow his father into the Royal Engineers, and instead took up a scholarship at New College, Oxford, where he obtained a first in mathematical moderations in 1897, and a first-class degree in chemistry in 1899.

When Arthur Guinness, Son & Co. Ltd, manufacturers of stout in Dublin, wanted to incorporate new scientific methods into their brewing process and decided to hire some bright young science graduates, Gosset was one of the first they hired, and in October 1899 he moved to Dublin to take up a job as a brewer at St James's Gate. In his early years there Gosset became familiar with various aspects of the brewing process, and in 1904 wrote a report for Guinness on 'The application of the law of error to the work of the brewery'. The report emphasised the importance of the use of probability theory in order to set exact values on the results of experiments in the brewery, and in particular recommended that a mathematician be consulted about analysing results of such experiments where only small samples were being observed. This led to Gosset spending a year's leave of absence (1906–7) in the biometric laboratory of Karl Pearson at University College, London, where he obtained the statistical foundations for much of his later work at Guinness. During this period, he was introduced to correlation coefficients and the large-sample theory which was extensively used by biometers at the time. He was aware, however, that modifications of the large-sample methods of Pearson would be necessary in order to deal with the special small-sample problems arising in the brewery.

William Sealy Gosset was a practical scientist and published twenty-two scientific papers while working for Guinness. The research and methods developed were motivated by problems in the brewery dealing with the production of stout, arising in response to variations in barley, hops and malt, and other experimental conditions. Gosset wrote under the modest pseudonym of 'Student'. Arthur Guinness, Son & Co. Ltd was then at the forefront in using applications of scientific methods to brewing, and emphasised secrecy to deny important information to its competitors. In particular, the company was not keen on its employees publishing scientific research, and insisted they use pseudonyms.

Gosset rediscovered the Poisson distribution in his first publication, entitled 'On the error of counting with a haemacytometer', which appeared in 1906 in Karl Pearson's journal *Biometrika* (vol. iv, 351–60). In this paper, which was motivated by the problem of the distribution of yeast cells in a liquid spread thinly over a grid, he gave new practical applications for this now classic probability distribution. However, it was Gosset's second publication, 'On the probable error of a mean' (*Biometrika*, vi (1908), 1–25), which has proved to be a landmark paper in the history of statistics. Gosset, like many other scientists at the time, was interested in how the mean of a sample might vary about the mean of a given population in an experiment – in particular when the sample size is small. In this paper, he derived the probability distribution of the standardised version of the sample mean given by z = (x-μ)/s, and gave tables for this z-distribution.

In about 1922 R. A. Fisher, motivated by the need to address a wider class of statistical problems, suggested using the statistic instead of z, and ever since it has been known as 'Student's t-distribution'. It has been for years one of the most frequently used tools of the statistician. Another very significant piece of work ('The probable error of a correlation coefficient', *Biometrika*, vii (1908), 302–10) was his investigation of the probability distribution of the small sample correlation coefficient for a bivariate normal distribution. Gosset was always very interested in agricultural experimentation, and in his later work made many valuable contributions to the design and analysis of experiments. He was a man of very wide interests in spite of his heavy workload and dedication to Guinness. However, among all his activities and contributions, it is the Student t-test that has won Gosset a unique place in the history of statistics and scientific method.

He married (16 January 1906) Marjory Surtees Phillpotts, sister of another Guinness brewer, in Tunbridge Wells, Kent. He remained with Guinness for all of his working life, residing in Blackrock, Co. Dublin, until 1935, when he moved to London to take up his appointment as head brewer of the new Guinness brewery at Park Royal in north-west London. He died of a heart attack on 16 October 1937, and was survived by his parents, wife, children (one son and two daughters), and one grandson. R. A. Fisher, the great statistician and mathematician, wrote in his 1939 tribute to Gosset that 'the untimely death of W. S. Gosset, at the age of sixty-one, in October 1937, has taken one of the most original minds in contemporary science'.

Philip J. Boland

Sources

R. A. Fisher, 'Student', *Annals of Eugenics* (1939), 1–9; W. S. Gosset, *Letters from W. S. Gosset to R. A. Fisher, 1915–1936* (with summaries by R. A. Fisher and foreword by L. McMullen) (1970); L. McMullen, 'Student as a man', *Studies in the History of Statistics and Probability*, i (1970), 355–60; E. S. Pearson, 'Student as statistician', *Studies in the History of Statistics and Probability*, i (1970), 360–403; idem, 'Some early correspondence between W. S. Gosset, R. A. Fisher, and Karl Pearson, with notes and comments', *Studies in the History of Statistics and Probability*, i (1970), 405–17; Stella Cunliffe, 'Interaction', *Journal of the Royal Statistical Society*, A, cxxxix, no. 1 (1976), 1–19; Churchill Eisenhart, 'On the transition from Student's z to Student's t', *American Statistician*, xxxiii (1979), 6–10; Joan Fisher Box, 'Gosset, Fisher and the t-distribution', *American Statistician*, xxxv (1981), 61–7; Philip J. Boland, 'A biographical glimpse of William Sealy Gosset', *American Statistician*, xxxviii (1984), 3, 179–83; *Student – a statistical biography of William Sealy Gosset*, based on writings by E. S. Pearson, ed. R. L. Plackett with G. A. Barnard (1990); Philip J. Boland, 'William Sealy Gosset – alias "Student" 1876–1937', *Creators of mathematics: the Irish connection* (2000), 105–12

Alicia Boole
(1860–1940)

AMATEUR MATHEMATICIAN

Alicia Boole was born on 8 June 1860 in Cork into an intellectually gifted family, third of five daughters of English parents: Prof. George Boole of QCC, distinguished mathematician and logician, and Mary Boole (née Everest; 1832–1916), author and pioneer in modern pedagogy. Ethel L. Voynich, novelist, was her youngest sister. She was a grand-niece of George Everest (1790–1866), surveyor general of India, whose name is commemorated by the mountain. The death of her father (1864) left the family impoverished, and her mother returned to England.

She remained in Cork and spent an unhappy childhood in the care of her maternal grandmother and her great-uncle, John Ryall (c. 1806–75), first vice-president (1845–75) and professor of Greek at QCC. About 1871 she was reunited with her family in London, where their straitened circumstances were lightened by a lively bohemian social life. She was educated at the school attached to Queen's College, London – where her mother held several positions including librarian and mathematics teacher – but had no mathematical training beyond the first two books of Euclid; however, c. 1888, under the stimulus of mathematician C. H. Hinton (1853–1907), her future brother-in-law, she experimented with wooden cubes and developed a clear grasp of four-dimensional geometry. Fascinated by the convex regular solids in four dimensions, she constructed on her own, by ruler and compass, cardboard models of the three-dimensional central-cross sections of all the six regular four-dimensional figures, introducing into English the term 'polytope' to describe them. At Hinton's request – due to his imminent departure from England – and jointly with H. J. Falk, she wrote the preface to, and completed, his treatise *A new era of thought* (1888).

While working as a secretary in Liverpool (1889), she married (1890) Walter Stott, actuary; they had a son and a daughter and Alicia gave up her mathematical hobby and devoted her energies exclusively to her family. Around 1900 her husband drew her attention to the work on central sections of the regular four-dimensional polytopes of Pieter H. Schoute (1846–1913), professor of mathematics at Groningen University in the Netherlands. She sent him photographs of her models and he invited her to collaborate with him, a partnership that lasted till his death; her exceptional powers of geometrical visualisation complemented his more conventional analytical approach. He persuaded her to publish her work (using her married name), *On certain series of sections of the regular four-dimensional hypersolids* (1900) and *Geometrical deduction of semi-regular from regular polytopes and space fillings* (1910) and they published jointly *On the sections of a block of eight cells by a space rotating about a plane* (1908). After his death she was invited to the tercentenary celebrations of Groningen University, which conferred on her an honorary degree (1914) and exhibited her models.

In 1930 she resumed her work, collaborating with the distinguished mathematician H. S. M. Coxeter (1907–2003), FRS, having been introduced to him by her nephew G. I. Taylor (1886–1975), applied mathematician, FRS. According to Coxeter, 'the strength and simplicity of her character combined with the diversity of her interests to make her an inspiring friend' (Coxeter, 259). They investigated the four-dimensional polytope of Thorold Gosset (1869–1962); she introduced new methods, discovered a great variety of uniform polytopes, and made two further important discoveries relating to constructions for polyhedra related to the golden section. R. R. Ball, in *Mathematical recreations and essays* (1947) described her methods as 'extraordinarily fruitful' (McHale, 262). She died on 17 December 1940 in a catholic nursing home. Her son, Leonard Boole Stott (1892–1963), OBE, was a pioneer in the treatment of tuberculosis and an inventor of great originality, devising a system of navigation based on spherical trigonometry, artificial pneumothorax apparatus, and a portable X-ray machine.

Her younger sister Lucy Everest Boole (1862–1905), chemist, was born on 5 August 1862 in Cork. Educated at the school attached to Queen's College, London, she never attended university but studied chemistry to become a dispenser in a pharmacy. She was appointed demonstrator (1891) and lecturer in chemistry (1893–1904) at the London School of Medicine for Women, where she was appreciated as a dedicated teacher. She collaborated and published jointly with Sir W. R. Dunstan (1861–1949), FRS. Her research centred on croton oil and other substances, and she became the first woman to be elected fellow of the Institute of Chemistry (1894). Despite suffering ill health for many years, she continued her work, which was her sole interest; she never married, and lived with her mother at 16 Ladbroke Road, Notting Hill, London. She died in December 1905.

Helen Andrews

Sources

'Plymouth lives', *Morning News*, 16 Nov. 1894; Mary Everest Boole, *Collected works,* ed. E. M. Cobham (1931); H. S. M. Coxeter, *Regular polytopes* (1948); N. T. Gridgeman, 'In praise of Boole', *New Scientist*, no. 420 (3 Dec. 1964), 655–7; Alexander Lawson, 'Miss [Lucy] Boole', *New Scientist*, no. 423 (24 Dec. 1964), 860; 'Obituary: Miss Boole' *Magazine of London Royal Free Hospital School of Medicine for Women* (1905), 454–5; Geoffrey [I.] Taylor, 'Amateur scientists', *Michigan Quarterly Review*, vol. viii, no. 2 (1969), 107–13; Desmond McHale, *George Boole: his life and work* (1985) (photo); L. S. Grinstein and P. J. Campbell (eds), *Women of mathematics* (1987); George Batchelor, *The life and legacy of G. I. Taylor* (1996) (photo)

Emily Anderson in 1961. © Dr Dagmar von Busch Weise.

Alicia Boole.

Image courtesy of University of Bristol Library, Special Collections (DM1718/A.98).

Agnes Mary Clerke.
Published in Lady [Margaret Lindsay] Huggins, *Agnes Mary Clerke and Ellen Mary Cerke: an appreciation* (1907).

Maude Delap.
Courtesy of Valentia Island Heritage Centre.

Alice Everett.
© Illustrated London News Ltd./Mary Evans.

Below, left:
Mary Gough at the Catholic University of America, Washington DC.
Courtesy of Jim Moore.

Below, right:
Margaret Lindsay Huggins.
Courtesy of the University of Chicago Library Special Collections Research Centre.

Kathleen Lonsdale in her laboratory.
© Pictorial Press Ltd./Alamy Stock Photo.

Kay McNulty around 1948.
Courtesy of Wikipedia Commons.

Below:
Helen Megaw in 1951.
Courtesy of the Cambridgeshire Collection, Cambridge Central Library.

Mary Mulvihill.
© Dara Mac Dónaill.

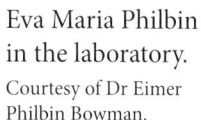

Eva Maria Philbin in the laboratory.
Courtesy of Dr Eimer Philbin Bowman.

Sheila Power (later Sheila Tinney) at the Institute for Advanced Study, Princeton, New Jersey, c. 1948–9.

Courtesy of the image collection of the Shelby White and Leon Levy Archives Center, Institute for Advanced Study, Princeton, New Jersey, USA.

Right:
Mary Ward in 1861.

Alice Everett

(1865–1949)

ASTRONOMER AND PHYSICIST

Alice Everett was born on 15 May 1865 in Blythswood, Glasgow, one of three daughters and three sons of Joseph David Everett (1831–1904), lecturer in natural philosophy at Glasgow University, and his wife Jessie, daughter of Alexander Fraser, presbyterian minister. She was two years old when her father became professor of natural philosophy at QCB. He was professor there for thirty years, training distinguished scientists such as John Perry and Joseph Larmor. Highly regarded as an educator, as a textbook writer, and as the main supporter of the introduction of metric units into physics, he was elected FRS in 1879; his pamphlet on the subject was internationally known and influential. On his appointment to QCB the family moved to Belfast, and Alice was educated at the co-educational Methodist College, Belfast.

In 1882 she attended lectures at QCB in preparation for the examinations of the RUI, eventually taking first place in the first-year scholarship examination in science, an event that caused the university authorities to consider the eligibility of women for scholarships (eventually granted in 1895). She entered Girton College, Cambridge (1886), where Elizabeth Welsh was mistress, and where Everett met Annie Maunder, with whom she became good friends. In 1889 she passed the mathematics tripos with honours. During her time at Cambridge she also sat and passed the RUI's examinations in mathematics and mathematical physics (1887) and was awarded an MA (1889).

After graduation, she was appointed as a 'lady computer' at the Royal Observatory at Greenwich, a routine job at a menial salary. She was assigned to the project of the astrographic catalogue – an international project, which aimed to survey the entire sky photographically and catalogue all stars brighter than eleventh magnitude. Other duties involved making observations in the transit department using the transit circle.

She joined the British Astronomical Association (1891), acted as its secretary (1893), and contributed papers on her observations of the total lunar eclipse of November 1891 and the Nova Aurigae of 1892. In November 1895, she began a three-year tenure as a scientific assistant at the astrophysical observatory in Potsdam, becoming the first woman to be employed in an observatory in Germany. Her duties were concerned primarily with the astrographic catalogue. In one year, 1897, she helped measure the positions of 22,000 stars. She left Germany in 1898 to take up a one-year position at the observatory of Vassar College, USA, and wrote two papers with Mary Whitney on observations of minor planets and a comet for the *Astrophysical Journal* (xx (1900), 47, 76). At the time it was difficult for women to acquire research positions and, despite applying to several American observatories, she returned to England in 1900. Her astronomical career was effectively over at the age of thirty-five.

Undaunted, she shifted her interests to optics and, in collaboration with her father, translated and edited Hovestadt's *Jena glass and its scientific and industrial applications* (1902). In the same year, her father communicated a paper by her to the Physical Society of London describing experiments on zonal observations in lenses. This was the first paper by a woman to appear in the society's journal (xviii (1903), 376). Her father died in 1904 and little is known about her career after this, until the outbreak of the first world war brought new opportunities; women were appointed to fill technical posts left vacant by men serving in the forces. After a year spent in the optical laboratory of the firm of Hilgers in London, she joined the National Physical Laboratory as a junior assistant in the physics division (1917), where she worked in the optical section. Her research duties concerned the design of optical instruments, photometry, and spectrophotometry, while she specialised in the calculation of aberrations in lens and mirror systems. She retired from her post in 1925, aged sixty, and began attending evening courses in practical wireless at the Regent Street Polytechnic, London, and then commenced research in the electrical engineering department of the City and Guilds College. She was among the founding members of the Television Society, established in 1927 to promote research into television. In 1933 she designed and patented, jointly with the Baird Television Company, an improved version of Logie Baird's 'mirror drum', the scanning device used in early transmissions. She was awarded a civil pension of £100 a year in 1938 in recognition of her contribution to physical science.

She died in London on 29 July 1949, aged eighty-four, leaving her scientific library to the Television Society.

Enda Leaney

Sources

Mary T. Brück, 'Bringing the heavens down to earth' in *Stars, shells, and bluebells: women scientists and pioneers* (1997), 70–71; Mary T. Brück, 'Alice Everett and Annie Russell Maunder: torch-bearing women astronomers', *Irish Astronomical Journal*, vol. xxi, nos. 3–4 (Mar.–Sept. 1994), 281–91 (portr.)

Maude Delap
(1866–1953)

Naturalist and marine biologist

Maude Jane Delap was born on 7 December 1866 at Templecrone rectory, Co. Donegal, seventh of ten children of the Rev. Alexander Delap and Anna Jane Delap (née Goslett). In 1874 the family moved to Co. Kerry on her father's appointment as rector of Valentia Island and Cahersiveen. She remained on Valentia all her life. As it was seen to be more important for her four brothers to gain good careers, she was educated mostly at home with her sisters. Her father's keen interest in natural history influenced her lifelong passion as a naturalist and marine biologist.

With her father and sisters, she collected plants and animals from the shore and, following her father's habit, began writing and sending specimens to the Natural History Museum in London. On the recommendation of Professor A. C. Haddon, Valentia, with its sheltered harbour and wide intertidal area, was chosen as a suitable site for a detailed marine survey by a group of eight English naturalists in 1895–6, led by Edward T. Browne. Maude and her sister Constance took an active part in the survey and are so acknowledged in the *Proceedings of the Royal Irish Academy* (1899), which published the results of the work. The survey's success rested on much of the work carried out by the two sisters. After the departure of the scientists, Maude and Constance continued the survey till 1898, taking sea temperatures and collecting plankton by tow-net from an open boat, which they rowed themselves. They sent on the preserved specimens to London, as well as detailed drawings and notes. Maude continued to correspond with Edward Browne, with whom she had fallen in love, till his death in 1937. He did not return her affection and married a colleague, but every year she sent him a box of violets on his birthday.

After the Valentia survey was finished, the sisters published two further papers on the plankton of Valentia Harbour for the periods 1899–1901 and 1902–5. Pursuing her interest in pelagic organisms, she undertook the task of breeding jellyfish in bell jars. These difficult and time-consuming experiments were a major contribution to the understanding of the complex life cycles of these fragile organisms, which can occur in either of two forms, medusa or hydra. Amongst others, she successfully reared *Chrysaora isosceles*, *Aurelia auritia*, and *Pelagia peria*, and published several papers in the fisheries reports and the *Irish Naturalist*. A list of her publications is in *Stars, shells and bluebells* (1997).

In 1906 Alexander Delap died. Some time before this, Maude was offered a post with the marine biological station in Plymouth. Her father's reaction was 'No daughter of mine will leave home except as a married woman' (Byrne, 1997). She herself, at the age of forty, may have thought it too late to leave. She remained on the island and moved with her mother and two sisters to Reenellen, an old house, where she set up her laboratory, 'the department', in one of the rooms. It was 'a heroic jumble of books, specimens and aquaria, with its pervasive smell of low tide', according to her nephew (ibid.).

Her last published paper (1924) refers to plankton collected between 1906 and 1910. Tow-netting was largely discontinued after this, although she still pursued studies in all things marine, identifying beached whales and birds, collecting and analysing specimens, and corresponding with museums in Dublin and London. In 1928 her scientific work was acknowledged when a rare sea anemone, *Edwardsia delapiae*, which she had discovered burrowing in eel grass on the shores of Valentia, was named after her. It was only recorded there again during the 1990s. The Linnean Society honoured her with an associate membership in 1936.

As well as her marine studies, she was a prodigious gardener, supplying vegetables for the family as well as augmenting their meagre income by growing and selling gladioli and lilies. She took an eager interest in the flora, fauna and local history of the whole area, contributing to Reginald Scully's *The flora of County Kerry* (1916) and publishing some papers in the *Kerry Archaeological Magazine*. With her sisters she was very much part of life on the island, helping to run the local cottage hospital and fisherman's hall. They were highly regarded and remembered for their charity and generosity. They kept an open house for visitors, especially welcoming their nieces and nephews.

Constance Delap (1868–1935), was born on 29 November 1868 at Templecrone rectory, Co. Donegal, the sixth and youngest daughter, and died on 4 June 1935 at home on Valentia. Although she had taken an active part in marine sampling and co-authored some papers on plankton and jellyfish rearing with Maude, it appears that her commitment to marine science was not as great as her sister's.

Maude died on 23 July 1953, the last survivor of the household, and was buried beside her sisters near Knightstown. Her large collection of specimens, mostly jellyfish, was left to her great-nephew John Barlee. Unfortunately, the preservative had not been renewed, and all that was left were jars of sludge. However, other specimens she collected are on display in the Natural History Museum in Dublin, including those presented by Edward T. Browne from the Valentia survey. A plaque was erected (1998) to her memory in Knightstown, Valentia Island.

Patricia M. Byrne

Sources

RIA Proc., xxi (1899), 667–854; Reginald W. Scully, *The flora of County Kerry* (1916); Robert Lloyd Praeger, *Some Irish naturalists: a biographical note-book* (1949); 'Obituary: Maude Jane Delap (1866–1953)', *Irish Naturalists' Journal*, xii (1958), 221–2; Timothy Collins, 'Some Irish women scientists', *UCG Women's Studies Centre Review*, vol. 1 (1992), 47; *Irish Times*, 3 Nov. 1997; 10 Aug. 1998; Anne Byrne, 'Untangling the medusa' in *Stars, shells and bluebells* (1997), 98–109

Harry Ferguson
(1884–1960)

ENGINEER

Henry George ('Harry') Ferguson was born on 4 November 1884 in the townland of Growell, near Annahilt, between Hillsborough and Dromore, Co. Down, third son and fourth child among eight sons and three daughters of James Ferguson, a prosperous farmer, and Mary Ferguson (née Bell). His mother was daughter of Joseph Bell, clerk of the union in Newry, Co. Down, and was half-sister of Elizabeth Gould Bell, and either a sister or half-sister of Margaret Bell, the first women to qualify as doctors in Ulster. Henry Ferguson (always known as 'Harry') attended the local schools till he was fourteen, when he left to work on the hundred-acre family farm. However, friction in his relationship with his strict and religious father intensified and, in 1902 after four years on the farm, he left home to work in Belfast as an apprentice in the garage business of his elder brother Joseph Bell ('Joe') Ferguson (b. 1879). He was increasingly fascinated by engines and by technology in general, and he took evening classes at the Belfast Technical College. The Fergusons' garage business was the biggest in Ireland by 1907. Harry began racing motorcycles and motorcars to publicise the business, and as a result of his risk-taking and love of speed he was known locally as 'the mad mechanic'.

Aviation was the great novelty of the day, and in 1909 Ferguson designed and built an aeroplane, based on descriptions of Blériot's monoplane in the magazine *Flight*;

at Hillsborough, Co. Down, on 31 December 1909 he became the first person to make a heavier-than-air flight in Ireland, and the first native of Britain or Ireland to build and fly his own monoplane. A replica of the plane is on display in the Ulster Folk and Transport Museum. Despite several crashes, including one in October 1910 which wrecked his plane and in which he was knocked unconscious, Ferguson devoted much of his time to improving his aircraft, and to increasingly ambitious flights at Magilligan strand, Co. Londonderry, and at Newcastle, Co. Down. His resultant lack of attention to routine work led to a rift between him and his brother, and in 1911 he set up his own business in Belfast – May Street Motors, later called Harry Ferguson Ltd; his engineering assistant Willie Sands remained with him most of his life, and was of considerable importance in helping turn Ferguson's brilliant designs into working machines. After Ferguson ceased to experiment with flight in 1911, he again collaborated with his brother Joe, in designing and building an innovative car, known to aficionados as the 'Fergus'; three were built. (The 'Fergus' was unsuccessful, largely because of production difficulties in the 1914–18 war and afterwards.) During the gun-running of April 1914, he made motor transport available for distributing arms landed for the Ulster Volunteer Force.

In the course of the first world war, it was apparent that the loss of manpower and even of horsepower, removed from farms to further the war effort, had left local agriculture in crisis at a time when more food than ever had to be produced. Ferguson, who had the agency to sell an early American-made tractor, was asked by the government to set up large-scale demonstrations in 1917 to show farmers how machinery, specifically ploughs, could improve yields while reducing labour costs. He saw at first hand the problems with the very rudimentary ploughs and other implements that were then available for tractors; his own early experience with horse-drawn machinery and with the back-breaking manual labour of traditional farming methods was useful, in that he appreciated that current models were still based on the concepts and physics of horse-drawn implements, and that engineers had not recognised the novel possibilities presented by tractor power. Ferguson began to sketch out designs in which the tractor and its implements functioned in mechanical terms as a unit. He also saw the importance of designing interchangeable implements to work with, rather than against, the motive power, and the need to provide easy but robust connections between tractor and implement. His own farming background led him to think in terms of light machines that would be useful on small farms and wet land, and as time went on, he realised that such machines would be relevant worldwide, where bigger tractors would have been too expensive for near-subsistence agriculturalists.

In 1917 he and Sands designed a plough for a tractor which was converted from the Ford Model T car, and a few years later, when Ford replaced this machine with the Fordson tractor, he went to Michigan to meet Henry Ford; Ford offered him a job, but at the time was unwilling to get involved in a partnership. Ferguson continued to improve the plough design, and in just two years came up with a two-point or duplex linkage, later modified into a three-point, triangular system, to enable implements to be attached to tractors. The revolutionary linkage almost completely eradicated a major cause of accidents, by making tractors much less likely to overturn if the plough was impeded in the soil; the force of the impact was transferred through the top link point and thence downwards, rather than forcing the front of the tractor upwards. Also, thanks to Ferguson's innovation, the tractor needed less weight to remain stable, and the plough could be lighter because it could be lowered deeper into the soil. In 1925 he set up a partnership with the American Shearman brothers and began manufacturing ploughs designed for Ford tractors, in America. After only a couple of years, however, the business was wound up when Ford stopped making tractors to concentrate entirely on cars. Once again, Ferguson was not discouraged by setback, and he continued to work on a radical new approach; he began to incorporate hydraulics into the linkage between his plough and its tractor, which would allow an automatic response to any mismatch between the force of traction or operation and the depth of work of the implement, or its draft. The new linkage was further improved by the inclusion of an easy-to-operate hydraulic lift and lowering mechanism, to allow the farmer to change the height of the plough without dismounting. Ferguson successfully patented plough draft control in June 1926, but had trouble interesting business backers, and there were also technical difficulties still to be overcome.

In 1933 Ferguson built his first tractor in his works in Belfast; the prototype was painted black, and thus known as the 'Black Tractor', to distinguish it from the much more famous later models which were always grey; it was later marketed as the 'Model A'. In 1936 he set up a partnership with David Brown of Huddersfield, and the production of the Ferguson Brown tractor began, with the Yorkshire company building machines and Ferguson both selling them and working on new designs. Although this was Ferguson's ideal type of business arrangement and at first a relatively successful venture, it lasted only two years, as David Brown wanted to make heavier, larger tractors, and – failing to change Ferguson's views – began to manufacture tractors to his own designs. Like almost every tractor made worldwide since Ferguson's patents were granted, however, the David Brown tractors were designed around the concepts introduced by Ferguson in 1917 and 1933.

It was at this time that Ferguson developed a partnership with Henry Ford. In October 1938, he demonstrated his 'Ferguson system', including his tractor, on Ford's estate in Michigan, and the two came to a gentleman's agreement (famously sealed with a handshake rather than a legal document), under which Ford would manufacture the tractor, and Ferguson would develop and sell it. Ferguson was unable to convince Ford that the tractor should be manufactured in Britain or Ulster; but of the 90,000 Ford Ferguson tractors produced by December 1941, many reached Britain before the second world war interrupted Atlantic shipping.

By 1947 the American plant had produced over 300,000 tractors; however, there were problems with Ford's new management, and Ferguson had already been making plans for the next stage of development. Despite the difficulties of obtaining financial backing and raw materials in post-war Britain, and after intense negotiations with government ministers and potential partners, Ferguson and the Standard Motor Co. began to manufacture tractors at Coventry in 1946. Sixteen TE (Tractor England) models were produced, selling hundreds of thousands of units, and associated implements; these were the world-famous grey machines that revolutionised world agriculture. Standard components, including bolts in just two sizes, were used in assembly. This helped speed up production and ensured that one Ferguson spanner could be used for almost all servicing and repairs. Known in Ferguson's home region as 'the wee grey Fergie', and in France as *le p'tit gris*, the tractor was for many farmers worldwide their first and only tractor; it quickly became indispensable and even beloved.

Though in many ways a difficult and driven man, and a very canny businessman, Ferguson was also a visionary, whose perhaps simplistic belief was that his system of agricultural mechanisation could produce 'for the first time in history, enough food to feed all the people of the world ... [and] a new wealth to enrich the world ... That is our ambition. That is the course to which I am wholly dedicated' (Ferguson, Dec. 1947, quoted in Kelly). Throughout his life he constantly urged governments to wipe out poverty by cutting costs of production, which would ultimately bring down prices. Although at times he seemed cocky and arrogant, he refused a knighthood for services to the Allies during the second world war, as he said he had only set out to assist the small farmer.

After Henry Ford's retirement (1943) and death (1947), his gentleman's agreement with Ferguson was first challenged by the Ford company, and then, when Ferguson refused to renegotiate, effectively repudiated, with Henry Ford II's approval. Ford started to manufacture a tractor, very closely modelled on the Ferguson system, and Ferguson's tractors were no longer made and distributed by Ford. Ferguson earnings in America dropped in one year from $59 million to $11 million. Ferguson had to set up his own manufacturing facility in America, and recreate a dealer network from scratch, and he filed lawsuits against Ford for infringing his patents and destroying his business; the case was one of the most complex on record and dragged on for four years. Ferguson, who claimed he pursued Ford as much on behalf of the small-scale inventor's rights against large corporations as on his own account, received in 1952 $9.25 million compensation, very considerably less than he had sought.

The following year, Ferguson sold his companies to Massey-Harris, a North American machinery company; as he received a very large proportion of shares in the newly created Massey-Ferguson Co., he became chairman but only held the post for a year before resigning on 7 July 1954 after disagreements over design changes. Once he was no longer involved so deeply in business operations, he turned his attention to a company which he set up to carry out research, and in particular he worked on the development of four-wheel drive and automatic transmission; he had always retained his interest in motor cars and wanted to improve safety. No major manufacturer was interested in Ferguson's prototype saloon car, which had advanced new features, but Ferguson's prototype of a four-wheel-drive racing car, codenamed the P99, was built and took part in several races. In 1962, after Ferguson's death, the famous racing driver Stirling Moss won the Oulton Park Gold Cup driving the P99. Ferguson's honours during his career included honorary D.Sc. degrees from QUB and Louvain, an honorary engineering degree from the University of Dublin, and fellowship of the Royal Society of Arts.

He married (1913), in Newry registry office, Mary Adelaide ('Maureen') Watson, daughter of Adam Watson, grocer, from Dromore, Co. Down; his brother Joe had previously been courting her and was unhappy to lose her; and her parents, who were Plymouth Brethren, were upset that she was marrying an agnostic. Throughout his life she was his most important supporter and advisor. On a holiday in Jamaica in 1957 with his wife he was shot in the leg by a burglar. His health slightly deteriorated from that point; he was subject to bouts of depression, and to insomnia. When he died in his bath on 25 October 1960 at his home in Stow-on-the-Wold, Gloucestershire, England, he was found to have taken an overdose of barbiturates; the jury at the inquest was directed to return an open verdict, since it was unclear whether he died as a result of an accident or by suicide. He was survived by his wife and their only child, a daughter.

Ferguson's place in history is secure; his innovative engineering designs, and his ability to get them produced affordably, altered farming forever. He has not been forgotten in his native Ulster; blue plaques mark his birthplace, his business premises, and the site of his flights; there is a memorial garden at his birthplace, and the University of Ulster's Engineering Village at Jordanstown is named in his honour. There are Ferguson museums in England and in Denmark; memorabilia trades at high prices and collectors vie for ownership of the little tractors.

Angela Murphy and Linde Lunney

Sources

WWW; Norman Wymer, *Harry Ferguson* (1961); *DNB*; Colin Fraser, *Harry Ferguson: inventor and pioneer* (1972); John B. Rae, *Harry Ferguson and Henry Ford* (1980); John Moore, *Motor makers in Ireland* (1982), 48–73; Bill Martin, *Harry Ferguson* (1984); Richard Hawkins, 'The Ferguson flying machine', *Irish Times*, 31 Dec. 1984; McRedmond; *DIH*; Bernard Crossland and John S. Moore, *The lives of great engineers of Ulster*, i (2003), 55–64; 'Ferguson P99 Climax', www.ultimatecarpage.com; Harold Gibson, 'Harry Ferguson, inventor and pioneer', www.lisburn.com/history/memotries/ferguson.html; George Field, 'The development of the Ferguson System', www.fergusonsociety.com; www.familysearch.org; 'Harry Ferguson: the man and the machine', www.ytmag.com; Raymond Kelly, 'They came from Dromore', www.raymondsoucntydownwebsite.com (internet material accessed Mar. 2007)

Erwin Schrödinger
(1887–1961)

PHYSICIST

Erwin Schrödinger was born on 12 August 1887 in Vienna, Austria, the only child of Rudolf Schrödinger, prosperous owner of a linoleum and oilcloth business, and the bilingual Georgine Emilia Brenda, daughter of Alexander Bauer, professor of chemistry, and his English wife, Emily Russell. The family placed great importance on education and Erwin was educated at home by tutors and his father, 'his friend, teacher and tireless partner in conversation' (*Dictionary of scientific biography*), who had a large library and a great interest in botany and art. In 1898, at the age of eleven, he went to the Gymnasium in Vienna, where the emphasis was on the classics. After entering the University of Vienna (1906), he began attending lectures in theoretical and experimental physics. He received his Doctor of Philosophy (Ph.D.) (1910) and joined the staff until the outbreak of the first world war, during which he served as an artillery officer on the Austro–Italian border. He also managed to continue his research and published his first paper on quantum theory (1917). He married (24 March 1920) Annemarie ('Anny') Bertel and, despite an unusually open marriage, she remained with him for the rest of his life. At this time, he was offered a poorly paid associate professorship in Vienna, which paid even less than Anny was earning as a secretary. He declined the position.

Due to the break-up of the Austro–Hungarian empire, a prospective professorship of theoretical physics at Czernowitz (now Chernivtsi, Ukraine) fell through. He proceeded to spend time (1920–21) at several universities – Jena, Stuttgart and Breslau (Wrocław) – before being appointed to the chair of theoretical physics at the University of Zürich (1921–7), where it is generally accepted his most productive research was carried out. Here he published his revolutionary work in a series of papers relating to quantum-wave mechanics and the general theory of relativity (1926). His partial differential equation, 'Schrödinger's wave equation', is the basic equation of quantum mechanics and changed the view of a particle description of an atom to a wave description. For this work he was awarded the Nobel prize for physics (1933), shared with his friend Paul Dirac.

On the retirement of Max Planck, the inventor of the quantum hypothesis, he was appointed professor of theoretical physics at the University of Berlin (1931), where Albert Einstein was one of his colleagues. After the advent of Adolf Hitler to power (1933), he spoke out repeatedly as a private citizen against the regime and by the end of the year had resigned his post and left Germany. Elected to a fellowship at Magdalen College, Oxford, he requested an additional post for an assistant, an Austrian colleague, Arthur March, with whose wife Hilde he fathered a daughter in 1934. During this period, he also spent time in Spain at the University of Madrid and at Princeton University. He was offered positions at both universities, but he declined the US offer, and the Spanish offer fell through on the outbreak of the Spanish civil war. Later that year he accepted a position at the University of Graz, Austria, longing to return to his own country. However, after the German annexation of Austria (*Anschluss*) in 1938 he was viewed unfavourably by the Germans for his previous Berlin resignation (1933) and was dismissed from his post just as he was preparing to leave the country. He fled to Rome and gratefully accepted an offer in a smuggled letter from Éamon de Valera of a position at the school of theoretical physics in the newly created Dublin Institute for Advanced Studies (DIAS). De Valera had trained in mathematics and was inspired to set up a school similar to the Institute for Advanced Studies in Princeton, where Einstein was a professor. The Dublin institute was to specialise in theoretical physics and Celtic studies. In order to establish its international reputation Schrödinger was suggested as a suitable first director by Edmund Whittaker, mathematics professor at Edinburgh, and previous teacher of de Valera.

After a year at Ghent, Belgium, Schrödinger arrived in Dublin (1939) and set up home at 26 Kincora Road, Clontarf, with an unconventional family arrangement of his wife Anny, Hilde March, and their daughter Ruth. Schrödinger was passionate about theatre and became part of Dublin's artistic and theatrical circles. He maintained close friendships with de Valera and with Pádraig de Brún, professor of mathematics at St Patrick's College, Maynooth.

Apart from Anny and Hilde, Schrödinger had relationships with many women during his life; while in Dublin he fathered two daughters by two different women (1944, 1946). Several of the relationships he pursued were inappropriate. In late 1926, while still at the University of Zürich, he tutored twin fourteen-year-old girls; their mother was friendly with Anny. Schrödinger groomed one of the girls over the coming years, often holidaying with the family. Their sexual relationship commenced just after her seventeenth birthday; an ensuing abortion is thought to have led to her later inability to have children. Such behaviour continued in Ireland. In summer 1940, Schrödinger and Anny holidayed at de Brún's cottage in Dunquin, Co. Kerry, where they were joined by De Brún's sister Margaret and her three daughters (their father Seán MacEntee was unable to join them). Schrödinger became infatuated with the youngest daughter, then aged twelve, and his behaviour drew a stark warning, likely from de Brún, to stay away from the child. Schrödinger recorded such encounters in his diaries and listed the child amongst the unrequited loves of his life. Past biographers have accounted for this behaviour as contributing to, or emanating from, Schrödinger's scientific genius, a view he personally propounded in his diaries.

While at DIAS, Schrödinger continued his work on quantum theory, general relativity, statistical mechanics, nuclear physics and probability theory and began publishing on unified field theory. Here he ran into disagreements with other scientists, most notably Einstein. An excellent teacher, he gave the first lectures on quantum theory in Ireland to staff and students of both Dublin universities. Often taking an idiosyncratic approach to research, in 1935 he proposed a famous theoretical experiment to demonstrate the limitations of quantum mechanics. He imagined that a live cat was locked into a steel chamber with a radioactive atom connected to a vial containing a lethal poison. If the atom decayed it would cause the vial to break and kill the cat. But when the chamber is shut the observer cannot know whether or not the atom has decayed and therefore the cat is both alive and dead at the same time. Schrödinger was questioned so often about this experiment that he was later said to have regretted that he had ever mentioned the cat.

As well as physics he was concerned with broader questions of philosophy, the origins of life and the place of humans in the universe. He endeavoured to make connections between physics and biology, and in February 1943 gave a series of three lectures at Trinity College Dublin (TCD) which were subsequently published as a book, *What is life?* (1944) and translated into six languages. These concerned the physical aspects of the living cell, specifically the relationship between quantum theory and genetics. Watson and Crick, discoverers of the double helix structure of DNA (1953), later acknowledged in a letter to Schrödinger that his book was most influential in their entering the field of molecular biology. His interest in science, philosophy and the classics was expressed in his book *Nature and the Greeks* (1954).

Many of his publications appeared in the *Proceedings of the Royal Irish Academy*, as well as the proceedings of the academies of science of Vienna, Berlin and the Vatican. He was a member of a number of academies of science and a fellow of the Royal Society, and was an honorary member (1931) and professor (1940) of the Royal Irish Academy (RIA); for the latter, he received a special grant from the Irish government until his position in DIAS was confirmed. Among others he received honorary doctorates from the University of Ghent (1939), National University of Ireland (1940) and Dublin University (1940) and also received the Medaglia Matteucci (1929) and the Max Planck medal (1937). In 1957 he was accepted into the German order *Pour le mérite*.

Schrödinger and his wife became Irish citizens in 1948, although they retained their Austrian nationality. There were numerous appeals from Austria, including one from the president, Karl Renner, for Schrödinger to return to his homeland, which he was unwilling to do while it was under Soviet occupation. Austrian neutrality (1955) prompted his retirement from DIAS, and he returned to his homeland in 1956 as professor in the University of Vienna. In 1957 he was proposed unsuccessfully as a candidate for the Austrian presidency. After a debilitating illness he died on 4 January 1961 and was buried in Alpbach, in the Tyrol. His posthumously published book *Meine Weltansicht* (1961; translated as *My view of the world* (1964)) expressed his own metaphysical point of view.

In his honour, the Schrödinger lecture series was inaugurated in 1995 in the Erwin Schrödinger lecture theatre, TCD. An *Irish Times* article by Joe Humphreys, published in December 2021, brought greater public attention to Schrödinger's grooming and abuse of underage girls. TCD responded by removing a statue of him from public view and renaming the Schrödinger lecture theatre. A portrait by Seán Keating, RHA, hangs in the school of theoretical physics, DIAS.

Patricia M. Byrne and Turlough O'Riordan

Sources

DIAS archives; Royal Irish Academy Library, Margaret MacDonnell papers, MS 12 Y 15, (includes text of talk given at TCD by Ruth Braunizer (née Schrödinger), 27 Oct. 2000); RIA Library, *Minutes of proceedings of the Royal Irish Academy* (1939–40), 1, 9; Armin Hermann, 'Schrödinger, Erwin' in Charles Coulston Gillespie (ed.), *Dictionary of scientific biography* (16 vols, 1970–80), vol. 12, 217–23; James McConnell, 'Erwin Schrödinger (1887–1961), Austro-Irish Nobel laureate', *Occasional Papers in Irish Science and Technology*, no. 5 (1988), 1–13; Walter Moore, *Schrödinger: life and thought* (1989); Charles Mollan, William Davis and Brendan Finucane (eds), *More people and places in Irish science and technology* (1990); *Irish Times*, 9 Feb. 1998; 11 Dec. 2021; Mark McCartney and Andrew Whitaker (eds), *Physicists of Ireland* (2003), 186–97; John Gribbin, *Erwin Schrödinger and the quantum revolution* (2012), 131–2; J. J. O'Connor and E. F. Robertson, 'Erwin Rudolf Josef Alexander Schrödinger', MacTutor, Apr. 2015, https://mathshistory.st-andrews.ac.uk/Biographies/Schrodinger/ (internet material accessed June 2003, Feb. 2025)

Emily Anderson
(1891–1962)

ACADEMIC, CODE BREAKER, MUSICOLOGIST
AND TRANSLATOR

Emily Anderson was born on 17 March 1891 at Taylor's Hill, Galway, second daughter of the four children of Alexander Anderson, professor of natural philosophy and later president of Queen's College Galway/University College Galway (QCG/UCG), and Emily Gertrude Anderson (née Binns) from Co. Limerick, daughter of a bank manager in Galway. (Anderson's siblings were Elsie (1890–1957), Alexander (1895–1967), who was awarded the Distinguished Flying Cross in 1920 and changed his name around 1924 to Arthur Andrews, and Helen (1902–37).) The Andersons were presbyterian and lived in the quadrangle at the heart of the university. Anderson's mother was active in reform organisations and, with her daughters, attended local suffrage meetings; they were founder members of the Connaught Women's Franchise League in Galway in January 1913. In 1920 Alexander Anderson published the first public suggestion of the existence of black holes ('On the advance of the perihelion of a planet, and the path of a ray of light in the gravitation field of the sun') in *The Philosophical Magazine*.

Anderson was educated privately by a Swiss governess who was fluent in French and German. She learned piano from an early age and at fourteen commenced a series of visits to Germany, before entering QCG in 1908; she won a literary scholarship after an exceptional performance in her first-year examinations, when she placed first in English,

French, German and Latin; in 1909 and 1910 she held the college's Browne scholarship, and in 1911 graduated Bachelor of Arts (BA) in French and German. She then specialised in German and undertook postgraduate work at the universities of Berlin and Marburg, likely working towards her doctorate; her studies were interrupted by the outbreak of the first world war. In 1915 Anderson was appointed modern languages mistress at Queen's College, Barbados. After working there for two years, she returned to Galway in 1917. She was the first person to hold the newly established separate chair of German in UCG, and radically modernised and extended the course to incorporate middle and old high German, literature and phonetics, and to include more works on the history of the language and its literature.

Anderson was approached in autumn 1917 about joining the British war effort. Although the manner of her recruitment remains unknown, her linguistic acumen and knowledge of mathematics, as well as her family's cultural identification with the United Kingdom (her brother fought in the war and was interned in a German prisoner-of-war camp in November 1917) probably contributed to her decision. Her father's friendship with Sir Joseph Larmor, the esteemed Cambridge University mathematician (where many intelligence operatives were recruited), may also have been a factor. In July 1918, she moved to London and joined MI1(b), the British army's cryptanalytic bureau. There, alongside a small group of women code breakers assembled within the Women's Army Auxiliary Corps, Anderson excelled at 'attacking' foreign diplomatic cable traffic, utilising her cultural knowledge and linguistic and mathematical skills. Between 1918 and 1920 Anderson divided her time between Galway, retaining her position at the university, and London, where she continued to work with MI1(b) and the Government Code and Cypher School (GC&CS). The GC&CS, established in November 1919, collected expert cryptanalysts who had worked on signal and military intelligence during the first world war. In January 1920, she formally joined GC&CS, resigning from UCG in June. Notionally a 'junior assistant' with the Foreign Office, Anderson worked on the cracking and analysis of Italian diplomatic communications. In 1927 she became head of the Italian diplomatic section, where she recruited and managed a team of expert linguists.

In addition to her work with the Foreign Office, in 1923 Anderson published an English translation of Benedetto Croce's *Goethe* from Italian, which had drawn extensively on German sources. Engaging with German sources and their Italian translations, this work not only refined Anderson's linguistic skills but also undoubtedly aided her cryptographic work. As Goethe had known both Mozart and Beethoven, it also served her later musicological research. In effect, she had commenced a dual life. Publicly she was a translator and musicologist, soon to be internationally recognised; her daily work as a leading cryptanalyst was concealed. Drawing upon her love of Germany and its culture, in her spare time she compiled and translated the collected letters of Mozart and his family. These were published in the three-volume *The letters of Mozart and his family* (1938) which collected over 900 letters, including a dozen newly discovered letters. She was the first scholar to treat seriously Mozart's sometimes scatological and nonsensical letters, which previous scholars had censored or omitted, using her cryptographical acumen to reveal the coded allusions in the letters.

From 1920 to 1926, she lived at the Forum Club in Grosvenor Place and then at the Lonsdale Club in Hampstead. Drawn to the relaxed, cosmopolitan nature of the latter leafy suburb she lived in a flat on Arkwright Road from 1926 to 1938, and then from 1938 at Ellendale Road, where she remained. Anderson adored playing the piano and acquired a Bechstein boudoir grand piano; in 1930, she passed the associate examination of the London College of Music.

As tensions grew across Europe in the late 1930s, Anderson's work provided insights into Italian diplomatic and naval planning across the Mediterranean. In 1939 Anderson was the sole woman at 'senior assistant' rank. Intelligence and code breaking capabilities were unified at Bletchley Park, where Anderson was stationed from August 1939 to July 1940. After Italy entered the war in June 1940, relevant British cryptologic and intelligence resources were collected into the Combined Bureau Middle East, opened at Heliopolis in Cairo, Egypt, later that year. Anderson sailed to Durban and traversed Africa to join the bureau in Cairo to be closer to those intelligence sources, enabling more rapid deciphering and analysis. She was head of the Italian military section, focussed on cracking codes used in diplomatic communications between Rome and Addis Ababa, capital of Ethiopia (then under Italian occupation), and within the Italian military command operating across East Africa. Leading a team in demanding conditions, Anderson cracked a series of Italian ciphers, revealing Italian battle plans for Libya and Egypt. This advanced and highly detailed intelligence made a significant contribution to ensuing British military successes in Libya and Ethiopia, and to the capture of hundreds of thousands of Italian troops.

As the Axis powers surrendered in North Africa, Anderson returned to England in May 1943, where she was assigned to the Government Communications Bureau in Berkeley Street, London. There she tackled German and Hungarian diplomatic codes (in the 1930s she had worked on Hungarian cipher books with Dilly Knox, a renowned expert in linguistic approaches to code breaking). A notoriously difficult language to master, Hungarian diplomatic codes were regarded as an especially taxing cryptographic challenge by the intelligence community. In July 1943, Anderson was made an officer of the Order of the British Empire (OBE, civil division) 'for services to the forces and in connection with military operations' (*London Gazette*, 13 July 1943). Her singular importance, and distinction as one of the few women working at the highest echelons, saw her referred to as 'Emily' in high-level British intelligence communications and correspondence.

Anderson's prowess emanated from her ability to translate and decrypt simultaneously. This was especially important in diplomatic intelligence analysis where, alongside linguistic precision and sophistication, nuance and emphasis are intrinsically important. She excelled in book-building and cypher-stripping as diplomatic signal intelligence deciphering became increasingly important as the cold war commenced. While she could be demanding of colleagues and collaborators, Anderson's austere façade hid her warm personality.

Post-war, Anderson resumed work on Beethoven's letters, collating and transcribing correspondence on visits to archives and collections. After thirty years in the British civil service, she retired in November 1950. Her unusually long tenure in the demanding intelligence field was enabled by the stimulation and freedom her linguistic and musicological research engendered, and her parallel careers drew on – and nurtured – overlapping skill sets. Anderson revelled in the challenge of unlocking Beethoven's hieroglyphical handwriting. Utilising approaches from her intelligence work enabled Anderson to conquer his (mostly Gothic) script, as well as the coded notes he composed to himself in marginalia. She deployed her palaeographic skills to identify patterns and repetitions, from which she could recognise letters, words and phrases. Anderson's three-volume *Letters of Beethoven* was published in October 1961. Universally praised and widely lauded by musicologists and antiquarians, it collected 1,570 letters, 230 of which had not previously been published. That year she also published an English edition of *Hebel's Bible stories*, translated from Swiss-German; she also wrote historical articles for various music journals. In recognition of her contribution to Germanic culture and music Anderson was awarded the Order of Merit, first class, by the West German government at a ceremony in Bonn in October 1962.

Anderson had commenced preliminary work on revising *The letters of Mozart and his family* before her death on 26 October 1962 at New End Hospital, Hampstead, London, from heart disease (the revised edition was completed by her friends Monica Carolan and Alexander Hyatt King). After her funeral on 1 November 1962 at Hampstead parish church, attended by leading figures from the intelligence community and the world of London classical music, Anderson's remains were cremated at Golder's Green. On her instructions no funeral urn, burial plot or monument were instituted.

Anderson's will made several philanthropic bequests. £1,685 went to the Royal United Kingdom Beneficent Association to help persons of reduced means in the Republic of Ireland. After other bequests to friends and family, a trust fund was established, under which one-third of the residual estate went to the Musicians Benevolent Fund and the remainder was willed to the Royal Philharmonic Association for the establishment of an international annual competition for violin-playing in London. The Emily Anderson prize for young violinists was duly established in 1967 by the Royal Philharmonic Society and continues to be awarded. The University of Galway is home to the Anderson Centre for Translation Research and Practice (established in 2021), while in 2017 the university's concert hall was renamed in Anderson's honour. Facing the entrance to the quadrangle where she grew up, the Emily Anderson concert hall hosts an annual concert in memory of one of the university's most distinguished alumni.

Turlough O'Riordan and Linde Lunney

Sources

General Register Office, birth cert.; Census of Ireland, 1901, https://www.census.nationalarchives.ie/; *Who was who … 1897–1916* [etc.] (1920); *London Gazette*, 13 July 1943; *Times* (London), death notice and obit., 29 Oct. 1962; *Irish Times*, 25 Jan. 1963; Mary Clancy, '"It was our joy to keep the flag flying": a study of the women's suffrage campaign in County Galway', *UCG Women's Studies Centre Review*, vol. 3 (1995), 99; Rosaleen O'Neill, 'Modern languages' in Tadhg O'Neill (ed.), *From Queen's College to National University* (1999), esp. 375–6; Alec Hyatt King, 'Emily Anderson', *The new Grove dictionary of music and musicians* (29 vols, 2001), i; Róisín Healy, 'The lives of Emily Anderson: Galway professor, music historian, and British intelligence officer', 20 Mar. 2017, https://mooreinstitute.ie/2017/03/20/lives-emily-anderson-galway-professor-music-historian-british-intelligence-officer/; Jackie Uí Chionna, *Queen of codes: the secret life of Emily Anderson, Britain's greatest female codebreaker* (2023); Daniel Leeson, 'Emily Anderson (1891–1962)', Music Associates of America, www.musicassociatesofamerica.com/madima/1993/thanksoldtimer.html; 'Emily Anderson: the only woman junior assistant at the formation of GC&CS in 1919', https://www.gchq.gov.uk/person/emily-anderson (internet material accessed Apr. 2008, June 2024)

Kathleen Lonsdale
(1903–71)

X-ray crystallographer and pacifist

Kathleen Lonsdale was born on 28 January 1903 in Charlotte House, Newbridge, Co. Kildare, youngest among ten children of Henry Frederick Yardley (d. 1923), an English-born former soldier and postmaster of Newbridge, and his wife Jessie Cameron, of Scots descent. Her early life was difficult: the family had little money and relations between her parents were strained. Four of her six brothers died in infancy; another brother, Fred Yardley, had to leave school to go out to work, but became a pioneering radio officer, who in 1912 received the last radio signals from the *Titanic*. Her mother was a forceful character, who brought her family up in baptist beliefs. Kathleen attended the Newbridge village school for a short time before her mother, worried about the political developments in Ireland, took the children to England in 1908. They settled at Seven Kings, Essex; Henry Yardley lived elsewhere and seldom visited them. Kathleen attended the local elementary school, then won a scholarship to the county high school for girls at Ilford (1914–19) and was the only girl who opted to take classes in physics, chemistry, and higher mathematics at the Ilford Boys School. She was a brilliant, determined student and was awarded the county major scholarship and the Royal Geographical Society's medal for achieving the highest marks in geography papers. At the age of sixteen she entered Bedford College for Women, London (part of the University of London), where she studied mathematics. She gained a University of London scholarship after one year and transferred from mathematics to physics, because she preferred experimental work.

In 1922 she placed first in the honours B.Sc. examination, obtaining the highest marks awarded in ten years, and came to the attention of the Nobel prize-winner W. H. Bragg, one of the examiners, who offered her a position on his research team at University College, London (UCL), and later in the Royal Institution. There she worked on X-ray diffraction of crystals of organic compounds, beginning with those of succinic acid, the di-basic acid first synthesised by Maxwell Simpson. With a fellow student, W. T. Astbury, she published in 1924, aged just twenty-one, 'Tabulated data for the examination of the 230 space-groups' in the *Transactions of the Royal Society*, a major contribution to crystallography. Yardley was awarded an M.Sc. (1924) and a Ph.D. (1927).

On 27 August 1927 she married Thomas Jackson Lonsdale, an engineering research student at UCL, and moved to Leeds, where he got a research assistantship. Somewhat unusually for the time, Thomas Lonsdale encouraged his wife to continue her scientific work, and she joined Leeds University chemistry department as a part-time demonstrator. There she made her most important contribution to chemistry by proving, by X-ray diffraction of crystals of hexamethylbenzene, that the benzene ring was flat. This had been a major topic of interest in chemistry for sixty years. She was also first to use Fourier analysis of X-ray patterns to study the structure of an organic molecule, another benzene compound, hexachlorobenzene. The Lonsdales' first child, a daughter, was born in 1929, and shortly afterwards the family returned to London. Another daughter and a son were born (1931, 1934), but she managed to continue her scientific research, working on calculations at home while the children were babies, then took a post at the Royal Institution as research assistant to Sir William Bragg and later to Sir Henry Dale. She worked on magnetic anisotropy in crystals and molecules and also pioneered techniques such as divergent beam X-ray photography for investigating the surfaces and structure of crystals.

She was awarded the degree of D.Sc. in 1936. In 1946 she was appointed reader in crystallography at UCL and was appointed professor of chemistry and head of the department of crystallography (1949), the first woman professor in UCL. She began her teaching career at the age of forty-three; her students generally found her lectures challenging at best, but Lonsdale's initiatives in undergraduate teaching of crystallography, particularly the practical aspects, were copied in other universities, and she shared with J. D. Bernal the teaching in an intercollegiate M.Sc. course in crystallography. She thus trained many of the next generation of crystallographers. During her time at UCL (1949–68) she was at last able to develop her own research group. Interests included photo-reactions and order-disorder transitions in the solid state, thermal vibrations and diffuse scattering in crystals, various pharmacological compounds, and the constitution of bladder and kidney stones. She also worked on synthetic diamonds. The tables that she had compiled with Astbury established the theoretical basis of structure analysis; her book *Simplified structure factor and electron density formulae for the 230 space groups of mathematical crystallography* (1936) contained an important development of that work, and she made further contributions to understanding and study of X-ray analysis of crystals by putting enormous effort into editing three volumes of the second series of *International tables for X-ray crystallography* (1952, 1959, 1962), for many years the standard handbooks in the field.

In 1943 she was an invited lecturer at the Dublin Institute for Advanced Studies summer school, along with Erwin Schrödinger, Max Born, and P. P. Ewald; the taoiseach, Éamon de Valera, attended all the lectures. She was a visiting professor in several American universities. In 1945, after the Royal Society held a postal poll of existing fellows on the possibility of women being elected, she and the biochemist Marjory Stephenson were chosen as the first female fellows of the Royal Society; she was a member of the council and vice-president of the Royal Society in 1960–61. She was awarded the Royal Society's Davy medal, its pre-eminent award in chemistry, in 1957 (she donated the prize money to a fund to establish a lecture in memory of W. H. Bragg). In 1968 she became the first female president of the British Association for the Advancement of Science; she received honorary doctorates of science and of law from the universities of Wales, Leicester, Manchester, Leeds, Dundee, Oxford and Bath. In 1956 she was appointed Dame Commander of the British Empire and, in 1966, a rare form of hexagonal diamond, found in meteorites and produced synthetically, was named 'lonsdaleite' in her honour.

After their marriage, both Lonsdales became quakers 'by convincement'; she identified strongly with quaker insistence on absolute opposition to war. She had been a committed pacifist since her experiences as a child during the first world war. At the beginning of the second, though as a mother of young children she would have been exempt from any wartime duties, she refused on conscientious grounds to register for employment or civil defence duties which would have helped the war effort and was fined £2. When she refused to pay the fine, she was committed to Holloway prison for one month in February 1943. While imprisoned, she had to do the usual prison work and experienced much of the rigour and privation of prison life, though she was able in the evenings to continue her scientific work on anomalous reflexions. As a result of her experiences, she became an advocate of prison reform, and was appointed an official visitor to a prison at Aylesbury and to Borstal. She travelled widely to speak at conferences and study prison conditions abroad. During the war she opened her home to refugees from Germany.

In later life, she became increasingly concerned about the role that science was being asked to play in military preparations, and helped found the Atomic Scientists Association. Dame Kathleen also helped establish the Pugwash movement to work for an end to armed conflicts, was a member of the East–West committee of the Society of Friends and attended conferences and meetings all over the world. Of her many articles and pamphlets on the religious case against war and militarism, the most notable publication was *Is peace possible?* (1957), published by Penguin Books, which supported total nuclear disarmament. She was a vegetarian and a teetotaller.

Kathleen Lonsdale did a great deal, and not just as a role model, to encourage young people, especially women, to take up science as a career. She took every opportunity to speak in schools, and published articles on the practical adjustments that society needed to make to enable professional women to contribute successfully and happily in both domestic and public spheres, as she herself had been able to do. In 1965 she moved with her husband on his retirement to Bexhill-on-Sea, Sussex, continuing to commute to London for five hours a day until her own retirement in 1968, when she became emeritus professor of UCL. She continued to work and publish, almost until her death in University College Hospital of bone marrow cancer on 1 April 1971. She was survived by her husband and her three children. In 1981 the chemistry building at

UCL was renamed the Kathleen Lonsdale building, and in 1998 the new Aeronautical and Environmental Building at the University of Limerick was also given her name. A plaque marks her birthplace in Newbridge. She is also commemorated by the British Crystallographic Association in an annual lecture named for her, and National University of Ireland, Maynooth, which gives a student prize named after her.

A full list of her many scientific papers and a partial list of her publications on her other interests can be found in Dorothy Hodgkin, 'Kathleen Lonsdale', *Biographical memoirs of fellows of the Royal Society*, xlv (1975), 478–84.

Linde Lunney and Enda Leaney

Sources

Dictionary of scientific biography; Dorothy Hodgkin, 'Kathleen Lonsdale', *Biographical memoirs of fellows of the Royal Society*, xlv (1975), 448–84 (photo); J. P. R. Ryan, *The chemical association of Ireland, 1922–36* (1997), 153–5; Charles Mollan, 'Kathleen Lonsdale', *Irish innovators in science and technology* (2002), 237–8 (photo); P. P. E. Childs and A. MacLellan, 'The stuff off diamonds' in Mary Mulvihill (ed.), *Lab coats and lace: the lives and legacies of inspiring women scientists and pioneers* (2009), 144–155; 'Commemorative plaque unveiling in honour of Dame Kathleen Lonsdale (1903–1971), Newbridge, Co. Kildare', www.witsireland.com; information from James Lunney, TCD

Mary Gough

(1892–1983)

Educator and mathematician

Mary (Sr Mary de Lellis; 'Maggie') Gough was born Margaret Gough on 15 February 1892 at the family home in Rickardstown, Kilmore, Co. Wexford, the eldest of the two daughters of Ellen (née Dunne) and Walter Gough. Both of local modest farm labouring families, they married on 14 October 1891 in Kilmore. Walter worked as a farm labourer and acquired five acres there. Gough and her younger sister Lizzie (b. 9 Nov. 1894) both attended a national school run by the St John of God order. 'Maggie' (as she was listed in the 1901 census) continued her education in a convent school in the vicinity.

Raised in the widespread poverty then enveloping the community, in August 1909 Gough emigrated to America with a group of other local women. They sailed on the *Irak* from Liverpool and joined the Sisters of Charity of the Incarnate Word congregation in San Antonio, Texas. Emerging from France in the seventeenth century, the congregation had expanded into America in 1866 and focused on teaching and serving the sick and indigent. Dressed in 'rich bridal attire and wearing veils and wreaths of orange blossom', on 24 July 1910 Gough and thirteen other Irish emigrant postulants (amongst a group of twenty-one) underwent investiture (*New Ross Standard*, 26 Aug. 1910). Gough took 'Mary de Lellis' as her name in religion, likely inspired by Camillus de Lellis (1550–1614), a priest canonised in 1746.

She professed her vows in 1911 while studying at the congregation's Incarnate Word College in San Antonio. (It had been founded as a school in 1881, later moving to the congregation's mother house at Alamo Heights, and by 1910 was offering bachelor's degrees in arts, literature and science as it transformed itself into a higher education institution.) Becoming a teacher, Gough taught initially at catholic elementary (primary) schools in Texas and Missouri. She then taught mathematics at St Mary's academy, a high school in Amarillo, Texas. In 1920 she gained a Bachelor of Arts (BA) in mathematics from the Catholic University of America (CUA), a pontifical university in Washington, DC. Gough studied at the university's Catholic Sisters College (CSC), which had been founded in 1911 as a residential institute staffed by academics from the university. This setting was congenial to women religious, who were dispatched there from many orders and congregations to undertake undergraduate and postgraduate degrees, drawn by CUA's pontifical accreditation and the CSC's residential setting.

Gough returned to teach mathematics at Incarnate Word College, where she remained for over twenty years, apart from various sabbaticals pursuing postgraduate research. She visited the University of Oklahoma for the second semester of 1921–2, returning to the Catholic University in 1922–3. She was awarded a Master of Arts (MA) in mathematics in 1923 for a thesis submitted to the CSC titled 'The representability of a number by an indefinite binary quadratic form', afterwards resuming her teaching at Incarnate Word College.

During summer 1927 Gough undertook research at the University of Texas. She then returned to Washington, DC, where she commenced her doctoral studies at the Catholic University (1927–31). There she was supervised by Aubrey Edward Landy (1880–1972), a Canadian-American mathematician. Landy supervised many women mathematicians (comprising eighteen of the twenty-eight Doctor of Philosophy (Ph.D.) dissertations he oversaw), including Euphemia Haynes (1890–1980) who, in 1943, became the first African American woman to gain a Ph.D. in mathematics. Gough earned her Ph.D. in 1931 with a thesis titled 'On the condition for the existence of triangles in-and-circumscribed to certain types of the rational quartic curve and having a common side'; her doctoral studies also comprised 'minors' in education and physics. She was amongst three other women religious awarded doctorates by the university that year, all supervised by Landy and addressing algebraic geometry. In common with most of the women earning their doctorates from the CUA in the 1930s, Gough obtained the degree with the intention of improving the quality and augmenting the range of teaching provided at catholic women's institutions, such as Incarnate Word College, which were then transforming themselves into 'four-year' colleges.

Gough returned to Incarnate Word College where she taught until 1943, followed by a year teaching mathematics at Incarnate Word Academy in St Louis, Missouri. After some ill health, and hospitalisation at St Anthony's Hospital, Amarillo, Texas, she transitioned to a desk job. For the next twenty years she was a treasurer and chief accountant at St Joseph's Hospital, Fort Worth, Texas, which the congregation owned and operated.

Although she never returned to Ireland, Gough remained in touch with her family. Her emigration, enforced by poverty, was emblematic of the paucity of opportunities for women in rural Ireland in the early twentieth century. Her religious life in America engendered her social mobility, which enabled her to become the first Irish woman to obtain a Ph.D. in mathematics. In 1964 Gough retired to live at St Joseph's convent, San Antonio, amongst other retired women religious. Losing her sight, and enduring the likely effects of dementia, she died there on 17 April 1983 and was buried in the Sisters of Charity of the Incarnate Word cemetery in the city.

Gough was a member of the American Mathematical Society and it is sometimes incorrectly claimed that she invented the term 'mathemaphobia'. In 2023 the Irish Mathematics Teachers' Association instituted the Maggie Gough competition, which tests the problem-solving skills of junior and leaving certificate students. South East Technological University launched a funded Ph.D. in STEM (science, technology, engineering and mathematics) the same year to mark Gough's achievement, part-funded by her descendants.

Turlough O'Riordan

Sources

Birth cert., parents' marriage cert., parents' death certs, https://www.irishgenealogy.ie/en/; *New Ross Standard*, 26 Aug. 1910; Elinor Tong Dehey, *Religious orders of women in the United States: accounts of their origin and of their most important institutions* (1913), 232–4, https://www.loc.gov/resource/gdcmassbookdig.religiousorderso-00dehe/?sp=324&st=image; Judy Green and Jeanne LaDuke, *Pioneering women in American mathematics: the pre-1940 PhD's* (2009), 52; *History of Mathematics*, vol. 34 (2009); Green and LaDuke, *Supplementary material for pioneering women in American mathematics: the pre-1940 PhD's* (2016), https://www.ams.org/publications/authors/books/postpub/hmath-34-PioneeringWomen.pdf; Judy Green and Jeanne LaDuke, 'Pioneers: the pre-1940s PhDs' in Janet L. Beery, Sarah J. Greenwald, Jacqueline A. Jensen-Vallin and Maura B. Mast (eds), *Women in mathematics: celebrating the centennial of the Mathematical Association of America* (2017), 42; 'The real first Irish woman with a doctorate in maths?', Mathematics Ireland blog, Jan. 2020, https://www.mathsireland.ie/blog/2020_01_cm; Colm Mulcahy and Mary Cunneen, 'Meet Maggie Gough, the forgotten Irish maths pioneer', RTÉ Brainstorm, 18 Oct. 2022, https://www.rte.ie/brainstorm/2022/1018/1329907-maggie-gough-sister-mary-de-lellis-maths-pioneer-ireland/; 'Maggie Gough competition', Irish Mathematics Teachers' Association, https://imta.ie/maggie-gough-competition/ (internet material accessed Feb. 2025)

John Stewart Bell
(1928–90)

Physicist

John Stewart Bell was born on 28 July 1928 in Belfast, second child among one daughter and three sons of John Bell and Annie Bell (née Brownlee) of Tate's Avenue, Belfast. Both families were of Scottish protestant extraction. Although his father had left school at twelve, his mother saw education as a route to a fulfilling life and encouraged her children. However, means were limited and only John was able to stay at school over fourteen years of age. He was educated at Old Ulsterville elementary school and Fane Street secondary school before attending the Belfast Technical College, where an academic curriculum, combined with practical courses, provided a sound basis for his future interests in practical and fundamental aspects of science.

His interest in books and science from an early age earned him the nickname 'the prof.' at home. At the age of sixteen (1944) he began working as a junior laboratory assistant in the physics department of QUB under its professors Karl Emelaus and Robert Sloane. Recognising his ability, they encouraged him to attend first-year lectures. The following year, with money saved from his job and some extra support, he enrolled for a degree course. A scholarship was later awarded, and he graduated with a first-class degree in experimental physics (1948), staying on to achieve a second degree in mathematical physics (1949). He was particularly interested in quantum mechanics, and encouraged by the crystallographer Paul Peter Ewald, who taught him in his last year at QUB, he applied for a position at the Atomic Energy Research Establishment at Harwell, near Oxford (1949). There he worked under Klaus Fuchs (later arrested for espionage, 1950) on reactor physics before moving to Malvern to work on accelerator design. Here he met Mary Ross, a member of the design group, and they began a collaboration that lasted his lifetime, marrying in 1954.

In 1951 he was given leave of absence to work with Rudolf Peierls in the department of mathematical physics at Birmingham University, where he developed his version of the CPT theorem of quantum field theory ('Time reversal in field theory', *Proc. Roy. Soc. Lond.* (1955), A 231, 479–95) for which, with some additional work, he later gained his Ph.D. (1956). Unfortunately, the same theorem was published simultaneously by the renowned physicists Gerhart Lüders and Wolfgang Pauli, who received all the credit. Bell returned (1954) to Harwell to a newly set-up group to study elementary particle physics. Unhappy with the gradually more applied nature of the group's work, he and Mary moved (1960) to CERN in Geneva, where they could both continue pursuing their research interests; she on accelerator design and he on high energy physics, accelerator physics, and what he called his 'hobby', quantum measurement theory.

He published around eighty papers in high-energy physics and quantum field theory. In 1964 he published his greatest contribution to quantum theory, 'On the Einstein Podolsky Rosen paradox' (*Physics*, 1, 195–200), what he called his 'non-locality theory', which showed the potential for detecting instantaneous communication between subatomic particles that are far apart. This deviates from Einstein's relativity theory, where nothing travels faster than the speed of light. Although his paper was at first ignored, it was taken on board by the physics community. The theory was experimentally tested and came to be known as 'Bell's inequality' or 'Bell's theorem', a proof of quantum theory that reopened to experiment the fundamental basis of physics. Henry Stapp of the Lawrence National Berkeley Laboratory, California, called his result 'the most profound discovery of science' ('Are superluminal connections necessary?', *Nuova Cimento* (1977), xl B, 191–205). Another of Bell's papers discredited an earlier 'proof' by von Neumann of the impossibility of adding hidden variables to the theory of quantum mechanics.

Bell's pioneering work had an enormous influence on subsequent developments in quantum theory, quantum experiments and quantum technology. A collection of his own views on quantum philosophy was published in *Speakable and unspeakable in quantum mechanics* (1987) and presented with humorous illustrations. A list of his publications is found in *Biographical memoirs of fellows of the Royal Society* (1999).

He received many honours in his life, mostly at the latter end of his career; FRS (1972), Reality Foundation prize (1982), honorary foreign member of the American Academy of Arts and Sciences (1987), the Dirac medal of the Institute of Physics (1988), honorary D.Sc. from QUB (1988) and TCD (1988), the Heineman prize of the American Physical Society, and the Hughes medal of the Royal Society (1989).

Unassuming and modest about his own work, he is remembered for his intellectual precision, integrity and generosity, as well as a keen Ulster sense of humour. An incisive critic, he could be irritated by those less rigorous in their views of quantum physics than himself. He was a frequent visitor to Belfast, where his family remained. His younger brother David, after studying at night, qualified as an electrical engineer and became a professor at Lambton College, Canada, where he wrote several textbooks.

John Bell died of a stroke at his home on 1 October 1990 in Geneva, aged sixty-two. The proceedings of a conference to commemorate his life's work were published in *Quantum [un]speakables from Bell to quantum information* (2002). The Institute of Physics, who had described him as one of the top ten physicists of the twentieth century, mounted a plaque commemorating his pioneering work and contribution to science on the old physics building of QUB (2002). According to Andrew Whitaker (1998), biographer of Bell, his work has 'changed our perception of physical reality and the nature of the universe'.

Patricia M. Byrne

Sources

Biographical encyclopaedia of scientists (1992); Andrew Whitaker, 'John Bell and the most profound discovery of science', *Physics World*, vol. xi, no. 12 (1998), 29–34; P. G. Burke and I. C. Percival, 'John Stewart Bell', *Biographical memoirs of fellows of the Royal Society*, xlv (1999), 45, 3–17; John Bradbury, *Celebrated citizens of Belfast* (2002), 10–11; Charles Mollan and Brendan Finucane, *Irish innovators in science and technology* (2002); QUB communications office media release, 7 May 2002; Andrew Whitaker, 'John Stewart Bell 1928–1990', *Physicists of Ireland* (2003) 273–81; Andrew Whitaker, 'John Stewart Bell', MacTutor, Aug. 2002, https://mathshistory.st-andrews.ac.uk/Biographies/Bell_John/ (accessed Feb. 2003)

Peter Rice
(1935–92)

STRUCTURAL ENGINEER

Peter Ronan Rice was born on 16 June 1935 at the Leinster nursing home, 26 Upper Pembroke Street, Dublin, son of James Patrick Rice, head of the Louth vocational education committee, and Maureen Rice (née Quinn), living at 11 Faughart Terrace, St Mary's Road, Dundalk, Co. Louth. Educated at Drogheda CBS and later at Newbridge, Co. Kildare, he had studied through the medium of Irish and considered joining the priesthood. He subsequently opted for engineering at QUB, where he graduated in 1956. He then took the Diploma of Imperial College, London (1958). Meanwhile, he was first engaged professionally (1956) by the London office of the distinguished English-born engineer-architect of Danish origin, Ove Arup. He became a permanent employee and later partner and director.

After two years of preparatory work with Arup, Rice was appointed resident and site engineer (1960–66) at the renowned opera house in Sydney, Australia, designed by the Danish architect Jørn Utzon. This largely curvilinear structure was the first of several iconic buildings with which he became directly associated; without his expertise in mathematical and artistic intuition the architect's intent might have been frustrated by conventional structural practice. Utzon's dramatic resignation from the Sydney project, partly for political reasons, increased pressure on Rice and his team, and its successful completion is testimony to how well he understood the ultimate physical possibilities of concrete, steel and glass as materials of quality as well as function. This distinguished him from many of his post-war contemporaries, including architects, who regarded function as the primary concern of building, at the cost of beauty and imagination. His reputation was established with the extraordinary Sydney project and its seemingly impossible roof angles, as indeed was the reputation of Utzon, who owed so much to Rice's brilliance.

In 1965 Rice married Sylvia Watson; they had a son and three daughters. His personal life was devoted to what leisure he could afford in a busy career of front-line architectural works, which frequently astonished both professional colleagues and the public alike for their innovation and daring. He enjoyed horses, football, botany and the epicurean pleasures of good alcohol. His Byronically romantic appearance, described variously as hirsute and bohemian, presented a disarming exterior which, when he held forth in a professional capacity, charmed his listeners for the confidence and certainty of his vision. His date of birth (16 June) may have inspired the sobriquet 'the James Joyce of civil engineering' and his renaissance artistic and mathematical genius that of 'the Benvenuto Cellini of [recent] European architecture', but Rice's name also became a byword for 'whatever next?' in public buildings over thirty years from the early 1960s to the 1990s. He was frequently compared with the great Victorian engineers, whose heroic achievements in visual and structural beauty have outlasted their age.

In 1963 Arup made him a partner in the formation of Arup Associates, a firm of many disciplines. Typically, Rice was at home in the execution of arts and education spaces, and latterly of bridges and of terminals for air and rail transport, modern versions of the pioneering temples of progress built by such spiritual forerunners as the Brunels. He also carried out engineering for purely commercial architecture, both as a team engineer and an independent designer. In 1966–7 he was visiting scholar at Cornell University, Ithaca, New York. Rice was engaged in 1973–7 as chief engineer of the remarkable external steel skeleton and colourful ducting of the high-tech modernist Centre Pompidou at Place Beaubourg in Paris, designed by architects Renzo Piano and Richard Rogers. In 1977 he formed a partnership with Piano, and in 1978 he became one of seventeen directors of Arup. He simultaneously conducted his own business in Paris, and in 1982 established Rice Francis Ritchie (RFR) Design Engineering with Martin Francis and Ian Ritchie, which notably built the frontages of the National Museum of Science, Technology and Industry at La Villette, Paris (1985). His French commissions were many – from Aerogare 3 at Charles de Gaulle airport in Paris to the airport terminal at Marseille, the TGV station roof at Lille and other grand public statements in steel and glass.

Fascinated by glass as an architectural material, Rice specialised in study of its technological and artistic potential, later co-authoring a book in French with Hugh Dutton, *La verre structurel* (Paris, 1990), subsequently translated into English as *Structural glass* (UK, 1995). He was engaged by leading clients of Arup in further high-tech architecture, notably by its leading English exponent, Norman Foster, who involved him in building the structural masterpiece of Stansted airport terminal in Essex (completed 1991) with its overwhelming sense of light and space. This building clearly indicates the proximity of architecture and engineering in new design, the borderline of which Rice increasingly overlapped, making him so desirable an associate of modern architects. He worked practically up to his death on major projects of world influence. Rogers engaged Rice again for his Lloyds Building in the city of London (1979–84), which showed obvious parallels with the Pompidou development in Paris, combining function with beauty in its familiar-looking exoskeleton.

Also in London he worked on the canopy of Michael Hopkins's Mound Stand at Lord's cricket ground (1985–7). He worked with Piano in Italy on various projects, including the Stadio Nuovo in Bari for the soccer world cup of 1990, and the design of portable buildings, including emergency shelters for the aftermath of natural disasters. They had also worked together on the De Menil Museum in Houston, Texas, and at Osaka in Japan built the elongated international airport terminal in which Rice devised the steel support trusses. For Johann Otto von Spreckelsen's vast Défense arch in Paris (1982–90), he designed the internal canopy entitled 'Nuages' (Clouds).

Among his last projects Rice built the Pavilion of the Future at Expo 92 in Seville, Spain. He was MICE (from 1973) and an honorary FRIBA (from 1988), as well as becoming MRIAI in 1990, having spent virtually his entire career outside Ireland. Rice's formidable honours list included gold medals of the French Society for the Encouragement of National Industry and the French Academy of Architecture. Finally, he was awarded an exhibition of his work in London in June 1992, with the RIBA gold medal, a distinctly rare event for a non-architect, and received much praise in the British press. Such accolades were given just in time: he was then fighting a terminal brain illness, which he kept at bay until weeks before he died in London on 25 October 1992, aged 57.

Patrick Long

Sources

Dennis Sharp, *Twentieth century architecture: a visual history* (1991), 410; *Times*, 26 Mar., 7 Aug., 7 Nov. 1992; *Irish Times,* 3 Nov. 1992; *Annual Reg., 1992*; *WWW*; Newmann; Muriel Emanuel (ed.), *Contemporary architects* (1994 ed.), 799–800; John Fleming, Hugh Honor and Nikolaus Pevsner, *The Penguin dictionary of architecture and landscape architecture* (1998); Dennis Sharp (ed.), *The illustrated encyclopedia of architects and architecture* (2001 ed.); Mary Mulvihill, *Ingenious Ireland* (2002), 230–31

Gerrit van Gelderen
(1926–94)

NATURALIST, WILDLIFE FILM-MAKER,
BROADCASTER AND AUTHOR

Gerrit van Gelderen was born on 26 August 1926 in Rotterdam, the Netherlands, eldest child of Johannes Gerardus van Gelderen, a local-authority employee who lived within the municipal park where he worked. Familiar from childhood with the park's wildlife, Gerrit went to secondary school in Rotterdam and assisted in surveying the plants and animals of the wildlife sanctuary at De Beer, outside the city, in the late 1930s. He witnessed the city's bombing in 1940, and its German occupation until 1945. Although he was forced to spend a year at a labour camp in Germany, some of his bitterest war memories included the military fortification of De Beer, and subsequently its post-war Europoort industrial development, polluting the Rhine–Maas delta. His other favourite nature reserve, the Biesbosch, adjacent to Dordrecht, was protected against the sea but became, in van Gelderen's opinion, homogenised into a sterile replacement of true wilderness.

After attending the college of art in the Hague, his impatience for adventure led him to hitch-hike through the environmental oases of post-war Scandinavia, working casually and selling units of his blood for cash. In August 1955, wanderlust eventually brought him to his adoptive homeland of Ireland, in response to an advertisement for commercial artists at Sun Advertising in Dublin. There he joined other foreign staff, whose continental design training was valued more highly than the Irish equivalent, particularly in areas such as aircraft drawing. Although struggling financially and socially in a strange country, he had discovered the bird life of a pre-industrialised landscape – a landscape he believed Holland had now lost. Travelling around Ireland's natural habitats, including the Great Saltee Island, a major bird sanctuary in Co. Wexford whose ornithological survey team was then mostly English, van Gelderen discovered a scant Irish public awareness of indigenous wildlife. He committed his future to celebrating and promoting it through his artistic talents, primarily illustration, photography, and, by extension, documentary film.

His future wife, Lize ('Lies') Henderson, of distant Scottish ancestry, also a naturalist, travelled from Rotterdam soon after his own arrival and agreed to settle in Dublin. Married in 1956, they occupied a flat in Edenvale, an old house with a large, wild garden at Conyngham Road, directly between the Phoenix Park and the River Liffey. Here they kept a Galway currach, in which they rowed downstream to the city centre. The garden became an eccentric outdoor laboratory, sufficiently tamed for van Gelderen to attract and photograph wildlife in action. As a result of this interest, an unexpected career opportunity arose in the early 1960s. His employment in advertising had been regular but erratic, moving from Sun Advertising (1958) to the *Irish Farmers' Journal* as cartoonist/illustrator, photographer and columnist, then (1960) to Janus Advertising. His distinctive graphic style (with crisp, at times extensive, captioning) charged potentially dry illustrative material with palpable energy. Using his equally individual cartooning talent, he criticised human destruction of the environment. At about the time Irish national television began regular broadcasting as Telefís Éireann in 1962, his wildlife hobby formed the basis of friendship and professional collaboration with the

Dublin supplier of his animal food, Parnell Street pet shop proprietor and environmentalist Éamon de Buitléar.

Having persuaded the infant Telefís Éireann to grant them a weekly programme on Irish wildlife entitled *Amuigh faoin spéir* ('Out under the sky'), van Gelderen and de Buitléar soon became household names, sharing the struggles and accolades of their surprising success. Van Gelderen's graphic and cartoon talents merged into rapid sketches on screen as de Buitléar spoke a commentary in English and Irish. Initially made in studio with live fauna, including a troublesome mute swan which van Gelderen had captured on the River Liffey for the first programme, the series ventured outdoors, filming largely in van Gelderen's own semi-wild garden. Ultimately, as their series gained in popularity (van Gelderen subsequently illustrating Justin Keating's *Telefís feirme* series), a studio Land Rover and outdoor crew were provided for more adventurous programming. Their work won them a prestigious Jacobs Award in 1967. They became inextricably linked in the public mind but agreed to follow separate careers when they outgrew their original working relationship. Success provided each with opportunities to work independently, van Gelderen setting his sights on challenging overseas environments.

In the mid-1970s, he created his own television series, *To the waters and the wild*. He filmed extensively in Ireland but also travelled to the USA, Canada, Iceland, Europe, Saharan Africa, the Middle East and India, depending greatly on sponsorship, available transport, and the frequent kindness of strangers. Braving extremes of climate and, for the sake of his independent career, risking every danger from drugs to guns and warring revolutionaries, he earned the international respect of his peers. He served on the executive of An Taisce, edited its journal, and illustrated and wrote articles for periodicals such as the youth magazine

Our Boys. Van Gelderen co-wrote several publications, notably *The Irish wildlife book* (1979), edited by Fergus O'Gorman, and wrote his autobiographical *To the waters and the wild: adventures of a wildlife film maker* (1985). The latter encapsulated his life as a travelling environmentalist, modestly recording his opinions, especially on his beloved Irish landscape and the carelessness of those who damage it through greed and ignorance. He included cartoons, gently aimed at hunters, polluters, politicians and developers, concluding pessimistically that 'it would have been nice' to end on a cheerful note. His autobiography reveals the agreeable, although determined, personality within, accepting the world as it is while doing his utmost to focus public attention on the vulnerable beauty of natural habitats. Emphasising the absence of political frontiers in nature, he underlined his philosophy of life.

Gerrit van Gelderen was a name and a voice instantly recognisable to a generation of Irish television viewers that did much to encourage many natives to appreciate the ecology of the country he had adopted as his own. He and Lize had four children: three sons – Merlin (1962), Finn (1968) and Oisín (1970) – and a daughter, Aoife (1964). They lived latterly at Twayblade, Sandyford, Co. Dublin, where he died suddenly on 28 February 1994, while recovering from a lung operation. He was cremated at Glasnevin cemetery.

Patrick Long

Sources

ITWW; Gerrit van Gelderen, *Doings* (1975); Fergus O'Gorman (ed.), *The Irish wildlife book* (1979); Gerrit van Gelderen, *To the waters and the wild: adventures of a wildlife film maker* (1985); Irish Life Viking Centre, Dublin, *The world of the vikings* (1987); *Irish Times, Irish Independent,* 2 Mar. 1994; *Kerry's Eye*, 3 Mar. 1994; *Wild Ireland*, Sept.–Oct. 2000; Éamon de Buitléar, *A life in the wild* (2004); information from Lize van Gelderen (widow)

Hilary Stevenson

(1947–94)

Food scientist

Hilary (Mary Hill) Stevenson was born on 12 January 1947 at Coleraine, Co. Londonderry, the only daughter of James Stewart Morrison, of a farming family, and Elizabeth Morrison (née Martin) of Coleraine. Her childhood was spent at Drumadaun, Seacon Road, in the townland of Ballyrashane, Coleraine, and she went to secondary school at Coleraine High School. She entered QUB, where she graduated with first-class honours in chemistry (1969) and agriculture (1970), after which she joined the Department of Agriculture for Northern Ireland (DANI) as agriculture inspector and lecturer at Loughry College of Agriculture and Food Technology. Interested in research she obtained an M.Sc. (1971) in food science and microbiology, when she was seconded to the University of Strathclyde, Scotland. In 1974 she was promoted to senior scientific officer for DANI and was transferred within the department to the agricultural chemistry research division. That same year she was also appointed university lecturer in the department of agriculture and food science at QUB, where she taught a wide range of courses, contributing particularly on food chemistry and human nutrition. In 1981 she was awarded a Ph.D. for studies in the mineral metabolism of poultry and was promoted to principal scientific officer for DANI.

As her career developed her research interests changed focus. Her M.Sc. research topic related to the vitamin content of peas before and after processing, but after her return from Scotland she began working on the absorption of minerals by sheep. During the 1970s she worked on poultry nutrition. She published numerous papers on the mineral metabolism of the laying hen, the protein nutrition of broilers, and nutrition and metabolism in the goose in *British Poultry Science* and *Journal of the Science of Food and Agriculture*. By the mid-1980s her research interests had turned to the science of irradiated food and it is in this area that she made her most enduring contribution. Irradiation sterilises food by bombarding it with low-level gamma rays, and it is claimed that chemicals (free radicals) produced by this process are potentially carcinogenic. Through her work on methods of detecting irradiated food (mainly poultry but also meat and shellfish), she became one of the most influential scientists in the world in this area, and in recognition of her work was awarded OBE (1993). She published over forty papers on this subject, many in the *International Journal of Food Science and Technology*. As well as co-editing *Food irradiation and the chemist* she also contributed to almost twenty books and was working on another, *Detection of irradiated food – current status* before her death. Collaborating with academics in Europe, the USA and South Africa, she led several international research programmes and was an active participant in conferences organised by the Atomic Energy Agency and the Food and Agricultural Organisation of the United Nations.

As a fellow of the Institute of Food Science and Technology, she was chairperson of its Northern Ireland branch and was an active member of the Nutrition Society. She was referee to *British Poultry Science* and contributed to its success by also sitting on the council of management and on the business committee. Remembered for her professionalism, integrity and enthusiasm, she set high standards for herself and her team of researchers.

A person of great humanity and compassion, she was a committed Christian who often put others before herself. Outside her work her interests were reading and walking. She married (11 September 1976) Noel Stevenson; they lived in Lisburn, Co. Antrim, and had no children. Committed to her work, she was influential in bringing an international conference on detection of irradiation to Belfast in 1994, four months before her untimely death. She had battled with a prolonged illness before she died on 5 October 1994 at the age of forty-seven.

Patricia M. Byrne

Sources

Times, 2 Nov. 1994; Queens College news-sheet, *Update*, no. 200 (19 Jan. 1995); *British Poultry Science*, xxxvi (1995), 173–4; *Webster's new world encyclopedia* (1992); information from Prof. Jack Pearce, Food Sciences Division, department of agriculture and rural development, QUB

John Lighton Synge
(1897–1995)

Mathematician and theoretical physicist

John Lighton Synge was born on 23 March 1897 in Dublin, youngest among one daughter and three sons of Edward Synge (1859–1939), then land agent in Kingscourt, Co. Cavan, and his wife Ellen Frances (1861–1935), daughter of the distinguished Irish engineer James Price. The Price family can be traced back to Sir William Stuart of Scotland who settled in Ireland in the early seventeenth century. In the male line, Synge's family can be traced back to the sixteenth century to Thomas Millington, 'corruptly called Singe of Bridgnorth' in Shropshire (K. C. Synge, 1937). According to tradition, the changing of the name from Millington originated with Henry VIII, who commanded a favourite choirboy to 'Singe, Millington, singe'. The present form, Synge, was well established by 1600 and it is pronounced to rhyme with 'sing'.

Synge's family were members of the Church of Ireland, and an incredible number of his distant ancestors attained high office in the church. Pre-eminent among them were his direct ancestor Edward Synge (1659–1741), archbishop of Tuam, and Hugh Hamilton (1729–1805), grandfather of Isabella Hamilton, Synge's great-grandmother. Hugh Hamilton – no relation to the mathematician Sir William Rowan Hamilton – 'was the most intellectual Irish bishop of the eighteenth century' (Synge, 1957), and wrote extensively, and with great distinction, on mathematics, physics and chemistry, and theology. Remarkably, Hamilton's academic career is almost identical to J. L. Synge's more than 150 years later. Interestingly, the family of Isabella's mother, Juliana Tisdall, can be traced back to the time of Henry VIII, to the McCrossans of the sept of Leix (Co. Laois) called O'Moore (or O'More), thus establishing a Gaelic strain in Synge's ancestry. Of J. L. Synge's more immediate relatives the most distinguished are, undoubtedly, his uncle John Millington Synge, the playwright and dramatist, and his daughter, Cathleen Synge Morawetz (1923–2017), an eminent applied mathematician and the first woman to hold the directorship of the famous Courant Institute of New York.

In stark contrast to so many of his illustrious ancestors Synge was an atheist, stating in his characteristic style: 'I am a protestant to the marrow of my bones, holding the essence of protestantism to consist, not in the recitation of this creed or that, but in the assertion of the right of the individual to hold his own views on all matters and express them as he thinks fit, with the prudential reservation that one does not preach vegetarianism (at least not too violently) in the lion's den' (Synge, 1957).

In 1903 the Synge family moved to Dublin, where J. L. Synge attended St Andrew's College (1911–15) and entered TCD in 1915; he won a foundation scholarship in mathematics at the end of his first year, probably an unprecedented achievement. In TCD he met Elizabeth Eleanor Mabel Allen, a history student who shared his religious and political beliefs; they married in 1918 in a registry office ('certainly not in a church', as he put it). He graduated in 1919 with a double senior moderatorship in mathematics and experimental physics and a large gold medal.

In January 1920, he was appointed lecturer in mathematics in TCD, and in the late summer of the same year left for Canada to join the University of Toronto as assistant professor of mathematics. It was soon after his arrival at Toronto that Synge became interested in Einstein's theory of relativity. His approach to the theory was the elegant geometrical and visual approach which Hermann Minkowski initiated in 1908; this geometrical approach was to become the most distinct characteristic of Synge's subsequent work in theoretical physics.

In 1925 Synge returned to Dublin to a fellowship and the Erasmus Smith chair of natural philosophy in TCD. Of his many contributions to differential geometry, dynamics, and relativity in the following five years, the most important paper was 'On the geometry of dynamics' (1926). In it, Synge regarded the configuration space of a dynamical system as a Riemannian manifold and used the method of tensor calculus throughout. A by-product of this work was the derivation of the all-important equation of the geodesic deviation. A major undertaking of Synge's during this time was the editing, with Professor A. W. Conway, FRS, of UCD, of the first volume of the mathematical papers of Sir W. R. Hamilton; it was published by the RIA in 1931.

In 1930 Synge was invited to head the newly established department of applied mathematics of the University of Toronto. Apart from a number of short visits to Brown University in Maryland and to Princeton University, and a brief appointment as a ballistics mathematician in the US Army Air Force during the war, he was to remain in Toronto till 1943. In 1933 he applied the theory of elasticity to investigate the problem of 'traumatic occlusion' connected with the physiological periodontal membrane; the result was a major paper 'On the tightness of the teeth, considered as a problem concerning the equilibrium of a thin incompressible elastic medium', a supreme example of mathematical modelling. A theorem, known now as Synge's theorem, on even-dimensional Riemannian manifolds, published in 1936, is acclaimed as 'one of the most beautiful results in global differential geometry of the twentieth century' (Frankel, 2004). Another important and influential paper on 'Relativistic hydrodynamics', published in 1937, became a classic; it was reproduced in the *Journal of General Relativity and Gravitation*, vol. xxxiv, no. 12 (2002), as one of the 'golden oldies' of relativity.

He moved to Ohio State University in 1943 to head the mathematics department for the following three years; the method of the 'Hypercircle', a precursor of today's 'finite elements method' in numerical analysis, was developed, with W. Prager, during this time. In 1946 Synge accepted an invitation to build up and head the mathematics department of the Carnegie Institute of Technology (latterly the Carnegie-Mellon University) in Pittsburgh.

Synge left America in 1948 to return permanently to his native Dublin as a senior professor in the school of theoretical physics of the Dublin Institute for Advanced Studies (DIAS); he officially retired in 1972 but continued his research, mainly on relativity, for another twenty years or so. What must be one of Synge's most remarkable achievements during these years is his paper on the 'Gravitational field of a particle' (1950); in it he was able, for the first time, to penetrate and explore in detail the region inside the Schwarzschild radius (what we call today a black hole). Synge's reputation as a relativist attracted research scholars, collaborators, and eminent visitors from all over the world, making DIAS one of the great centres in relativity theory.

Synge made outstanding contributions to widely varied fields: classical mechanics and geometrical optics, gas dynamics, hydrodynamics, elasticity, electrical network and antenna theory, mathematical methods, and, above all, differential geometry and Einstein's relativity theory. He published eleven books, including the extraordinary semi-popular book *Kandelman's Krim*, and over 200 papers, the last one at the age of ninety-two; it was, appropriately enough, on geometry. The complete list of his published work can be found in *General relativity* (Ó Raifeartaigh, 1972). Every book and every paper is a remarkable work of art, characterised by his striking clarity of expression and the sheer beauty of his prose, and, of course, by Synge's geometric spirit. He was also a superb lecturer.

The almost universal geometrical approach to the theory of relativity in the last forty years or so is due primarily to Synge's influence, especially to his two epoch-making books on the special and general theories of relativity, which were published in the late 1950s. It is on record, for example, that the outstanding relativist Sir Roger Penrose was drawn into the field of relativity after reading Synge's books. In 1972 Synge himself said: 'If you were to ask me what I have contributed to the theory of relativity, I believe that I could claim to have emphasised its geometrical aspect' (Synge, 1972).

Synge was the recipient of many honours throughout his long life. Member (1926) and president (1961–4) of the RIA, fellow of the Royal Societies of London (1943) and of Canada (1932), and honorary fellow of TCD, he was awarded honorary doctorates from the University of St Andrews (1966), QUB (1969), and the NUI (1970), the Tory medal of the Royal Society of Canada (1943), and the Boyle medal of the RDS (1972). The Royal Society of Canada and the University of Toronto founded mathematics prizes in Synge's name, and in 1992 TCD, his alma mater, founded the J. L. Synge public lecture and the J. L. Synge prize in mathematics, given in alternate years.

Synge died on 30 March 1995, exactly one week after his ninety-eighth birthday. His mind was lively and vivid to the very end of his life, reading avidly and thinking about mathematical problems. He was a kind and generous man who helped and inspired several generations of students. In old age he suggested that a significant part of his epitaph might read: 'He encouraged younger men'. Alas, there is no tomb for an epitaph, Synge having bequeathed his body to the medical school of TCD. But his students, and those who were fortunate to come in contact with him, will always remember him with gratitude, admiration, and the deepest respect.

Petros S. Florides

Sources

K. C. Synge, *The family of Synge or Sing* (1937); J. L. Synge, *Kandelman's Krim: a realistic fantasy* (1957); idem, *Geometry and physics* (Boyle Memorial Lecture, 1972); L. Ó Raifeartaigh (ed.), *General relativity: papers in honour of J. L. Synge on his 75th birthday* (1972); P. S. Florides, 'Professor John Lighton Synge, FRS (obituary)', *Irish Mathematical Society Bulletin*, xxxvii (1996); idem, 'John Lighton Synge' in A. Whitaker and M. McCarthy (eds), *Irish physicists* (2002); Th. Frankel, *The geometry of physics: an introduction* (2nd ed., 2004); personal knowledge

Ernest Walton
(1903–95)

SCIENTIST, EDUCATOR AND NOBEL PRIZE LAUREATE

Ernest Thomas Sinton Walton was born on 6 October 1903 in Abbeyside, Dungarvan, Co. Waterford, elder of two children of the Rev. John Arthur Walton and Anna Elizabeth Walton (née Sinton). His father, a methodist minister, was born in Cloughjordan, Co. Tipperary, and his mother in Richhill, Co. Armagh. His sister Dorothy Letitia was born in 1905, a year before the untimely death of his mother. John Walton later married Mary Elizabeth Kirkwood, and their only child, James Kirkwood, was born in 1919. Because methodist ministers at that time moved residence about every three years, the Walton family lived in thirteen different locations in Ireland between 1901 and 1995: eight of them in counties that became part of Northern Ireland in 1920.

The requirement to move house so frequently influenced the manner in which Ernest Walton pursued his primary and secondary education. After kindergarten in Banbridge, Co. Down, he attended Cookstown Academy for a period before entering Methodist College, Belfast, as a boarder (1915–22). There he excelled in science and mathematics. Having acquitted himself with distinction, he entered TCD in the autumn of 1922 on foot of an entrance scholarship (sizarship) and a scholarship from Co. Armagh, where the family resided from 1919 to 1922. After a remarkable undergraduate career in physics and mathematics, Walton graduated in 1926 with a double first and a large gold medal in experimental science. He remained in Trinity for a further year to pursue a master's degree in hydrodynamics and was duly awarded an M.Sc. as well as the McCullagh prize in 1927.

Having gained an overseas scholarship from the royal commissioners for the great exhibition of 1851, Walton was accepted as a research student in Trinity College, Cambridge, in the autumn of 1927 under the supervision of Ernest Rutherford, the director of the Cavendish Laboratory. Mindful of Rutherford's earlier experiments on the transmutation of nitrogen into oxygen when bombarded with alpha particles (charged nuclei of helium atoms) from radio-isotopes such as radium, Walton suggested the possibility of using artificially produced beams of swift charged particles to induce nuclear transmutations. The challenge was to generate such particles with the requisite energy by accelerating them across an electric potential difference (voltage) which Walton had estimated to be of the order of at least a few million volts. Walton's research initially focused on the generation of high-energy electrons through acceleration in a circular electric field. Although the experiment was unsuccessful, his research laid the groundwork for the development of the betatron in later years. He then switched his efforts to the linear acceleration of positive ions.

It was about this time in 1928 that George Gamow applied wave mechanics to the problem of alpha particle emission from radioactive substances. He argued that alpha particles of much lower energies could tunnel through rather than jump over the very high potential energy barrier surrounding the nucleus. John Cockcroft, a colleague in the Cavendish, saw that Gamow's theory could be applied in reverse. The possibility of getting particles *into* the nuclei of atoms, using voltages that could be relatively easily handled in a laboratory, thus became a tantalising reality.

At Rutherford's instigation, Cockcroft and Walton joined forces. Working in concert, they succeeded in effecting nuclear disintegration by artificial means in 1932. Walton was the first to witness the birth of this new era of accelerator-based experimental nuclear physics when, on 14 April of that year, he observed the disintegration of Lithium nuclei bombarded with protons accelerated across 700,000 volts. Two alpha particles were produced, along with the release of an enormous surplus of energy which conformed exactly to Einstein's relationship between energy and mass, $E=mc^2$, where E is energy, m is mass, and c is the velocity of light.

The significance of the experiment was threefold: first, it pioneered a new branch of physics in which artificially accelerated particles were used to initiate nuclear interactions in a controlled way; second, the experiment verified the predictions of the new wave mechanics; and, third, it was the first direct verification of Einstein's mass/energy relationship in a nuclear reaction in which the destruction of a very small amount of matter released a large amount of energy. The experimental approach adopted by Cockcroft and Walton is still used in many of the accelerator laboratories throughout the world.

On the academic front, Walton was awarded his Ph.D. in 1931. He remained in Cambridge till 1934 to investigate further aspects of nuclear transmutation with the support of a senior research award from the department of scientific and industrial research (1930–34) and a Clerk Maxwell scholarship (1932–4). Thereafter, he could have gone to any number of leading laboratories throughout the world but chose instead to return in 1934 to his alma mater as a fellow of TCD in the physics department.

In the same year (23 August), Ernest Walton married Freda Wilson, also of the methodist faith, who was a former school colleague and daughter of the Rev. Charles Wilson and Annie Wilson (née Elliott). She was a qualified kindergarten teacher who trained under the National Froebel Union and taught for a time at the Bishop Foy school in Waterford. Their four children, Alan, Philip, Marion and Jean, all pursued careers in science. Their first-born, Winifred Ruth, died in infancy.

Much had changed in Ireland during Walton's seven-year absence in Cambridge. During that time, the efforts of government had been directed mainly to establishing the institutions of a new state in a world economy that was depressed and turbulent. Trinity College continued to be a hostage to poverty and stress, with little more than a trickle of public financial support. Funding for research was minimal, laboratory space was scarce, teaching and examination loads were heavy, and administrative duties were onerous. Throughout the war years (1939–45), the situation deteriorated further in the physics department with the departure to England of Robert Ditchburn, the Erasmus Smith's professor of natural and experimental philosophy and head of department, to assist in the war effort. This reduced the teaching staff to three. In addition, the little research time that was available was directed to a range of national problems identified by the emergency research committee set up by the government, mostly to deal with shortages such as domestic and motor fuel.

In 1941 Walton was asked by C. P. Snow of the British ministry of labour and national service to participate in scientific war work. After much soul-searching, Walton declined the invitation, having judged Ireland's needs to be his greater priority. Later, he was contacted by Sir James Chadwick with an unusual and quite mysterious request to know if he would participate in 'war work' in the United States, which subsequent clarification identified as the Manhattan project. Walton was not keen on going but, nevertheless, consulted the provost, E. H. Alton, who refused permission, citing the needs of the already hard-pressed physics department to be the more important.

Walton's reluctance to participate in war work was not based solely on pacifist principles. He often argued that he would like to be a pacifist but would none the less have difficulty with that position in certain circumstances. His sensitivities on the issue of nuclear weapons had been heightened by the press coverage following the Cockcroft/Walton experiment (1932), which raised moral issues in the public mind with regard to the potential military applications of their experiment. At that time he pointed to the discovery of the neutron in 1932 and the demonstration of fission of uranium when bombarded with neutrons in 1938 as the two key experiments that underpinned the development of the bomb.

Post-war, Walton was strongly committed to minimising the threat of nuclear war and banning the bomb: hence his membership and presidency of the Irish Pugwash group, whose goal was precisely along those lines. He did, however, admit the possibility of a just war, when fought justly. Overall, Walton's approach to life was guided by the fundamental principles of his methodist faith as handed on by his parents, and he lectured widely on the relationship between science and religion.

Ditchburn remained in England after the war, and in 1947 Walton was appointed the Erasmus Smith's professor and head of department, a post that he held till his retirement in 1974. During his tenure the physics department grew in size to accommodate the sustained post-war increase in student numbers. As a lecturer, Walton was unrivalled in the way in which he could present even the most complicated concepts in simple, readily understandable terms, often aided by demonstrations, which reflected the same level of ingenuity that characterised his experimental work in Cambridge.

Although funding for research would remain wholly inadequate throughout the whole of his professional life, Walton worked on a number of scientific projects, delivered occasional lectures on linear accelerators, and published a number of papers. He was an ardent promoter of science teaching and research in Ireland, which had been largely neglected since the foundation of the state. In a letter to Éamon de Valera in 1957, Walton stressed the need for a strong scientific foundation on which to build prosperous industries and to increase agricultural output and made several practical proposals to achieve this aim. His proposal predated the initiative of Seán Lemass and T. K. Whitaker in 1959 to establish a strong manufacturing sector in Ireland, based on foreign direct investment. In hindsight, Walton clearly foresaw the advent of the knowledge economy which, decades later, continues to transform global society.

Throughout his career Walton was honoured in many ways. The 1951 Nobel prize for physics was awarded jointly to Walton and Cockcroft 'for their pioneer work on the transmutation of atomic nuclei by artificially accelerated atomic particles'. Walton's award, to date (2005), remains the only Irish Nobel prize in science. Other honours included election to the RIA (1935); the Hughes medal of the Royal Society of London (1938); honorary doctorates from QUB (1959), the Gustavus Adolphus College in Minnesota (1975), the University of Ulster (1988) and Dublin City University (1991); the naming of the Walton Causeway Park in Dungarvan and the Walton Building in Methodist College, Belfast, in his honour; and a plethora of other testimonials of his outstanding achievements as an educator and scientist.

It was appropriate that Ernest Walton returned in his twilight years to Belfast, the city that nurtured his early interest in science. Having attained the summit of his early ambition, he led a long and contented life, which inspired several generations of physicists, students and colleagues alike. He died on 25 June 1995 in Belfast and was buried in Deansgrange cemetery in Dublin. The family bequeathed all his papers and correspondence to the manuscript library, TCD. His portrait (by Thomas Ryan, RHA) hangs proudly in the entrance of the Physical Laboratory, recently renamed the Fitzgerald Building.

Vincent McBrierty

Sources

Walton MSS, Manuscript Library, TCD; V. J. McBrierty, *Ernest Thomas Sinton Walton (1903–1995)*; *Irish scientist* (2003)

Helen Megaw
(1907–2002)

CRYSTALLOGRAPHER

Helen Dick Megaw was born on 1 June 1907 at 44 Northumberland Road, Dublin, the eldest child and one of five daughters and two sons (along with Thomas and Alice (twins), John, Margaret, Annie and Sarah) of Robert Megaw, a lawyer and professor of common law at King's Inns, Dublin, and Annie McElderry, a mathematics teacher at the Rutland School, Dublin. Robert Megaw, a member of the Orange Order, became a king's counsel (KC) and served a term (1921–5) as a member of the Northern Ireland parliament for Antrim. His was a family of high achievers, and he had high expectations for his children.

Helen Megaw was educated at Alexandra College, Dublin, from 1916 to 1921, when the family moved to Belfast, where she continued her education at Methodist College before being sent to Roedean School, near Brighton. There she first read W. H. and W. L. Bragg's *X-rays and crystal structure* (1915). She matriculated at Queen's University Belfast (QUB) before winning a Todd memorial scholarship that allowed her to move to Girton College, Cambridge, to read chemistry, physics and mineralogy for the natural sciences tripos. On graduating in 1930, she began postgraduate work at the Cavendish Laboratory, Cambridge, with the Irish polymath Desmond Bernal, himself a student of W. H. Bragg. Bernal led a group devoted to groundbreaking uses of X-ray diffraction to investigate the structures of crystalline, amorphous and molecular matter, the understanding of which became the key to some of the most important advances in twentieth-century science. Megaw's colleagues and friends in Bernal's group included Dorothy Hodgkin, who became the first British woman to win a Nobel prize, for determining the structure of vitamin B12.

Crystallography at Cambridge was a rare area of research where men and women contributed on an equal basis. Megaw used X-rays to study thermal expansion and determined the crystal structure of hydrargillite (gibbsite), an aluminium hydroxide. She grew ice crystals from both normal and heavy water using an original method that involved encapsulating the water in a thin-walled glass tube and cycling temperature around the freezing point. Megaw and Bernal inferred that there were two types of hydrogen bonds, one where the hydrogen was close to oxygen (as in hydroxides), the other where it oscillates between two positions between a pair of oxygens (as in water). Megaw's method was also used by British chemist Rosalind Franklin to grow crystals of DNA in a mother liquor.

In 1934, having been awarded a doctorate from Cambridge, Megaw spent a postdoctoral year with Austrian-American chemist Herman Mark at the University of Vienna, followed by a year with physical chemist Francis Simon at the Clarendon Laboratory in Oxford, before becoming a schoolteacher in 1936 at Bedford High School and then at Bradford Girls Grammar School. In 1943 she accepted an invitation to join Philips Lamps Ltd in Mitcham, Surrey, for classified research on barium titanate ($BaTiO_3$), a recently discovered ferroelectric ceramic that had important potential applications. She determined its tetragonal perovskite-type crystal structure and showed that ferroelectricity disappeared when the structure became cubic at a phase transition above room temperature. Her name is permanently associated with barium titanate, which later became the mainstay of a multibillion-dollar industry. After the second world war, in 1945, she joined Bernal at Birkbeck College, London, where he had been appointed professor of physics. The following year, however, Megaw became a fellow (and later a life fellow) of Girton College. She resumed work at the Cavendish Laboratory as associate director of crystallography and eventually became a lecturer in physics in 1959. For the Festival of Britain, the great forward-looking exhibition organised on the south bank of the Thames in 1951, Megaw served as scientific consultant to the exhibition's festival pattern group. The group co-ordinated contributions from various industries that promoted products featuring crystal structure diagrams sourced from Megaw and the pattern group, as did the furnishings and tableware in the festival's Regatta restaurant.

Megaw's interests in crystallography were centred on two of the large families of inorganic oxide minerals related to perovskite and feldspar; their crystal structures include periodic arrays of octahedra or tetrahedra of oxygen anions which share corners or edges, and each contain a metal cation. Megaw had the remarkable gift of being able to visualise these structures in three dimensions from any angle and could see how small tilts or twists of the linked oxygen units propagated throughout the structure and determined its spatial symmetry. Together with her skill at collecting and analysing the X-ray diffraction patterns recorded on special photographic film (with no aid from digital computers), she succeeded in establishing a body of precise information on oxide minerals which has had a durable impact on earth science. Feldspars are the major constituent of the Earth's crust, but under the enormous pressures and temperatures prevailing in the Earth's mantle, dense oxide minerals with the perovskite structure are ubiquitous, and they are now believed to account for most of the volume of the Earth.

Megaw authored numerous influential books and journal articles, published *inter alia* in *Nature*, *Proceedings of the Physical Society* and *Proceedings of the Royal Society*, as well as *Ferroelectricity in crystals* (1957) and *Crystal structures: a working approach* (1973). She was the first woman and fifty-second recipient, in 1989, of the Roebling medal, the highest honour awarded by the Mineralogical Society of America. Megaw Island in Antarctica is named in her honour, as is the orthorhombic perovskite mineral Megawite ($CaSnO_3$). She was awarded a doctorate in science (D.Sc.) by Cambridge University in 1967, and an honorary doctorate by QUB in 2000. The citation for the latter, delivered by Ruth Lynden-Bell, recalled that Megaw was one of a number of women attracted to the newly emerged field of X-ray crystallography: 'In those pioneering days preparation of crystals and collection of data was more difficult and more skilled than it is today … there were no computers and the detailed calculations which lead from the brightness of spots on a photographic plate to a three-dimensional crystal structure were all done by hand. Dr Megaw was one of the pioneers in this field' (Lynden-Bell).

After her retirement in 1972, Megaw moved to the family home in Ballycastle, Co. Antrim, where she lived with her sister. She maintained a passion for crystallography and was often seen back in Cambridge. Megaw never married, believing the life of a professional scientist to be incompatible with the role of wife and mother. She was kind and generous with her time, especially with students, on one occasion assisting one of her former postdoctoral researchers, Mike Glazer, in revising an article after it received severe criticism from a peer reviewer; some years later she revealed that she had been the peer reviewer. Megaw was resolute in her scientific and political opinions, which were at odds with those of many of her colleagues in

Bernal's group. She was a lifelong and enthusiastic amateur botanist.

Helen Megaw died of a stroke on 26 February 2002 at 22 Dunamallaght Road, Ballycastle, Co. Antrim. Her personal papers and research notes are deposited in the Girton College archive, while the Victoria and Albert Museum also holds a collection of her papers, largely related to her work with the Festival of Britain.

J. M. D. [Mike] Coey

Sources

Ruth Lynden-Bell, 'Dr H. Megaw: citation for honorary degree of Doctor of Science', *Crystallography News: British Crystallographic Association*, no. 75 (Dec. 2000); Elizabeth Lomas, *Guide to the archive of art and design, Victoria and Albert Museum* (2002), 178; Mike Glazer, 'Helen D. Megaw (1907–2002)', *Crystallography News: British Crystallographic Association*, no. 81 (June 2002); Robert Olby, 'Bernal, John Desmond', *Oxford dictionary of national biography* (2004); A. M. [Mike] Glazer, 'Megaw, Helen Dick', *Oxford dictionary of national biography* (2006); idem, 'Helen D. Megaw (1907–2002) and her contributions to ferroelectrics', *IEEE Transactions on Ultrasonics, Ferroelectrics and Frequency Control*, vol. 68, no. 2 (Feb. 2021), 334–8 (photos), doi: 10.1109/TUFFC.2020.3035268; Andrew P. Brown, 'J. D. Bernal: the sage of science', *Journal of Physics: Conference Series*, 57 (2007), 61–72; Helga Kaschl, 'Helen Dick Megaw: kristallografin, naturwissenschaftlerin, fotografin, dichterin', https://www.schreibfrauen.at/startseite/helen-dick-megaw/; Richard Froggatt, 'Helen Dick Megaw', *Dictionary of Ulster biography*, https://www.newulsterbiography.co.uk/index.php/home/viewPerson/1919 (internet material accessed June 2024)

Eva Philbin
(1914–2005)

Chemist and university professor

Eva Maria Philbin was born on 3 January 1914 in Ballina, Co. Mayo, the elder of two daughters of George Ryder, a postman and later a publican, and his wife Kate (née Donegan). Eva attended the Convent of Mercy in Ballina and then went to UCG to study science. Graduating with a first-class honours B.Sc. (1936) and an M.Sc. (1937), she took up a post in the chemistry department as an assistant to Professor Thomas Patrick Dillon, a pioneer in the study of the chemistry of carbohydrates of seaweeds. Two years later, she became chief chemist in two Galway companies, Cold Chon and Hygeia. During the war years, raw materials for industry and daily life were difficult to come by, and Ryder's research into possible uses of natural materials such as seaweed was regarded as potentially important.

Eva Ryder married John 'Jack' Madden Philbin (d. 1998) on 28 April 1943 in St Andrew's church, Westland Row, Dublin; he was an accountant and later a company secretary. The ceremony was performed by Jack's relative, Fr William Joseph Philbin, later a bishop. Most married women at the time did not work outside the home (until 1973 women civil servants were obliged to resign if they married), but Philbin took a job in 1945 as demonstrator in the department of chemistry in UCD, working with Professor Thomas Sherlock Wheeler on the chemistry of natural substances. Philbin's work and her many papers published with Wheeler and others undoubtedly enhanced the international reputation of chemistry in UCD, although the generally low level of funding for basic science in the 1950s and 1960s hindered the establishment of research programmes. She was promoted to assistant lecturer (1949) and college lecturer (1955) and was awarded a Ph.D. in 1954 for work on the Wessely–Moser rearrangement reaction in certain flavonoids and on the Baker–Venkataraman transformation, used in the synthesis of flavones. Philbin held a research fellowship in 1955 at the Eidgenössische Technische Hochschule in Zürich, Switzerland, where she developed a research interest in the stereochemistry of flavonoids.

In acknowledgment of her research and publication record, she was awarded the degree of D.Sc. in 1957 and became one of the first women science professors in UCD when appointed professor in organic chemistry in 1961. After Wheeler's death in 1962, she became head of the department of chemistry in the following year. She often sought well-qualified graduates from elsewhere to come to work in UCD and bring with them new ideas and enthusiasm. Even more important than her own research was her encouragement and training of generations of chemistry students, supporting the development of the chemical and pharmaceutical industries in Ireland in the 1960s and 1970s. Her contribution to chemistry as a profession was considerable: a foundation member and later a fellow of the Institute of Chemistry of Ireland, she was elected vice-president (1964) and president (1966–8), the first woman in the role. Philbin served on the councils of the Chemical Society and of the Royal Institute of Chemistry, having been elected a fellow of the latter in 1954. She was elected MRIA in 1957, one of the first women scientists in the RIA, and served for a number of years on its council and as senior vice-president. In the Academy's bicentenary history, Philbin provided the article on 'Chemistry'. In 1964 she narrowly missed being elected to the senate of the National University of Ireland. She was a member of the first

National Science Council (from 1967) and of the Nuclear Energy Board in 1973. Philbin was an important pioneer and role model for young women who wanted to work in science; ambitious and able, she had nonetheless managed to be polite to newspaper interviewers in the 1950s who archly talked of 'girl chemists' and their marriage prospects.

She retired in 1979 from her professorship, though she continued to take an interest in research and in the department of chemistry. To mark her seventy-fifth birthday in 1989, former colleagues and friends produced a festschrift of 115 papers, mainly on the chemistry of flavonoids and related topics. Her academic work was only part of Philbin's life; as well as looking after her own family, one of whom had special needs, she also made a lasting contribution to the provision of education and care for children with mental and physical disabilities. She worked for years with various charities and support bodies, was honorary treasurer of the National Association for the Mentally Handicapped of Ireland and was chairman of the influential Consultative Council on Mental Handicap (1970–75).

Eva and John Philbin had two daughters and a son. She died in the Ailesbury Nursing Home, Dublin, on 24 June 2005. The Institute of Chemistry of Ireland established the Eva Philbin award and annual lecture series in her honour.

Linde Lunney

Sources

General Register Office, birth cert.; *Irish Independent, passim*, esp.: 30 Apr. 1943; 18 June 1955; *Irish Times, passim*, esp.: 3 June 1970; 25 June, 9 July 2005; *Report of the President, University College Dublin 1978–79*, 125–6; Dervilla M. X. Donnelly, foreword to *Papers dedicated to Eva Philbin, MRIA, on the occasion of her 75th birthday*, published as part of *Proceedings of the Royal Irish Academy*, lxxxix, section B, (1989); Patrick J. Lindsay, *Memories* (1992), 38; 'Jordan website', www.myheritage.com (accessed Feb. 2013)

Kay McNulty

(1921–2006)

PIONEERING COMPUTER PROGRAMMER

Kathleen Rita ('Kay') McNulty was born on 12 February 1921 in the townland of Feymore, Creeslough, Co. Donegal, the third of six children (three boys and three girls) of James McNulty (1890–1977) and his wife Anne or Annie (née Nelis). Around 1908 James McNulty emigrated from Creeslough to Philadelphia and trained as a stonemason. Involved in Clan na Gael, he returned to Creeslough in 1915 to take part in the struggle for Irish independence. He became commandant of the Doe battalion of the Irish Volunteers, which, owing to confusion and poor communications, took no part in the 1916 rising. After the rising, he continued to recruit and organise Volunteers, and also worked with the local Sinn Féin club, helping to establish Doe Cooperative Society in Creeslough in 1920. In an attempt to seize guns from the home of a protestant JP in early 1919, McNulty was shot and seriously wounded. After a slow recovery, he returned to active service with the IRA and organised the sabotage of a railway bridge outside Creeslough (7 February 1921); fifteen British soldiers were injured in the resulting derailment. Arrested the day after his daughter was born, he was imprisoned in solitary confinement in Derry jail, under threat of execution, until released in the general amnesty of December 1921. He opposed the Anglo–Irish treaty and, unwilling to recognise the new government of the Irish Free State, returned to Philadelphia in 1923 to join a brother in a construction business; his wife and family travelled to America in October 1924. He was successful in his business, working with John B. Kelly, father of Princess Grace of Monaco, and was involved in the construction of important government buildings. He returned to Ireland in 1966 and died in Creeslough in 1977.

The household in Chestnut Hill, Philadelphia, was Irish-speaking, and Kay first learned English from her two older brothers (she remembered her prayers in Irish for the rest of her life). She attended the parish grade school and then Hallahan Catholic Girls' High School, where she was an excellent student. Chestnut Hill College offered her a scholarship, and she graduated in spring 1942, having majored in mathematics. By then the US army had a pressing need for mathematicians to produce ballistics calculations and, with a scarcity of trained men, McNulty was one of a number of women taken on to work as 'computers' at the Moore School of Electrical Engineering at the University of Pennsylvania.

Calculating missile trajectories, using the desk calculators and tables then available, took each woman about forty hours, and hundreds of such calculations were required. McNulty and another woman were trained to use a recently built differential analyser machine (an analogue device, reliant on mechanical operations), which speeded up calculations. A much more sophisticated machine, designed on quite novel principles, using electrical circuits to execute calculations, was being developed in great haste at the army's Aberdeen Proving Ground in Maryland. In June 1945, McNulty was one of six women selected to work on this room-sized ENIAC (Electronic Numerical Integrator and Computer). For the next few months, the women collaborated with the engineers who were still working on the design and construction of ENIAC; there were no manuals, only design blueprints, as the machine was still incomplete.

McNulty and others devised the processing routines that enabled the machine to carry out calculations, more or less establishing the ways in which artificial intelligence subsequently developed. ENIAC had no memory capabilities: its programmes had to be input manually, using punch cards and realigning wiring and switches, for each calculation. McNulty is credited with suggesting the concept of subroutines, in which the master programmer element of the instructions to the machine was set to trigger the reuse of sections of code, enabling the logical circuits to carry more capacity. Once they began to perform calculations on the actual machine, McNulty and her colleagues became expert in diagnosing problems and finding where the machine's physical wiring or some of the 17,468 vacuum tubes or 5,000,000 hand-soldered connections had failed, as they did at first every few hours.

The public launch of the ENIAC machine as the first general-purpose electronic digital computer took place on 15 February 1946, causing great excitement in the scientific and business communities, as the potential importance of such machines was already evident. The event, however, relegated the women programmers to the role of hostesses, and official reports and early histories of computing made no mention of female operators. Tellingly, as mid-century America reversed the gains made in wartime by women in employment, science and public engagement, some contemporary observers even regarded the women in the project as 'refrigerator ladies': models employed to stand elegantly in front of machines that they did not understand. (Even in 1986, five of the women who had first programmed the 'beast' were not invited to the fortieth anniversary celebration of the birth of the electronic computing age. Kay McNulty was there, and gave an address, but did so as the widow of one of the men who had developed ENIAC.

Only as the 1980s ended was the women's contribution to the development of computer systems acknowledged and celebrated.)

On 7 February 1948 Kay McNulty married John Mauchly. Her parents were not present and were deeply upset by her decision to marry a non-catholic, fourteen years her senior, who had a son and a daughter by a first marriage. John Mauchly was one of the engineers chiefly responsible for designing the hardware of ENIAC; his first wife, also a gifted mathematician, had worked with him, but drowned while on holiday in 1946. Mauchly was also suffering chronic illness, hereditary haemorrhagic telangiectasia (which all but one of his and Kay's five children inherited), necessitating constant vigilance and frequent hospitalisation; he later developed diabetes.

Until her marriage, McNulty had continued to work on ENIAC through 1947 and 1948, testing the device during its reassembly after a move to the Aberdeen Proving Ground. It is possible she was also involved in its development into a machine with a rudimentary capacity to store an operating system. In her autobiography, Kay noted without comment that her new husband gave her a cookbook on their honeymoon, and that she was thereafter expected to be the family cook; she left paid scientific work on her marriage.

McNulty's possible contribution to developing technology and information systems after her years on ENIAC is now difficult to trace. She may have provided some suggestions in discussions of her husband's pioneering work on the first computer designed for commercial use, UNIVAC, built by his company, Eckart-Mauchly. However, the couple were increasingly preoccupied by legal tussles over patents (which they lost) and difficulties with Mauchly's security clearance and spent considerable time in disputes with former colleagues and attempts to establish companies and new projects. For the rest of her life, Kay was bitter about how the industry and the government treated her husband and ardently defended his work and his claims to priority in the computer revolution. In 2002, she was able to accept John Mauchly's posthumous induction into the National Inventors Hall of Fame.

Kay and John Mauchly had four daughters and a son. While rearing her children, she volunteered in youth and church organisations and did some supply teaching in elementary schools. John Mauchly died on 8 January 1980. Kay married again on 27 December 1985; her second husband was a successful, Italian-born photographer, Severo Antonelli. Her years with him were busy and enjoyable, with travel and social engagements, until he developed Parkinson's disease. He died after two difficult years on 14 December 1995.

In her later years, Kay McNulty Mauchly Antonelli was lionised as one of the invisible women scientists rediscovered in the late twentieth century and developed considerable skills of communication and presentation as she was sought out to attend conferences and functions to discuss and record the role of the women pioneers of information science. Her online autobiography captures some of the excitement of the wartime work for which she became famous. In April 1999 she and an ENIAC colleague went on a lecture tour in Ireland, and were filmed for a feature documentary, *Oh Kay computer* (1999). She revisited Creeslough for the first time since 1924 and met many of her relatives there. During her visit, a prize for the best student in computer science was established in her honour at Letterkenny Institute of Technology.

In 1997 she and her five female colleagues were inducted into the Women in Technology Hall of Fame. After suffering from cancer, she died on 20 April 2006 in Wyndmoor, Pennsylvania. A computer science building was renamed in her honour in Dublin City University in 2017.

Linde Lunney

Sources

Donegal News, 16 Jan. 1954; 30 Apr. 1999; *Irish Times*, 30 Nov. 1998; 30 Apr. 1999; Kay McNulty Mauchly Antonelli, *The Kathleen McNulty Mauchly Antonelli story*, 26 Mar. 2004, https://sites.google.com/a/opgate.com/eniac/Home/kay-mcnulty-mauchly-antonelli; Walter Isaacson, *The innovators* (2014); Hayley Williams, 'Invisible women: the six human computers behind the ENIAC', 10 Nov. 2015, www.lifehacker.com.au/2015/11/invisible-women-the-six-human-computers-behind-the-eniac/; 'Kay McNulty, ENIAC superhero', 22 Aug. 2016, codelikeawoman.wordpress.com/2016/08/22/kay-mcnulty-eniac-superhero/; 'Kathleen "Kay" McNulty Mauchly Antonelli', memorial no. 136819670, www.findagrave.com; (internet material accessed Oct. 2020)

Dan Bradley
(1928–2010)

Physicist

Daniel Joseph ('Dan') Bradley was born in Derry city on 18 January 1928, the son of John Columba Bradley, a Post Office worker, and his wife Margaret (née Keating), one of ten daughters of farming stock, originally from near Cashel, Co. Tipperary. He was the second-born of four surviving children, with an elder sister and two younger brothers. The family home was at 12 Ewing Street, Derry. Dan's grandfather, William John Bradley, was head postman for the Derry postal area and an alderman (1920–23) in the first catholic-majority Derry corporation.

After completing the first and second parts of the technical school examinations in electrical engineering, Dan worked for three months as a telegraph boy, during which time he failed the clerkship entry examination for the Post Office. He subsequently enrolled at Lumen Christi High School, Derry, where he obtained his secondary-school senior certificate (1945), surprisingly not taking physics, but with a satisfactorily high standard to warrant a university scholarship. As the scholarship was insufficient to cover all costs, he did not take up a place at QUB but instead with a king's scholarship enrolled at St Mary's teacher training college in Belfast.

After graduation in 1947, he taught at the Long Tower primary school in Derry. While in various teaching posts in Derry (1947–53), he studied part time for a B.Sc. special degree in mathematics with the University of London.

On receipt of his degree, he moved to London, where he taught science and mathematics at various independent and London county council schools. In October 1953, he enrolled at Birkbeck College to study part time for the B.Sc. special physics degree, and was a Ravenscroft exhibitioner (1954–7) and college exhibitioner (1956), obtaining his degree in 1957 at the top of the class.

At the start of the 1957–8 academic year, he obtained an assistant lectureship at Royal Holloway College, enabling him to undertake a Ph.D. research programme under the supervision of Professor Sam Tolansky, FRS. The topic of his chosen research programme was the scanning Fabry-Perot interferometer. In the late 1950s there was considerable interest in developing such scanning techniques to add versatility and simplify the recording of emission spectra for application in spectroscopy. Many of the approaches were slow and cumbersome, and resulted in reduced finesse and resolution. Bradley developed a simple mechanical scheme where one plate was fixed and the other moved, with the moving plate mounted on a brass tube and moved parallel to this on springs. He also used photomultiplier detection, and with scanning rates of up to 1 kHz allowed real time detection of spectral line emission with high resolution.

At Royal Holloway, he met Winifride O'Connor, a 1951 botany graduate from the University of Liverpool, who was also an assistant lecturer. They married in 1958 and had five children: Sean (b. 1959), Mairead (b. 1960), Donal (b. 1960) (who became a distinguished physicist and was elected FRS (2004) and appointed CBE (2010)), Ronan (b. 1965) and Martin (b. 1972).

Bradley submitted his Ph.D. thesis, 'A high resolution interference spectroscope', in August 1961, and alluded to the potential of the device in earth satellite observations. At the beginning of the 1961–2 academic year he was appointed to a lectureship in the instrument technology group in the physics department at Imperial College in London. Broadening his research on the applications of the Fabry-Perot, with the coming of the laser era he was quick to realise that, although suitable for diagnosis of continuous operating lasers, the scanning Fabry-Perot configurations he had developed were totally unsuitable for investigations of nanosecond Q-switched lasers and the laser-generated plasmas they produced. He rapidly expanded his research programme to utilise gated or swept electro-optic image intensifiers in combination with fixed-gap Fabry-Perots, and widely investigated new, efficient, highly reflecting coatings for operation in the ultraviolet. With the superior angular dispersion of the Fabry-Perot and the increased luminosity over grating dispersers, he realised that these compact devices were highly suitable for astronomical spectroscopy from both balloons and rockets.

With an increasing international reputation, Bradley was promoted to a readership at Royal Holloway in 1964. He continued research and development on Fabry-Perot devices and their applications, and introduced a particularly novel, narrow-gap, hence exceedingly broad free-spectral range device, which was later used to tune short-pulse, broadband lasers and was successfully commercialised. Although he maintained a major interest and published widely on solar spectroscopy, his principal interests were increasingly directed towards ultra-fast electron-optical technology, laser development, diagnostics and applications.

His appointment as professor and head of the department of physics at QUB, remarkably only five years after obtaining his Ph.D., afforded him the opportunity to establish one of the most influential and largest laser research groups worldwide, with research outputs punctuated by many world firsts. In addition to innovative advances in tuneable narrow-line lasers for spectroscopy, Bradley was particularly noted for the development of the passively mode-locked, flashlamp-pumped dye laser, which allowed wavelength tuneable pulses of picosecond duration to be generated. He clarified the role of the saturable absorber (ultra-fast light gate) in the mode-locking process, showing that with solid-state lasers it was the lifetime or open time of the gate that determined the pulse width, while with the dye laser, pulses substantially shorter than the absorber lifetime were generated because saturable gain played a vital role in reducing the tail of the pulse after saturable absorption had removed the front. Pulses of a few picoseconds (10^{-12}s) were routinely achieved, and Bradley was also instrumental in the formation of one of the first laser spin-out companies, helping establish Electro Photonics Ltd in Belfast, who rapidly commercialised the outputs from the research group. Bradley was also internationally distinguished for his innovation and development of the pulsed electron-optical streak camera that allowed the only technique for the direct measurement of picosecond and sub-picosecond (femtosecond) optical events.

Bradley had lobbied for and had hoped that a government-funded national laser facility could be established in Northern Ireland. However, the increasing instability and political violence of the early 1970s effectively negated any possibility of that. By 1973 he also had concerns for the well-being of his young family, leading him to accept the chair of optics at Imperial College that October.

At Imperial, Bradley set about establishing another laser group of major international importance from small beginnings. He initiated major programmes on e-beam excitation of gaseous excimer and exciplex lasers for VUV (vacuum ultraviolet) generation, as well as mode-locked, semiconductor lasers for application in communication and switching. He expanded his dye laser work to mode-locked, continuously operating systems and at various times held the record for the shortest pulses achieved. To record and use the pulses from continuously operating mode-locked lasers, he developed the concept of the synchroscan streak camera, a continuously sweeping streak camera, where the high-voltage, sinusoidal sweeping of the electron image of the fast optical pulses was synchronised with the pulses emitted by the laser. When recorded on a phosphor screen, much like the concept of the scanning system of an old television tube, the pulses were precisely located on top of each other, greatly increasing the sensitivity of the device, while exhibiting sub-picosecond resolution. Together, the streak camera and the mode-locked continuous dye laser represented a powerful piece of ultrafast technology and diagnostics that Bradley applied extensively to investigating the picosecond relaxation dynamics of various molecular species. He also saw great potential in application to systems of biological importance.

Bradley's time was increasingly being called upon outside his research, and in 1976 he was appointed head of the department of physics at Imperial. He was also chairman of the Science Research Council (SRC) steering committee for the Joint Laser Centre, an institution where he had always been a vociferous proponent. He was delighted when the facility was approved in October 1975, with him serving as chairman of the SRC laser facility committee (1976–9). Throughout 1979, however, Bradley had become increasingly frustrated by administrative problems, in particular those relating to the processes and limits on promotion and appointment of junior staff. He also had wished to be more actively involved in laboratory investigations and was planning his future research strategy when his term as head of department ended. Despite this, it was surprising when he announced he would take up the newly established chair in optical electronics at TCD in October 1980.

Bradley had firm ideas on his research directions as he set out to establish his new group and research facility at Trinity. He planned application of mode-locked semiconductor lasers to optical communication and optical logic and a major effort on the application of ultra-fast laser technology to investigate dynamical processes in biological molecular species. Although he succeeded in obtaining considerable external funding to support this, internal funding for major projects was difficult to come by. Nominated by the provost, Professor Bill Watts, in 1981, he became bursar of Trinity. By the latter part of 1983, Bradley's group was growing, was in well-established laboratories, and was beginning to publish in the areas designated above, but on 21 October 1983 Bradley suffered a severely debilitating stroke.

As a result, his mobility was restricted and his speech severely impaired, and he retired in 1984. He still continued to travel extensively and participate at numerous national and international conferences. In time, illness restricted his travels and in his later years he was cared for in a residential home in Dublin, where he died on 7 February 2010.

In a relatively short but stellar career, Dan Bradley published more than 160 scientific papers and co-wrote more than 200 conference presentations. He supervised more than sixty Ph.D. students. His extensive contributions to the field were recognised through numerous international awards. He received the Thomas Young medal and prize of the Institute of Physics (1975), was elected a fellow of the Royal Society (1976), received the royal medal of the Royal Society (1983), the C. H. Townes medal of the Optical

Society of America (1989) and the Cunningham medal of the RIA (2002). Awarded honorary D.Sc. degrees from the University of Ulster (1983) and QUB (1986), he was a fellow of the Institute of Electronic and Electrical Engineers, the Optical Society of America and the Institute of Physics, and a member of the RIA. He also presented the prestigious Scott lectures in physics at the Cavendish Laboratory at the University of Cambridge in 1977. A bench was placed in his memory outside the Fitzgerald Building at TCD.

James Roy Taylor

Sources

United States patents 3761614, 3973117, 4021693 and 4327285; *Belfast Telegraph*, 1 July 1969; M. H. Key, *Adventures in laser produced plasma research* (2006); Donal Bradley, 'Dan Bradley: physicist, entrepreneur, teacher', presentation at QUB, 25 June 2014; E. C. Finch, *Three centuries of physics in Trinity College Dublin* (2016); J. R. Taylor, 'Daniel Joseph Bradley, 18 January 1928–7 February 2010', *Biographical memoirs of fellows of the Royal Society*, lxiii (2017); family history provided by Professor Donal Bradley, FRS

Sheila Tinney
(1918–2010)

MATHEMATICAL PHYSICIST

Sheila Christina (née Power) Tinney was born on 15 January 1918 in Galway city, fourth daughter of Michael Power (1885–1974), professor of mathematics in UCG (1912–55), and Christina Power (née Cunniffe), who also had a son and later another daughter. Michael Power's mathematical interests included the theory of complex functions; towards the end of his career, he and his daughter were able to attend the same international mathematical colloquia. He had several roles in the governance of UCG and the NUI. A keen angler and golfer, he was captain in 1925 when Galway Golf Club raised money to buy and lay out its new course. Christina Power died in 1930, leaving a family of six children, including two sets of twins, all under fifteen; Sheila was twelve.

Sheila Power attended the Dominican College, Taylor's Hill, Galway, and then went to St Mary's Dominican Convent, Cabra, Dublin, where she took her leaving certificate examinations in 1935. Unusually, she took honours mathematics, one of only eight girls in the country to do so and had the highest marks in geometry and also in Latin of all Irish girls in that year. Even more unusually, Power opted to study mathematics, first in UCG for a year, then in UCD, from where she graduated BA (1938) with a first-class degree in mathematical science, and MA (1939). Her results were so outstanding that she was awarded an NUI travelling studentship prize; she went to the University of Edinburgh to work on a doctorate. Her supervisor was the celebrated physicist and mathematician Max Born; Power worked with him on the stability of crystal lattices and was awarded a Ph.D. by Edinburgh in 1941. Previously believed to have been the first, she was in fact the second Irish woman to receive a doctorate in mathematical sciences, after Mary Gough. Her first paper, based on her thesis, appeared in 1942.

In 1941 she was appointed to an assistant lectureship in UCD, at the age of twenty-three, and also held a part-time fellowship in the Dublin Institute for Advanced Studies (DIAS). A year later, she was the only woman attending an international colloquium in the institute, at which the Nobel prize winner Paul Dirac lectured on quantum electrodynamics. This was a topic on which Power herself lectured and published several papers. She was promoted to statutory lecturer in 1945. From September 1948 to June 1949 she took leave of absence to go on a fellowship to the Institute for Advanced Study in Princeton, New Jersey, where she worked on aspects of nuclear physics. Colleagues there included Albert Einstein and Freeman Dyson. While visiting New Jersey, Power went horse-riding but was thrown off when the horse was startled by a snake; the resulting concussion was the worst injury she sustained in a lifetime of participation in sporting activities such as mountaineering and skiing.

Erwin Schrödinger, director of DIAS, described her as among the 'best equipped and most successful of the younger generation of theoretical physicists in this country', and in 1949, on her return to Dublin, Power was one of the first four women to be elected to full membership of the RIA, along with Phyllis Clinch (a UCD colleague), Eleanor Knott and Françoise Henry; she later served on the council of the academy (1975–6). After her marriage in the summer of 1952 to Sean Tinney (d. 2003), an engineer who held senior positions in the ESB, Sheila took her husband's name and became known professionally as Sheila Tinney. She retained her connection with DIAS as a research associate (1954–7) and became an associate professor in mathematical physics in UCD in 1966. However, the heavy teaching load with which Tinney coped throughout her career (she taught engineering as well as science students) meant that there was little time for new research, and probably – given that she was teaching large first-year undergraduate classes as well as postgraduates – little energy left, even for developing her existing interests.

A charming and strikingly attractive woman, Tinney was also a gifted and dedicated amateur musician; music was very important to her, as part of her heritage from her mother, and was very much a family affair. Her son Hugh Tinney became a celebrated professional pianist, and one of her two daughters, Ethna, was also a concert pianist and producer of music programmes for RTÉ. Mary Catherine Tinney, Sean Tinney's sister, was an enthusiastic musician as well as one of Ireland's first women career diplomats. Sheila Tinney retired from UCD in 1978. Her husband was president of the Royal Dublin Society (1995–7), but by then Sheila Tinney was suffering from Alzheimer's disease, and she eventually had to move into a nursing home, where she spent the last nine years of her life. She died in the Molyneux Home, Dublin, on 27 March 2010.

Linde Lunney

Sources

Aberdeen Journal, 12 July 1941; Tadhg Foley (ed.), *From Queen's College to National University* (1999), 169–72; *A century of scholarship: travelling students of the National University of Ireland* (2008); *Irish Times*, 26 June 2010; J. J. O'Connor and E. F. Robertson, 'Sheila Christina Power Tinney', MacTutor, Apr. 2015, https://mathshistory.st-andrews.ac.uk/Biographies/Tinney/ (accessed Jan. 2016)

James Dooge
(1922–2010)

ENGINEER, HYDROLOGIST AND POLITICIAN

James Clement Ignatius ('Jim') Dooge was born on 30 July 1922 in Grange Road West, Birkenhead, near Liverpool, the only son of Denis Dooge, marine engineer, and his wife Veronica (née Carroll). The Dooges were a family of engineers, most notably Jim's grandfather, John Publins Dooge (1862–1954), of Barranisky, Co. Wicklow, who worked for thirty-two years with the Burma Railway Company before returning to Ireland in 1921 and becoming a long-serving Fine Gael representative on Dún Laoghaire borough council and Dublin county council, acting as chairman of both.

Jim Dooge was educated in Liverpool before his family moved to Dún Laoghaire, Co. Dublin, where he attended the local CBS and became fluent in Irish. Entering University College Dublin (UCD) in 1939 with first place in the Dublin County Council university scholarship competition, he graduated B.Sc. and BE (Civil) with first-class honours in 1942, winning the Pierce Malone scholarship. He played hockey for Monkstown, engaged in amateur theatrics, and was active in local debating societies and the Irish Film Society. While in UCD, he met Marie Veronica ('Roni') O'Doherty from Belfast and married her in 1946; they lived first in Booterstown, Co. Dublin, and had two sons and three daughters.

Dooge's interest in hydrology (hydraulic engineering dealing with floods, drought, rainfall and evaporation) dated from his appointment in 1943 as assistant engineer on the design and survey of river improvements with the Office of Public Works (OPW). He joined the hydrometric design section of the Electricity Supply Board (ESB) in 1946 and conducted studies for hydroelectric schemes. His research was published in professional and scientific journals from the late 1940s and yielded a stream of prizes from the Institute of Civil Engineers of Ireland (ICEI) and also an ME from the National University of Ireland (NUI) in 1952.

Attracted by family connections and the party's support for economic planning, he joined Fine Gael in 1947 and was installed as constituency secretary by local TD Liam Cosgrave. Elected to Dublin county council in 1948 and Dún Laoghaire borough council in 1950, Dooge served as chairman of Dublin county council (1950–51 and 1953–4). His catholic faith nurtured a social conscience that was not very evident during his local government career, where he attracted notice as a notably able, but fairly conventional Fine Gael representative.

In 1954 he took leave of absence from the ESB and resigned from local government to become a research associate at the University of Iowa's world-renowned institute of hydraulic research. After taking an M.Sc. there in fluid mechanics and hydraulics, he returned to Ireland in 1956 and resumed at the ESB as senior design engineer with responsibility for hydraulic model experiments. In recognition of his internationally acclaimed research, he was appointed professor of civil engineering at University College Cork (UCC) in 1958 and moved to Bishopstown, Cork. Focusing on the unit hydrograph method for modelling rainfall run-offs in river catchments, he helped pioneer the application of mathematical systems theory to hydrology. The model outlined in his 1959 paper 'A general theory of the unit hydrograph' represented a fundamental advance in unit hydrograph principles and won the Horton award of the American Geophysical Union, helping to establish Dooge's international reputation.

Shouldering a heavy teaching workload to deter accusations of being distracted by his renewed political activism, he was successively elected a Fine Gael senator on the labour panel (1961–9) and the industrial and commercial panel (1969–77). His learned speeches, mainly on economics and education, fell on deaf ears, but he believed that technical seanad criticisms informed subsequent legislation. (While serving as president of the ICEI (1968–9), he negotiated its merger with Cumann na nInnealtoirí and shepherded the required legislation through the oireachtas.) Eager to base himself nearer to the political cockpit, he returned to Dublin in 1969 when he was appointed professor of civil engineering in UCD. He lived thereafter in Monkstown, Co. Dublin.

The new Fine Gael leader, Dooge's mentor Liam Cosgrave, nominated him for leas-chathaoirleach of the seanad (1965–73) and relied on him to formulate party policy, until they became semi-estranged in 1966 over Dooge's association with Fine Gael's emergent progressive wing. Advocating social pluralism and mildly redistributionist economic policies in implicit opposition to Cosgrave's cautious leadership, Dooge unsuccessfully proposed that the party rename itself 'Fine Gael – The Social Democratic Party' at the 1968 ard-fheis.

Despite tensions between Fine Gael's liberal and conservative factions, Dooge was respected across the party and crucial to its underdeveloped national organisation, as academic commitments restricted him to a covertly influential backroom role. (Conversely, his political interests led him to turn down a number of prestigious academic appointments abroad.) He was sensitive to suggestions that he had been disloyal towards Cosgrave, who continued to seek his advice and included him in negotiations for the joint general election manifesto with the Labour party in 1973. Upon the ensuing election of the Fine Gael–Labour coalition, Dooge became cathaoirleach of the seanad, an undemanding role that he performed with aplomb for the next four years.

Following the coalition's general election defeat in 1977, he retired from the seanad to concentrate on his still-flourishing academic career, eventually accumulating some 100 publications as sole author and over fifty as joint author. Regarded as an inspirational lecturer, he disseminated his hydrological knowledge widely. The most comprehensive elaboration of his theories on systems hydrology – which likened hydrological phenomena to a mechanical network obeying predictable rules – was his 1973 publication *Linear theory of hydrologic systems*, which enduringly influenced the management of water resources worldwide. Unlike some promoters of linear theory in hydrology, he readily acknowledged the inherent randomness of water flow and fretted that many of his academic colleagues suffered from a lack of practical engineering experience. He was instrumental in bringing together hydrological knowledge from both sides of the iron curtain during the cold war, initially establishing an informal international network of water scientists and engineers, which later developed into a commission within the International Association for Hydrological Sciences.

Regularly lecturing abroad and acting as a consultant to aid agencies, he made a leading contribution to international cooperation in hydrological research, particularly in eastern Europe and China. Also keen to encourage inter-disciplinary research, he was among the first to urge hydrologists to collaborate with atmospheric and oceanic scientists in monitoring the earth's climate and was, in 1978, involved in some of the earliest discussions on climate change. He was president of the International Commission on Water Resources Systems (1971–5) and of the International Association of Hydrological Sciences (1975–9); chairman of the scientific advisory committee of the World Climate Impact Studies Programme (1980–90); secretary general (1980–82) and president (1993–6) of the International Council for Science; and secretary (1978–81) and president (1987–90) of the Royal Irish Academy (RIA).

The liberal takeover of Fine Gael following the succession of Garret FitzGerald as leader in 1977 drew Dooge back into politics, particularly since he and FitzGerald had grown close while serving together in the seanad in 1965–9. Valued by FitzGerald as a more considered foil for his own quicksilver intellect, Dooge was pre-eminent within the urbane, extra-parliamentary inner circle that drove Fine Gael's transformation into a professionally run party. Dooge's report, as chairman of the election committee, on candidate selection and vote management, provided the blueprint for Fine Gael's sweeping gains in the 1981 general election. In tandem with Alexis FitzGerald, another of Garret FitzGerald's confidants, Dooge oversaw policy formation and scriptwriting, and assisted Garret FitzGerald in negotiating coalition agreements with the Labour party in 1981 and 1982.

Offered the foreign affairs portfolio in the June 1981 coalition cabinet, Dooge accepted, while foreseeing that his elevation from outside the oireachtas would infuriate the mass of Fine Gael deputies jealous of FitzGerald's unelected personal clique. There would have been an open mutiny had it been known that FitzGerald was guided by his wife, Joan FitzGerald, who argued that Dooge was the only candidate he could trust in such a sensitive portfolio. Before formally assuming his position, Dooge had to be appointed to the seanad as a taoiseach's nominee in August 1981 and ratified as minister by the reconvened dáil in October. Until then, he could not draw a ministerial salary, use a state car or attend cabinet meetings, and was accompanied at diplomatic negotiations by an acting foreign minister. Moreover, FitzGerald's ill-advised attempts to resolve the hunger strikes in Northern Ireland caused immediate complications.

The unrest within Fine Gael accompanying Dooge's appointment faded thanks to his obvious merit and diligent cultivation of backbenchers; it helped that he was strikingly unassuming for such an accomplished man. Lauded by Foreign Affairs officials, he conducted a cunning rearguard action against British attempts to reform the common agricultural policy, and upheld Ireland's neutrality during discussions on European Economic Community (EEC) security. Yet he was barely three months in office when FitzGerald's government fell in January 1982.

Rebuffing FitzGerald's pleas to run for the dáil in the February general election (in which the coalition was defeated), Dooge topped the poll for the NUI seanad panel in April, doing so again in February 1983, and resumed as a key member of FitzGerald's campaign team for the November 1982 general election that returned the Fine Gael–Labour coalition. Citing his fading eyesight, but probably in acknowledgement of the opposition within Fine Gael to his reappointment, Dooge ruled himself out of FitzGerald's second cabinet (no minister has since been chosen from outside the dáil). His influence waned thereafter, as FitzGerald became increasingly dependent on his media handlers. He served as government leader in the seanad (1983–7), ensuring that it dealt with more legislation than any previous seanad.

Declining the offer of an EEC commissionership, Dooge accepted FitzGerald's nomination (July 1984) as chairman of an EEC committee established to propose ways of advancing progress towards European unity. Little was expected of the so-called 'Dooge committee', and in September the West German government attempted unsuccessfully to replace Dooge with a more prestigious figure. His subtle chairmanship defied the critics and won Ireland significant kudos by providing cover for the French government's integrationist agenda. Speedily completing its work, the committee's report (March 1985) forensically clarified the parameters of the debate and provided a politically realistic basis for the intergovernmental negotiations that produced the Single European Act (1987), a far-reaching advance for the EEC.

Dooge did not seek re-election to the seanad in 1987 and retired definitively from politics. Resigning his UCD professorship in 1984, he concentrated on water ethics and developing climate change models, first with his team of researchers at the department of engineering hydrology in University College Galway (UCG) and then at the Centre for Water Resources in UCD from 1988. He was chairman of the organising committee of the second world climate conference (1990) and also chaired the inaugural world conference on water (1992); held in Ireland, the 1992 conference formulated the 'Dublin principles', a set of internationally accepted principles governing water management.

A founding father of modern hydrology, he was showered with academic distinctions, including eight honorary doctorates, the international prize in hydrology (1983), an honorary professorship at the East China Technical University of Water Resources (1986), the Bowie medal of the American Geophysical Union (1986), the International Meteorological Organisation prize (1999), the Prince Philip medal of the Royal Academy of Engineering (2005), and the RIA gold medal (2006). Amongst others, he was a foreign member of the Accademia Patavina (Padua) and of the academies of science for Poland, Russia and Spain, and a fellow of the Institution of Civil Engineers (London), the Royal Academy of Engineering, the American Society of Civil Engineers and the American Geophysical Union.

Regularly visiting Italy, he relished its art, food and wine. In retirement, he remained active with St Vincent de Paul, the Refugee Trust and the pastoral council for Blackrock parish. Having all but completed his memoirs, Jim Dooge died in his Monkstown residence on 30 July 2010 and was buried in Deansgrange cemetery. His personal papers are in UCD Archives, and his will disposed of €1.1 million.

Terry Clavin

Sources

Irish Independent, passim, esp.: 1 July 1950; 13 Feb. 1956; 6 July 1960; 2, 25 July 1981; *Irish Times*, passim, esp.: 19 Mar., 25 July 1964; 15 May 1968; 2 Dec. 1975 (profile); 9 Mar., 17 May, 20 Dec. 1985; 29 June 1987; 28 Aug. 2010 (obit.); *Irish Press*, passim, esp.: 8 May 1964; 12 May 1982; *Nusight*, Apr. 1970; *Sunday Independent*, 8 June 1975; *Magill*, July 1981; Dec. 1982; Oct. 1983; Sept. 1985; Report of the president, University College Dublin (1983–4), 133–4; *Guardian*, 29 Sept. 1984; Vincent Browne (ed.), *Magill book of Irish politics* (1984), 185, 373; Patrick Keatinge, *A singular stance: Irish neutrality in the 1980s* (1984); Raymond Smith, *Garret: the enigma* (1985), 12, 377–9, 402; Stephen O'Byrnes, *Hiding behind a face: Fine Gael under FitzGerald* (1986); James Dooge, 'The role of the seanad' in Patrick Lynch and James Meenan (eds), *Essays in memory of Alexis FitzGerald* (1987), 133–59; Patrick Keatinge and Anna Murphy, 'The European Council's ad hoc committee on institutional affairs (1984–85)' in Roy Pryce (ed.), *The dynamics of European union* (1987), 217–33; Michael Burgess, *Federalism and European Union: political ideas, influences and strategies in the European Community* (1989), 186–90; Garret FitzGerald, *All in a life* (1991); J. P. O'Kane (ed.), *Advances on theoretical hydrology: a tribute to James Dooge* (1992); Elizabeth Shaw, *Hydrology in practice* (1994), 375; Stephen Collins, *The Cosgrave legacy* (1996); Kathleen Meenan, '1984: the end of Eurosclerosis' in James Dooge and Ruth Barrington (ed.), *A vital national interest: Ireland in Europe, 1973–1998* (1999), 55–65; Paddy Harte, *Young tigers and mongrel foxes* (2005); 'Professor James Dooge', *Ingenia*, issue 24 (Sept. 2005), https://www.ingenia.org.uk/articles/professor-james-dooge-freng/; Obituary, *International Association of Hydrological Sciences*, https://iahs.info/About-IAHS/Awards/International-Hydrology-Prize/International-Hydrology-Prize-Winners/JCI-Dooge/; Garret FitzGerald, *Just Garret: tales from the political frontline* (2010); 'Interview by Caroline Stephenson: Jim Dooge' in Barbara Sweetman FitzGerald (ed.), *'The widest circle': remembering Michael Sweetman* (2011), 127–30; *Sunday Times* (Irish ed.), 9 Oct. 2011; Thomas Hennessey, *Hunger strike: Margaret Thatcher's battle with the IRA, 1980–81* (2014); Ronald Cox and Dermot O'Dwyer, *Called to serve: presidents of the Institution of Civil Engineers of Ireland, 1835–1968* (2014), 142–3; www.wmo.int/pages/mediacentre/news/obituary_dooge_en.html (internet material accessed Apr. 2016); information from Bruce Misstear

John Scott
(1940–2012)

BIOCHEMIST

John Martin Scott was born on 20 May 1940 in Dublin, the son of Martin Scott, an engineering inspector in local government, and Clare Scott (née Doran), who was a nurse before her marriage. He had one sister, and grew up in Churchtown, Co. Dublin, but attended Garbally College, Ballinasloe, Co. Galway, probably his father's old school.

In 1962 John graduated with a B.Sc. in biochemistry from UCD, and then moved to TCD to work for a Ph.D. He took up a junior lectureship in TCD in 1965, and from 1966 to 1968 had his first sabbatical period in the USA as National Institutes of Health (NIH) international post-doctoral fellow in the University of California, at Berkeley. He had three further sabbatical periods during his career, two in the USA and one in London.

Shortly after returning from his first sabbatical, Scott became friends with Donald Weir (regius professor of physic in TCD from 1977). Weir credited Scott with showing him, in a tremendously fruitful collaboration over thirty years from 1969, how biochemistry can elucidate the problems encountered in clinical medicine. The two men quickly established a research group of scientists and clinicians, with specialisms in nutrition and biochemistry, a group which gained the reputation of being able to move with equal commitment between laboratory bench and bedside. Scott was appointed to a personal chair in experimental nutrition in TCD in 1978.

His main focus throughout his career was on folates, a group of compounds with shared structure and equivalent biological activities, that collectively make up one of the B vitamins essential to health. Folates are derived naturally from food sources such as green leafy vegetables. The synthetically produced, commercially available precursor molecule, folic acid, is an important source of folate. Scott's early work was on the role of polyglutamate forms of folates in microbial and mammalian cells. This work gave an understanding of how folates are retained in cells and how excretion and breakdown of folate molecules occur. With Weir he also carried out research on the form of megaloblastic anaemia caused by deficiency of folate or the closely associated vitamin, B12. Together Scott and Weir and their group elucidated the general biochemical mechanism of the classical demyelination of the spinal cord and clinical neuropathy seen in vitamin B12 deficiency, but not in folate deficiency.

Researchers had recognised since the 1960s that a maternal micronutrient deficiency (most likely of folates) in pregnancy could cause neural tube defects (NTDs) in the foetus. NTDs include spina bifida and anencephaly and cause high infant mortality or serious lifelong disabilities. Up to the 1970s, Ireland's rate of such NTDs was one of the highest recorded in Europe; with nearly eight babies out of 1,000 born with NTDs. In the early 1990s two important clinical trials (an international trial coordinated by the UK Medical Research Council (1991) and a Hungarian trial (1992)) demonstrated conclusively that maternal supplementation with folic acid before and during early pregnancy would greatly reduce the risk of having an NTD-affected pregnancy.

Years before that result was published, Scott and Weir's team, in collaboration with the Health Research Board and Dublin maternity hospitals, had made substantial contributions to the subject by organising the collection (1986–90) of more than 56,000 blood samples from Irish women in early pregnancy. Most women at the time in Ireland did not take nutritional supplements and there was little or no fortification of foods, so, crucially, these data reflect a baseline situation. Using this biobank, bloods from eighty-four mothers who had delivered babies with NTDs were identified, and the team was able to demonstrate that affected mothers had lower folates in red blood cells than non-affected mothers, and that having a red blood cell folate concentration above a specified concentration was greatly protective against having an NTD-affected pregnancy. The work was published in a significant and forthright paper 'Folate levels and neural tube defects. Implications for prevention' in the *Journal of the American Medical Association* (1995). The paper, which has been cited over 500 times, had immediate and lasting impact. Twenty years later, it formed the basis for a World Health Organization guideline: 'Optimal thresholds for serum and red blood cell folate concentrations in women of reproductive age for prevention of neural tube defects' (WHO 2015).

In another highly influential paper, published in the *Lancet* in 1996, Scott and his team published results showing that the bio-availability of naturally occurring folates was rather poor, compared to the uptake of the synthetic vitamin (folic acid). They demonstrated that the protective red blood cell folate concentration noted earlier, which was well above levels that resulted in clinical deficiency, could not easily be reached by eating dietary folates but only with supplements and fortified foods. Scott also demonstrated that an ongoing intake of small amounts of folic acid, such as the amount that could be added to fortified foods, would, over time, allow a protective blood concentration to be achieved. The work provided support for calls to add folic acid to foodstuffs, particularly to fortify bread, so that the cohort of women of childbearing age who might fall pregnant unexpectedly would be at least somewhat less at risk of an NTD pregnancy. Campaigns led in due course to the mandatory fortification of foods with folic acid in the USA, Canada and over seventy other countries worldwide.

Scott's team engaged with collaborators in the National Institutes of Health (NIH) in the United States to study the role of folic acid in NTDs. With these collaborators, he worked on strategies to establish the level of supplementation, whether taken voluntarily and individually, or in fortified food, which seemed likely to be optimal in preventing NTDs. He and his team also researched the possible positive or negative implications of treating whole populations with supplementary folic acid. His collaborative work in TCD and in associated institutions such as St James's Hospital and the University of Ulster, examining the risks and benefits of increasing folic acid consumption in various populations and for many health outcomes, led to scores of publications, presentations, applications for research funding and clinical trials. Even for someone unacquainted with the field, the titles of the team's publications, appearing every few months in the 1990s, convey the scope of their studies, as well as the sense of excitement, urgency and enthusiasm for discovery which characterised this period of Scott's career.

Scott served on the UK's Department of Health Expert Advisory Group, which in 1992 unanimously recommended food fortification, and was a member of the Irish Food Safety Authority but was disappointed that the UK and Ireland continued to refuse to fortify food. Scott's team also worked to disprove several of the concerns which opponents of fortification put forward to justify their position: published papers on pregnancy complications, cardiac problems and the development of cancers broadly found no increased risks due to folate supplementation. Research showed that the incidence of NTDs was unchanged in countries where voluntary supplementation was recommended, compared with the USA and Canada, where there were indeed fewer affected pregnancies thanks to mandatory fortification of flour. Overall, a very great deal of credit for the worldwide understanding of the requirement for folic acid to prevent NTDs must go to the work of researchers from Trinity's Schools of Biochemistry and Medicine, led for thirty years by John Scott.

Largely in collaboration with colleagues in the NIH, Scott and his team looked at possible genetic differences between women which might lead to less successful metabolism of nutrients such as the folates and other B vitamins, and towards the end of his career, he examined the influence of genetic makeup on whether or not individuals experienced changes to blood pressure after riboflavin therapy. Even after retirement age, Scott continued his research and collaborated on major work to examine the role in pregnancy and otherwise of vitamin B12; the group reported in 2009 that maternal blood status of vitamin B12 is likely to be an important additional factor in causing maternal risk for having an NTD-affected pregnancy. He was also interested in orofacial clefts and was involved in the collection in Ireland of a biobank of DNA from patients with clefts, which was used with other internationally collected samples to confirm the involvement of previously unidentified genes. The study was published in *Nature Genetics* in 2010.

Alongside an internationally recognised research career, Scott was also involved in the administration of his discipline, serving on national, European and American scientific committees. He was elected to fellowship of TCD in 1973 and was a member of the RIA from 1984. Serving as bursar of TCD (1977–80), at a time of considerable change and development in the college, he was also a member of the board of St James's Hospital for more than twenty years. Scott received many awards in recognition of his outstanding contributions to science, medicine and human welfare, such as the degree of Doctor of Science (1981) by TCD and honorary degrees from the University of Ulster and from Universidad San Pablo, Madrid. He received the TCD Provost's award for outstanding contribution to teaching and learning, and was the first non-American to receive the Lederle award from the American Society of Nutritional Science. In honour of Scott's achievements, TCD in 2016 established three John Scott fellowships for Ph.D. students to research in biochemistry.

On 6 July 1966 Scott and Isabel Finnegan were married in Dublin; they had a son and a daughter. His wife predeceased him in 2010, and John Scott suffered increasingly poor health for the last couple of years of his life. He died on 29 December 2012 in St Luke's Hospital, Rathgar, Dublin.

Anne Molloy and Linde Lunney

Sources

A. V. Hoffbrand and D. G. Weir, 'Historical review. The history of folic acid', *British Journal of Haematology*, 113 (2001), 579–89; John M. Scott, 'Addition of vitamin B12 to folic acid supplements to optimise the prevention of spina bifida and other Neural Tube Defects', Report for SHINE; *Irish Times*, 31 Dec. 2012; 1 Jan. 2013; 'Death of professor John Scott, distinguished researcher', www.cleft.ie/?p=508; 'Our alumni. Interview Donald G. Weir', www.tcd.ie/alumni/alumni/interviews/donald-weir.php; A. Victor Hoffbrand, 'Professor John Scott, folate and neural tube defects', *British Journal of Haematology*, 164 (2014), 496–502; 'How does a university change the world? The origins of folic acid fortification of foods', www.tcd.ie/research/about/history/the-origins-of-folic-acid-fortification-of-foods.php; 'Folate (folic acid), health policy and the consumer', Impact Case Study, University of Ulster; Research Excellence Framework, impact.ref.ac.uk/casestudies2/refservice.svc/GetCaseStudyPDF/1019; Newsletter School of Biochemistry and Immunology, www.tcd.ie/Biochemistry/assets/pdf/Alumni_Newsletter_2016-17.pdf (internet material accessed Dec. 2018)

Mary Mulvihill
(1959–2015)

SCIENCE COMMUNICATOR

Mary Rita Mulvihill was born on 1 September 1959 in London, the eldest of three daughters of Joe Mulvihill, a clothing manufacturer from Co. Carlow, and Maureen Mulvihill (née McGrath), a radiographer from Co. Clare. The family lived in London for four years before returning to Ireland to live in Rathfarnham, Co. Dublin.

Mulvihill received her primary and secondary education at Sancta Maria College, Ballyroan, Co. Dublin, showing an early interest in science (her aunt Kitty was a science teacher). In order to take chemistry in the leaving certificate she attended classes at Coláiste Éanna, a Christian Brothers boys' school, as the subject was not offered in her girls' school. Mulvihill studied genetics at Trinity College Dublin (TCD), where she was awarded a scholarship that allowed her to study for several months at Ann Arbor University, Michigan, USA. She graduated with a B.Sc. in genetics (1981), following which she took an M.Sc. in statistics and operations research (also at TCD) and later enrolled at the same university for a doctorate, studying the genetics of performance in thoroughbred horses. In 1983, however, Mulvihill left university to work as a research officer in genetics with An Foras Talúntais (the Agricultural Institute).

During this period, Mulvihill began developing wider cultural interests, taking a course in creative writing and writing poems and sketches of possible plays that reflected her feminism and radicalism, as well as her disposition towards scientific inquiry. In 1987 she turned to journalism as a career, studying for a graduate diploma in journalism at the National Institute of Higher Education, Dublin (now Dublin City University (DCU)). On graduating in 1988 she became a freelance science journalist, which she remained until her premature death in 2015. Her early journalism activities included a decade as co-editor of *Technology Ireland* magazine, a role she used to encourage many other freelance journalists specialising in science and technology.

From the late 1980s Mulvihill wrote and presented science radio programmes on RTÉ Radio 1 and Lyric FM and contributed science items to current affairs and other programmes. She developed a distinctive voice and innovative approaches to science storytelling, as indicated in the titles and topics of programmes she devised and presented, which included *Up'n'atom*, a weekly magazine series; themed series such as *The perfect pint*, exploring fluids, from ready-mixed concrete to shampoo to bull's semen, *Chopped, pickled and stuffed*, about the Natural History Museum, and *Washed, peeled and dried*, about the National Botanic Gardens; and documentaries, including *Pedals and pebbles*, a geological tour of Dublin by bicycle, and *Time, please*, a history of time and timekeeping in Ireland.

Over a span of twenty years Mulvihill was a frequent contributor to the *Irish Times*, first as a writer of news reports and features for the news pages, and later as an occasional columnist for 'An Irishwoman's diary' and the science page. From her earliest newspaper articles she eschewed the standard science reportage of covering recent discoveries and supposed breakthroughs. Instead, she approached current research topics through allusions to everyday, historical and social contexts. Mulvihill also pursued her commitment to increasing media coverage of science through active membership of the Irish Science Journalists' Association.

Mulvihill's conviction that science and invention deserved greater recognition in the telling of Irish history, particularly when accomplished by women, threaded through her work. In April 2015, she used the career of the Strabane-born astronomer Annie Maunder (born Annie Russell) to highlight the long history of discrimination against women in science. Mulvihill's column (which turned out to be her last contribution to the *Irish Times*) was a biographical article of Russell who, with her astronomer husband Edward Walter Maunder, undertook expeditions in the 1890s to several continents to observe solar eclipses. Describing her expedition to India, Mulvihill recounted how Russell had designed her own camera, which she used to 'capture an image of a streamer from the sun's corona that was 10 million kilometres long, the longest that had then been seen' (*Irish Times*, 9 Apr. 2015). The photograph was, however, published under her husband's name, as happened for many female scientists at that time.

Mulvihill also advocated for greater representation of women in science and technology. A founding member of Women in Technology and Science (WITS), she served as the organisation's inaugural chairperson (1991–3). She contributed her professional skills to WITS, editing two collections of biographical essays on Irish women that were published by the organisation: *Stars, shells and bluebells: women scientists and pioneers* (1997) and *Lab coats and lace: the lives and legacies of inspiring Irish women scientists and pioneers* (2009). Mulvihill encouraged and mentored many early-career researchers, particularly women, in communicating publicly about their scientific work. From the mid-1990s she also organised events and published a newsletter under the banner Science@Culture, reflecting her interest in locating science as part of culture and strengthening its public visibility. Film screenings, public talks and panel discussions were among the events in which science was brought into conversation with literature, drama, politics and ethics. The Science@Culture newsletter, which provided information on a wide variety of public science-related activities, was published as a solo voluntary enterprise in changing formats over fifteen years.

Gathering materials for her magnum opus was a continuing activity over six years. She corresponded, foraged and travelled widely to assemble what became *Ingenious Ireland: a county-by-county exploration of Ireland's marvels and mysteries* (2002). This 500-page mix of encyclopedia, topography, dictionary of biography and gazetteer, has the scope of a life's work rather than the undertaking of someone at a relatively early stage of her writing and publishing career. In this project and in her wider work, 'she roamed freely over – and delved deeply into – the earth sciences, astronomy, chemistry, physics, mathematics, biology, ecology, archaeology, medicine and engineering' (Sheridan, 182); '[*Ingenious Ireland*] combines the range and authority of an encyclopaedia with the intimacy that comes with a single authorial voice' (Sheridan, 187). The book came to be widely appreciated as a reference work and it found a new life and wider readership on its well-received republication in 2019.

From *Ingenious Ireland*, Mulvihill spun-off a local guide – *Ingenious Dublin* – and scientific walking tours and audio guides to aspects of the country's and capital's scientific heritage and natural habitat. Tours included introductions to the stone used in selected Dublin buildings and the fossils they bear; the audio guides included one to the National Botanic Gardens. Mulvihill was an enthusiastic guide, willingly taking groups on tours of places of scientific interest but also recruiting other guides to support the enterprise. She was engaged by various scientific and other agencies to write and edit texts, and to train staff in public communication. She wrote a history of the School of Cosmic Physics at the Dublin Institute for Advanced Studies and explanatory notices for a historical exhibit mounted by Dublin Port and Docks Board, among other such commissions. Mulvihill ran communication courses for Met Éireann and for Teagasc (the successor to her former employer, An Foras Talúntais) and in 2002 was appointed to a newly established government advisory body, the Irish Council for Bioethics.

Mulvhill was a voracious reader, covering a wide span of literature far beyond her professional interest in science. She and friends set up a book club in 1988, well before such groups became a widespread phenomenon; the club was still running thirty-five years later. A keen cyclist, hill walker and observer of nature, she applied her environmental consciousness to her own modest lifestyle. She urged radical rethinking of our consumer habits, including doing things very deliberately by halves – reducing the amount of washing powder and shampoo used, for example – in *Drive like a woman, shop like a man: greener is cheaper* (2009).

Mulvihill married physicist Brian Dolan in 2002 and together they observed the night skies, walked the hills and mountains of his native Scotland and undertook a journey to the Galapagos Islands that was extravagant by her terms, but undertaken in homage to her scientific hero, Charles Darwin.

Mary Mulvihill died of cancer in Dublin on 11 June 2015. A science communicator who worked in many formats and media, she also played a prominent role in promoting women's involvement in science and technology and was a tireless advocate for increasing public awareness of Ireland's scientific heritage. The house she shared with

Dolan and in which she lived from 1987 now bears a plaque commemorating her as 'science journalist – pioneer in science communication', the first such commemoration of a science communicator among the more than seventy plaques erected by the National Committee for Commemorative Plaques in Science and Technology. The Mary Mulvihill Association has sought to maintain her legacy through a student science media award, an annual Science@Culture talk and the republication of *Ingenious Ireland*. Mulvihill was also honoured posthumously with a DCU alumni award for outstanding achievement in societal impact. Her collected papers, including materials used for *Ingenious Ireland*, are held in DCU Archives.

Brian Trench

Sources

Dublin City University (DCU) Archives, Mary Mulvihill collection; *Irish Times*, 9 Apr. 2015; Cormac Sheridan, 'The stories that she told: Mary Mulvihill (1959–2015)' in Brian Trench, Pádraig Murphy and Declan Fahy (eds), *Little country, big talk: science communication in Ireland* (2017), 181–94; information from Nóirín Mulvihill (sister) and Brian Dolan (husband)

John Byrne
(1933–2016)

ACADEMIC AND COMPUTER SCIENTIST

John Gabriel Byrne was born in Dublin on 25 July 1933, the only son of Thomas Brendan Byrne and Doreen (née Lawlor). His father, a Trinity College Dublin (TCD) engineering graduate of 1924, worked for Dublin county council for most of his life. Byrne's great-grandfather, Anthony Scott (1844–1919), and his grandfather, Thomas Joseph Byrne, both spent much of their careers as architects involved in the development of public housing. This family history of public service, engineering and architecture had a strong influence on Byrne, who attended Loreto High School Beaufort, Rathfarnham, followed by Belvedere College, Dublin, where, perhaps somewhat surprisingly given his future career, he concentrated on classics. He entered TCD in 1952 and spent the first year studying French, Latin and Greek and attending lectures in physics and chemistry, while at the same time preparing for the special mathematics entrance examination required at that time for admission to engineering. Byrne was tutored in mathematics by the renowned lecturer Victor Graham, to whom he always remained very grateful; they remained close friends until Graham's death in 1991.

Byrne graduated top of his class from TCD's school of engineering in 1956, with first-class honours. He briefly worked in Birmingham for the engineering firm then constructing Croke Park's new Hogan stand before he applied for and received a bursary to attend Imperial College

London in 1956, where he took a diploma in concrete technology and first heard about digital computers. Byrne returned to Dublin in 1957 to begin his doctoral studies at TCD with William Wright, who had just been appointed to the university's chair of civil engineering. His doctoral thesis, which was concerned with the mathematical modelling of the torsional stresses in hollow reinforced concrete beams, involved solving a large number of partial differential equations. While attending a conference in London, Byrne heard of Bernard Carré, a mathematician who had developed a programme for solving the type of equations with which Byrne was working. It was his first practical experience of digital computers and programming, which would ultimately form the basis of his career. Byrne was conferred with his Ph.D. in 1961 and was appointed to a junior lectureship at TCD in 1963, initially funded by the graduate school of engineering studies, and then as an established lecturer in the school of engineering from 1965. He was elected a fellow of TCD in 1969 and appointed to the first chair of computer science in 1973.

Together with Wright, Byrne arranged for the purchase in 1962 of TCD's first computer, an IBM 1620. Computing studies at the university, driven by the school of engineering, took off immediately and the department of computer science was established in 1969 with Byrne as its head. He remained as head of the department for thirty-two years, apart from a brief interlude of three years at the end of the 1980s when he served as dean of the then-faculty of engineering and systems sciences. The department of computer science grew from three academic staff in 1969 to twenty-two a decade later; by the time Byrne stepped down as head of the department in 2001, the academic staff stood at almost sixty in what had become the school of computer science and statistics. There was a corresponding increase in technical, administrative and support staff, all of which was overseen by Byrne virtually single-handedly.

Byrne's vision and drive firmly established TCD as the leader in the development of computer science as an academic discipline in Ireland. He pioneered several short courses in computing aimed at those working in business and industry, as well as several degree programmes. The Master of Science (M.Sc.) in computer applications, launched in 1963, was the first master's degree in computing in Ireland and among the first in Ireland and Britain (it was also one of the very earliest taught masters programmes in TCD), while Byrne also introduced the first full-time undergraduate programme in computing in 1966 when a computer engineering stream was added to the engineering degree; the first graduates emerged in 1970. A Diploma in Systems Analysis followed in 1968, while a Diploma in Computers in Education, aimed at teachers, was inaugurated in 1973. In what was a major innovation for TCD, a successful part-time evening Bachelor of Science (B.Sc.) degree was introduced in 1970, catering to both the public and private sectors. Attuned to shaping the department's teaching and research to national needs, Byrne utilised government funding aimed at transforming the skill sets of Ireland's labour force to establish undergraduate degrees in computer science (1969) and information and communications technology (ICT) (1997). He collaborated with the university's arts faculty to introduce an innovative degree in computer science, linguistics and either French or German.

Byrne was also alert to the importance of European funding, particularly under the European Commission's European Strategic Programme on Research in Information Technology (ESPRIT), established in the early 1980s. He facilitated the formation of a number of research groups that brought together academics working in similar areas and actively encouraged participation by his department's staff, creating a critical mass that boosted applications for larger research grants. Though not directly involved in the establishment of campus companies that were spun out from the department of computer science, Byrne fostered an encouraging and supportive environment.

Byrne's contribution to laying the foundations for Ireland's development as a major European – if not global – centre for ICT is difficult to overstate. One of the rate-limiting steps for the emerging technology sector globally was (and remains) the lack of an appropriately skilled workforce; Byrne developed educational programmes that built a base of skilled professionals, thereby playing a major part in attracting ICT businesses to Ireland from the early 1970s. Byrne was also an active member of various committees in both the Industrial Development Authority (IDA) and Enterprise Ireland, where his skills in identifying future industrial trends were very much to the fore. While the IDA had identified electronics as a fruitful sector for Ireland to attract foreign direct investment, its initial focus was on manufacturing. Byrne and others thought that software and ICT services were likely to be future growth areas, providing the IDA with the critical evidence that helped lay the groundwork for Ireland's emergence as the European headquarters of many of the world's largest ICT companies in the early 2000s.

Byrne pursued many interests outside of academia, including horse racing, genealogy, architecture, mathematics and history, particularly the history of computing. His impressive collection of early computing books, documents, slide rules, software, instruments and machines were donated to TCD and form the basis of the John Gabriel Byrne Computer Science Collection. In 1985 Byrne curated a special exhibition in the university library's

Long Room, titled 'Computing through the ages', to coincide with TCD's hosting of the International Federation for Information Processing's annual conference. His work on the exhibition prompted him to develop an innovative digital version of the library's catalogue of books acquired prior to 1872, then only available in printed format. Working with students, Byrne's catalogue (which is still in use) necessitated the development of a bespoke optical character recognition (OCR) system, was completed in five years and listed approximately 165,000 books in at least fourteen different languages.

Byrne retired from TCD in 2003, aged seventy. He had belonged to the old style of university professor and head of department for life, with a style of leadership that might best be characterised as benevolent dictatorship. He ran his department virtually single-handedly for over thirty years and never sought or wanted any credit, acting in what he felt were the best interests of the department, its staff and its students. Painfully shy, he eschewed the limelight. His shyness belied a deeply caring nature for his students and colleagues, whom he would go out of his way to assist if they found themselves in difficulty – always quietly and with a minimum of fuss. An ardent feminist, he was a mentor and strong supporter of the few women in TCD's department of computer science. He never married and left a bequest to TCD's student hardship fund in his will.

John Byrne died on 16 April 2016 at Newtownpark House nursing home, Blackrock, Dublin. Considered the 'father of computing' in Ireland, Byrne was driven by a devotion to TCD and a belief in the value of public service (*Irish Times*, 19 Dec. 2019). His contribution to the development of Ireland's ICT sector continues to resonate.

Jane Grimson

Sources

William Wright and John G. Byrne, 'M.Sc. course in computer applications at Trinity College', *Computer Bulletin*, vol. 8, no. 2 (Sept. 1964), 51–3; *Observer*, 29 June 1986; John V. Luce, *Trinity College Dublin: the first 400 years* (1992); Ronald Cox, *Engineering at Trinity* (1993); Ray Mac Sharry and Padraic White, *The making of the Celtic tiger: the inside story of Ireland's boom economy* (2000); Tony White, *Investing in people: higher education in Ireland from 1960 to 2000* (2001); John G. Byrne, 'The Trinity College Dublin 1872 online catalogue' in Simone Marinai and Andreas Dengel (eds), *Document analysis systems vi: proceedings of the 6th international workshop, DAS 2004, Florence, Italy* (2004), 17–27; Interviews with John Byrne (2011), Irish Life and Lore collection, https://www.irishlifeandlore.com/product-category/recordings/thematic/education/; William E. Vaughan, *The old library: Trinity College Dublin, 1712–2012* (2012); Higher Education Authority (Van Vught report), *A proposed reconfiguration of the Irish system of higher education* (2012), http://hea.ie/assets/uploads/2017/04/International-Panel-Report-on-Reconfiguration.pdf; John Byrne and Michael Fewer, *Thomas Joseph Byrne: nation builder* (2013); Timothy R. Jackson (ed.), *Frozen in time: the Fagel collection in the Library of Trinity College Dublin* (2016); *University Times*, 23 Oct. 2016; Chris J. Horn (ed.), *Professor John Byrne: father of computing in Ireland. Reminiscences* (2017); Jane Grimson, 'Trinity Monday memorial discourse on John Gabriel Byrne', 9 Apr. 2018, https://www.tcd.ie/media/tcd/secetary/pdfs/discourses/2018_John-Gabriel-Byrne.pdf; *Irish Times*, 19 Dec. 2019; Dictionary of Irish architects, 1720–1940, https://www.dia.ie/architects/view/4764/SCOTT%2C+ANTHONY; 'The Victor Graham award', Irish Applied Maths Teachers' Association, https://iamta.ie/victor-graham-award/ (internet material accessed Nov. 2024)

Anne Kernan
(1933–2020)

Academic and particle physicist

Anne Kernan was born on 15 January 1933 in Glasnevin, the second of four children (along with Denis, Úna and Gerard) of Frederick Kernan, a civil servant, and Annie Connor, living at 242 Griffith Avenue, Drumcondra, Dublin.

Although neither of her parents were scientists, Kernan wrote that 'they both influenced me in that direction … Scientists were heroes' (*American Scientist*, 1986). She chose to attend the Dominican College on Eccles Street, Dublin, so that she could study physics and later specialised in the subject during her undergraduate studies at University College Dublin (UCD, B.Sc., 1950–53). Awarded a first-class degree, she was the only woman in her class and remained at UCD to pursue a Ph.D. in particle physics. Part of her doctoral research was conducted at the University of Rochester, New York, supported by a scholarship from the American Association of University Women (1954–5), which enabled her to study particle interactions at the Brookhaven Laboratory Cosmotron on Long Island, New York. Her Ph.D., on the interactions of protons and kaons, was awarded in 1957.

Kernan was then hired as an assistant lecturer at UCD (1958–62) and worked in the nuclear emulsion group situated in Earlsfort Terrace. Although her research was based on the standard emulsion particle detector technology of the time, Kernan stayed abreast of the latest experimental techniques, giving a seminar to the Dublin Institute for

Advanced Studies in the 1961–2 academic session on the analysis of data from bubble chambers by digital computers, a recent technological innovation.

In 1962, with the aid of a Soroptimist foundation fellowship, Kernan moved to America to perform research at the Lawrence Radiation Laboratory (now Lawrence Berkeley National Laboratory) in the University of California at Berkeley. American facilities were world-leading at the time, allowing physicists to study the proliferation of particles that ultimately led to the hypothesis of quarks as the fundamental ingredients of matter. Whilst at Berkeley, first as a postdoctoral researcher with the Linear Accelerator Centre at Stanford University (1966–7), and subsequently as an academic at the University of California, Riverside, Kernan and her collaborators made many measurements of different baryon species and kaon decays.

Kernan joined Riverside in 1967 as a lecturer, becoming associate professor in 1968 and the first woman to gain tenure in the department. She was influential in establishing the experimental high-energy physics group there and was awarded a full professorship in 1970, later becoming chair of the physics department (1973–6).

In 1973 Kernan changed her research focus to CERN, the European Centre for Particle Physics, in Geneva, Switzerland. She joined experiments at CERN's Intersecting Storage Rings facility which enabled her to perform more detailed studies of particle production and to explore effects due to the strong force at higher energies. Following the discovery of the charm quark in America in 1974, Kernan led her team in searches for charm particle production at the facility, finally observing a charmed baryon produced by the strong force for the first time in 1979.

In the late 1970s, CERN scientists developed techniques to build a colliding beam facility with sufficient energy to search for W and Z bosons, the particles posited to convey the weak force (the weak and strong forces are two of the four fundamental forces known to physics). Kernan led Riverside to become one of nine founding institutions of UA1, one of the two experiments situated there in 1978. Led by particle physicist Carlo Rubbia, UA1 operated between 1981 and 1990. The W and Z bosons were discovered in early 1983, earning Rubbia and Simon van der Meer, whose innovations enabled the facility to be built, the Nobel prize for physics in 1984. In light of her contributions to the experiment, Kernan was invited by the prize recipients to attend the award ceremony.

Kernan's own research interests centred on tests of the strong force and the production of particles containing heavy quarks. Hopes were high at the time that UA1 might also be able to discover the unseen top quark, a fundamental constituent of matter, and Kernan's group were tasked with constructing a small, precise silicon vertex detector necessary to identify it. The unrealistic timescales and challenging technology of the project, combined with the inexperience of her team, led to Kernan calculating 'the odds of pulling it off were at best one in a hundred' (Taubes, 213). She accepted the challenge and won substantial funding from the US Department of Energy, but after months of effort it proved impossible to build a working detector. The experience did not discourage Kernan, who established a laboratory at Riverside to develop silicon detectors for other experiments where the top quark could be discovered.

In 1986 Kernan changed her research focus back to America. She joined the DZero experiment at Fermilab, Illinois, which was under construction at what would become the most powerful particle physics facility in the world. Her group contributed to many aspects of the experiment; the high voltage system, the trigger system and the design and construction of a silicon microvertex detector for the second period of DZero data-taking. Kernan resumed her exploration of heavy particles with DZero and members of her group were part of the team that discovered the top quark there in 1995.

In parallel to working on DZero, Kernan became the vice-chancellor for research and dean of the graduate division (both 1991–4) at Riverside, with responsibility for all graduate students and graduate recruitment. She was the first woman to serve in these positions and retired in 1994.

In addition to her research, Kernan served on many advisory committees supporting the particle physics community: the science and education advisory committee for Lawrence Berkeley laboratory, the Fermilab Programme advisory committee, the Department of Energy high-energy physics advisory panel and American Physical Society (APS) committees on the status of women in physics and on the international freedom of scientists. Elected a fellow of the APS (1975) and the American Association for the Advancement of Science (1987), Kernan served as APS councillor (1985–9) and councillor of the society's division of particles and fields (1993–5). She was awarded an honorary Doctor of Science (D.Sc.) by UCD in 1995. Kernan donated funds to establish the Anne Kernan Endowment, used to support annual graduate student awards in Riverside's department of physics and astronomy. She also awarded a bursary fund to Dominican College to reward student academic excellence in the pursuit of science (2007–19).

Kernan was known amongst her peers as an accomplished and successful physicist with a knack for 'being at the right place at the right time' (Smith, correspondence with author), and as a strong and innovative leader who was kind, generous and supportive. She was an advocate for women in science – on one occasion not only funding a research trip to CERN for an undergraduate she had never met, but meeting her at the airport on her arrival and even withdrawing money from her own bank account to tide the student over until her funds were paid. Outside work Kernan enjoyed skiing, cooking and the arts, and frequently hiked with her brother Gerard when he lived in California in the 1960s and 1970s. After retirement she lived with her sister Úna in Massachusetts. She died on 11 May 2020 in Panama City Beach, Florida.

Tara Shears

Sources

Dublin Institute for Advanced Studies, annual report 1961–2 (1962), 18, https://dair.dias.ie/id/eprint/72/1/DIAS__Annual_Report__1961-1962.pdf; Gary Taubes, *Nobel dreams: power, deceit and the ultimate experiment* (1987), 213; 'Seventy-five reasons to become a scientist', *American Scientist*, vol. 76, no. 5 (Sept.–Oct. 1988), 459; Natalie Roe, 'How an early boost made a big difference', 19 May 2014, https://diversity.lbl.gov/2014/05/19/natalie-roe/; Francesco Lacava, 'The UA1 experiment', 3 Feb. 2017, https://www.roma1.infn.it/~lacava/UA1_Experiment.pdf; *Irish Times*, 30 May 2020; Marguerite Norris, 'A tribute to Anne Kernan from Dominican College', 22 June 2020, https://dominican-college.com/News/A-tribute-to-Anne-Kernan-from-Dominican-College/91600/Index.html; Darlene Mason, 'Anne Kernan: in memoriam', University of California, academic senate, https://senate.universityofcalifornia.edu/in-memoriam/files/anne-kernan.html; information from John Ellison, Darrell Smith (internet material accessed June 2024)

Index

A

abiogenesis 65
Accademia Patavina (Padua) 232
Actonian Prize 87, 107
Adare, Lord 33
agnosticism 63, 64
agricultural machinery xxiii, 143–6
Alexander, John 27
Alexandra Basin, Dublin 95
Alton, E.H. 199
American Academy of Arts and Sciences 175
American Geophysical Union 227–8, 232, 233
American Mathematical Society 172
American Physical Society (APS) 175, 256
American Scientist 253
American Society of Civil Engineers 233
American Society of Nutritional Science 240
Anderson, Alexander 156
Anderson, Alexander (Arthur Andrews) 156, 157
Anderson Centre for Translation Research and Practice 162
Anderson, Elsie 156
Anderson, Emily Gertrude (*née* Binns) 156
Anderson, Emily xiii, xxii, xxiii–xxiv, 156–62
  Goethe (Croce), translation of 158
  Hebel's Bible stories 161
  Letters of Beethoven 161
  Letters of Mozart and his family, The 158, 161

Anderson, Helen 156
Andromeda Galaxy 93
Ann Arbor University, Michigan 241
Annals of Science 6
Anne Kernan Endowment 256
Antonelli, Severo 214
Arago Medal 81
Armagh Observatory 28, 122
Armstrong, Sir W.G. 117
Art Industry Exhibition (1853) 40–1
Arthur Guinness, Son and Company Limited 52, 127–8, 129
artificial intelligence (AI) xii, 212
Arup Associates 178, 179
Arup, Ove 177, 178
Ashmolean Museum, Oxford 6
Astbury, W.T. 164, 165
  'Tabulated data for the examination of the 230 space-groups' 164
astronomers, obituaries of 107
Astronomical Society 108, 115
astronomy 27–8, 71, 85–8, 243
  see also Clerke, Agnes Mary; Everett, Alice; Parsons, William
Astronomy and Astro-Physics 86
Astrophysical Journal 107, 136
Astrophysical Observatory Potsdam 136
astrophysics 86, 105–8
Atomic Energy Agency 187
Atomic Energy Research Establishment 174
Atomic Scientists Association 167
aviation 142–3
Aylesbury Prison 167

B

Babbage, Charles xiv, 111, 112, 116
bacteriology xiii, 65, 66
Baird, Logie 137
Baird Television Company 137
Baker–Venkataraman transformation 208
Ball, R.R., *Mathematical recreations and essays* 133
'Balmer lines' 106
Bank of Ireland 123
barium titanate research 203–4
Barlee, John 140
Barlow, Revd William 33
Barrington, Croker 45
Barrow navigation 38
Barthololinus, Erasmus 28
Barton, James 93
Bastian, Henry Charlton 66
batteries 11, 12
Bauer, Alexander 150
Bauer, Emily (*née* Russell) 150
Bedell, William 6
Bedford College for Women, London 163
Beethoven, Ludwig van 158, 160–1
Belfast Technical College 142, 173
Bell, Annie (*née* Brownlee) 173
Bell, David 175
Bell, Elizabeth Gould 142
Bell, John 173
Bell, John Stewart xi, xiv, xx, xxii, 173–6
   'On the Einstein Podolsky Rosen paradox' 174–5
   Quantum [un]speakables from Bell to quantum information 176
   Speakable and unspeakable in quantum mechanics 175
   'Time reversal in field theory' 174
'Bell's inequality' ('Bell's theorem') 175
Bell, Joseph 142
Bell, Margaret 142
Bell, Mary (*née* Ross) 174
Berch, C.R. 6
Beresford Bridge, Dublin 95
Bernal, John Desmond xxvi, 165, 202–3, 204, 206
Biesbosch National Park 182
biochemistry xxiii, 235–6
Biographical memoirs of fellows of the Royal Society 168, 175
Biometrika 128, 129
Birch, Thomas 6
bird sanctuary 183
Birkbeck College, London 204, 217
Birmingham and Midland Institute 64
Birmingham University 174
Birr Castle, County Offaly 12, 48, 50, 93, 115
black holes 156, 192
Blériot, Louis 142
Bletchley Park 159
Blood, Bindon 93
Boland, Revd John 44
Boole, Alicia (*later* Stott) xvii–xviii, xix, xx, 20, 131–3
   Geometrical deduction of semi-regular from regular polytopes and space fillings 132
   New era of thought, A (Hinton), preface to 132
   On certain series of sections of the regular four-dimensional hypersolids 132
   On the sections of a block of eight cells by a space rotating about a plane 132
Boole, George xiii, xiv, xix, 14–23, 70, 131
   'Claims of science, The' (lecture) 16–17
   'Exposition of a general theory of linear transformations' 15
   Investigation of the laws of thought on which are founded the mathematical theories of logic

and probabilities, The 17, 18, 22
Mathematical analysis of logic, The 15–16, 22–3
'On a general method in analysis' 15
Studies in logic and probability 16, 17
'Symbolical logic, being an essay towards a calculus of deductive reasoning' 23
Treatise on the calculus of finite differences, A 20
Treatise on differential equations 19–20
unpublished papers 23
Boole, John 14
Boole Library, UCC 23
Boole, Lucy Everest 20, 133
Boole, Margaret (*later* Taylor) 21
Boole, Mary 70
Boole, Mary (*née* Everest) 20, 21, 23, 131
Boole, Mary (*née* Joyce) 14
Boole Papers 23
Boolean algebra 22–3
Born, Max 166, 224
Borstal 167
Bowen, Ira A. 107
Bowie Medal 232
Boyle, Alexander 44
Boyle, Catherine (*née* Fenton), Countess of Cork 1
Boyle, Richard, 1st Earl of Cork 1, 6
Boyle, Robert x, xiii, xx, xxiv, 1–8
 'Boyle lectures' 7–8
 Certain physiological essays 3
 Cold 4
 Colours 4
 'Essay on nitre' 3
 Excellency of theology, compared with natural philosophy 5
 Experiments, notes etc. about the mechanical origin of qualities 5
 Medicina hydrostatica 5

 New experiments physico-mechanical, touching the spring of the air and its effects 3, 4
 Occasional reflections 5
 'Of the study of the book of nature' 2
 Origin of forms and qualities 4
 Sceptical chymist, The 4
 Seraphic love 5
 Some considerations about the reconcileableness of reason and religion 5
 Usefulness of natural philosophy 3–4, 5
Boyne viaduct 39, 93–4
Boys, Sir Charles Vernon 111, 112
Boyton, Charles 27
Bradley, Daniel Joseph (Dan) xiv, xx, 216–22
 'High resolution interference spectroscope, A' 217
Bradley, John Columba 216
Bradley, Margaret (*née* Keating) 216
Bradley, William John 216
Bradley, Winifride (*née* O'Connor) 217
Bragg, Sir William H. 164, 165, 166, 202
Bragg, W.H. and Bragg, W.L., *X-rays and crystal structure* 202
Bray, County Wicklow 42, 44
Breslin, John J. 102
brewing 127–9
Brewster, Sir David 48
 Memoirs of the life, writings and discoveries of Sir Isaac Newton 48
Brinkley, John, Bishop of Cloyne 27, 28
Bristol College 74
British Admiralty 103
British Army, MI1(b) 157–8
British Association for the Advancement of Science 30, 71, 116, 124
 Lonsdale as first female president 166

Mallet's seismic experiments 53–4
'On the electrodynamic induction machine' (Callan) 11
'On the scientific use of imagination' (Tyndall) 63–4
Stokes and 75, 78, 81
British Astronomical Association 108, 136
British Crystallographic Association 168
British Museum 86
British Poultry Science 187
Bromhead, Sir Edward 14–15
Brookhaven National Laboratory 253
Brougham (Broom) Bridge x, 32–3
Brouwer, L.E.J. 32
Brown, David 145–6
Brown University, Rhode Island 191
Browne, Edward T. 138, 139, 141
Browne Scholarship 157
Bunsen, Robert Wilhelm 59, 78
Burma Railway Company 226
Burnell, Jocelyn Bell xvi
Burnet, Gilbert, Bishop of Salisbury 6
Burnett Lectures 80
Busk, George 61
Butt Bridge, Dublin 95
Byrne, Doreen (*née* Lawlor) 247
Byrne, John Gabriel xii, xx, 247–51
Byrne, Joseph 52
Byrne, Thomas Brendan 247
Byrne, Thomas Joseph 247

C

C.A. Parsons and Company 118
Callan, Denis 9
Callan, Margaret (*née* Smith) 9
Callan, Nicholas Joseph xiv, xx, 9–13
　'On the electrodynamic induction machine' 11
Cambridge Electricity Company 117
Cambridge Mathematical Journal 15
Campbell, John Frances 78
Campbell-Stokes recorder 78
canals 38, 39, 52
Carlisle Bridge, Dublin 95
Carnegie Institute of Technology 192
Carolan, Monica 161
Carré, Bernard 248
Casey, M.T., 'Nicholas Callan' 13
Catholic Sisters College (CSC) 170
Catholic University of America (CUA) 170, 171
Catterson Smith, Stephen 41
Cauchoix, R.A. 122
Cavalier, Jean 6
Cavendish Laboratory, Cambridge 196, 202, 204, 222
Cayley, Arthur 15, 16, 18, 19
Central Bank of Ireland 104
Centre Pompidou, Paris xxiii, 179, 180
Centre for Water Resources, UCD 232
CERN xi, xin1, xiv, 174, 254–5, 257
　Intersecting Storage Rings facility 254
　UA1 Experiment 255
C.H. Townes Medal 221–2
Chadwick, Dr 100
Chadwick, Sir James 198
Charles de Gaulle Airport 179
ChatGPT xii
Chemical Society 208
Chestnut Hill College, Philadelphia 211
Chien-Shiung Wu xvin5
Christian Brothers 101
Church of Ireland 34, 189
City and Guilds College 137
Clan na Gael 102, 210
Clarendon Laboratory, Oxford 203
Clausius, Rudolf 59, 90
Clerke, Agnes Mary xv, xx, 85–8, 106–7
　Dictionary of national biography 87–8

Familiar studies in Homer 88
Herschels and modern astronomy, The 88
Modern cosmogonies 87
Popular history of astronomy during the nineteenth century, A 86
Problems in astrophysics 87
scientific biographies 85–6, 87–8
System of the stars, The 87
Clerke, Aubrey 85
Clerke, Catherine Mary (*née* Deasy) 85
Clerke, Ellen Mary 88
Clerke, John William 85
climate change 229–30, 232
Clinch, Phyllis xvii, 224
Cockcroft, John xxii, 196–7, 199, 200
Codner, Maurice 119
Coghlan, Brian et al. 113
Cold Chon 207
Coleridge, Samuel Taylor 31, 34
Colleges (Ireland) Bill (1845) 16
Collier, John 100
Combined Bureau Middle East, Cairo 159
comets 62, 106, 136
computers/computer science xiv, 23, 111–13, 248–50
 see also Byrne, John Gabriel; ENIAC; Ludgate, Percy Edwin; McNulty, Kathleen Rita (Kay)
Connaught Women's Franchise League 156
Consultative Council on Mental Handicap 209
Contemporary Review 64
Conway, A.W. 191
Conway, Edward xxvi
Conwill, John 57
Cooper, Edward Joshua 122
Cornell University, Ithaca 179
Corporation for the Propagation of the Gospel in New England 5
Cosgrave, Liam 227, 228–9

Courant Institute, New York 190
Cox, R.C., *Robert Mallet FRS 1810–1881* 56
Coxeter, H.S.M. 132–3
CPT theorem of quantum field theory 174
Craigmore viaduct 39
Crick, Francis xvin5, 154
Crimean War 53
Croke Park, Hogan stand 247
cryptanalysis (code breaking) 157–8, 159–60
crystallography xv–xvi, xvin5, 165, 202–6
Cubitt, William 42
Cullen, Paul, Cardinal 44, 68
Cumann na nInnealtoirí 228
Curie, Pierre and Marie 107

D

Dale, Sir Henry 165
Dargan, Elizabeth 37
Dargan, James 37
Dargan, Jane (*née* Arkinstall) 38, 44–5
Dargan, Patrick 37
Dargan, Selina 37, 44
Dargan, William xx, xxii, 37–46
Darwin, Charles xx, 61, 68, 245
 On the origin of species 60
Dashkova, Princess Ekaterina Romanovna xvii
De Beer wildlife sanctuary 182
de Brún, Pádraig 152, 153
de Buitléar, Éamon 184
de la Rue, Warren 107
De Menil Museum, Houston, Texas 180
De Morgan, Augustus 15, 16, 23, 35
de Valera, Éamon 152, 200
de Vere, Aubrey 33
de Vere, Ellen 33
Deansgrange Cemetery 201, 233
Deasy, Rickard 85

Dedekind, Richard 18
DeepSeek xii
Défense Arch, Paris 180
Delamater Iron Works, New York 102
Delap, Revd Alexander 138, 139
Delap, Anna Jane (*née* Goslett) 138
Delap, Constance 138, 140
Delap, Maude Jane xix, xx, 138–41
Denvir, Cornelius 9
Department of Science and Arts xxi, 64
Departmentof Agriculture for
    Northern Ireland (DANI) 186
Derby Crown Glass Company 118
Descartes, René 2
Devoy, John 102
Dewar, Sir James 87
diamagnetism 59–60
Dictionary of Irish Biography (*DIB*)
    xxiv, xxivn16, xxvi
Dictionary of national biography (*DNB*)
    69, 87
Dictionary of scientific biography 150
Dillon, Thomas Patrick 207
Dirac Medal 175
Dirac, Paul 151, 175, 224
Disney, Catherine 33
Ditchburn, Robert 198, 199
DNA, structure of xvin5, 154
Doe Cooperative Society 210
Dolan, Brian 245
Donkin, William 18
Dooge, Denis 226
Dooge, James Clement Ignatius (Jim)
    xx, 226–33
  'General theory of the unit
      hydrograph, A' 227–8
  Linear theory of hydrologic systems
    229
Dooge, John Publins 226
Dooge, Marie Veronica (Roni) (*née*
    O'Doherty) 226
Dove, Heinrich 59
Dowden, Edward 21
Dowden, John 21

Draper, John William 62
du Bois-Reymond, Emil 59, 63
Dublin City University (DCU) 200
  Alumni Award, Mulvihill and 246
  McNulty Computing Building 215
Dublin County Council 226, 227, 247
Dublin Industrial Exhibition 122
Dublin Institute for Advanced Studies
    (DIAS) xiv, 152, 153, 154, 155
  School of Cosmic Physics 245
  School of Theoretical Physics 192
  seminar by Anne Kernan 253–4
  Summer School 166
  Tinney, Sheila and 224, 225
Dublin Photographic Society 123
Dublin Port Authority (Ballast Board)
    94
Dublin Port and Docks Board 94–5,
    245
Dublin Principles 232
Dublin University 21, 22, 51–2, 53,
    55, 95, 154
  see also Trinity College Dublin
    (TCD); University of
    Dublin
Dublin University Experimental
    Science Association 72
Dunsink Observatory x, 28, 32, 33,
    34, 35, 122
Dunstan, Sir W.R. 133
Dutton, Hugh and Rice, Peter, *Verre
    structurel, La* (*Structural Glass*)
    179
dynamics 30–1, 36
dynamo, self-exciting 12
Dyson, Freeman 224
DZero Experiment 255–6

E

earthquakes 53–4
East China Technical University of
    Water Resources 232

Eckart-Mauchly Computer Corporation 213
Edgeworth, Maria 33–4
Edinburgh Review 85
Edmondson, George 58
Edwardsia delapiae (sea anemone) 140
Eidgenössische Technische Hochschule 208
Einstein, Albert 151, 152, 153, 163, 224
   mass/energy relationship $E=mc^2$ 197
   theory of relativity xiv, 174, 191, 192, 193
Electric Boat Company 103
electricity 9–11, 65
Electricity Supply Board (ESB) 224, 227
Electro Photonics Limited 219
electromagnetic induction 10, 12
electromagnetic theory of light 71, 82, 91
Elswick Engine and Ordnance Works 117
Emelaus, Karl 173
emigrants/emigration xxi, xxv, 169, 171, 210–11
Emily Anderson Concert Hall 162
Emily Anderson Prize 161–2
Encyclopaedia Britannica 11, 85–6, 88, 107
Engineer 54
engineering 97–100
ENIAC (Electronic Numerical Integrator and Computer) xviii, 211–13, 214
Enterprise Ireland 250
entropy, concept of 90
Essex Bridge, Dublin 94, 95
European Economic Community (EEC) 231, 232
European Organization for Nuclear Research *see* CERN
European Strategic Programme on Research in Information Technology (ESPRIT) 249

Evans, William 39
Everest, Sir George 20, 131
Everest, Revd Thomas 20
Everett, Alice xvii, xxv–xxvi, 135–7
Everett, Jessie (*née* Fraser) 135
Everett, Joseph David 135, 136
evolution/evolutionists 60–1, 63, 66
Ewald, Peter Paul 166, 173
Expo 92 Seville 180

F

Fabry-Pérot interferometer 217, 218
Faithorne, William 6
Falk, H.J. 132
Faraday, Michael 10, 59, 60
Farrell, Thomas 41
Fastnet lighthouse 52
Fenian Brotherhood 101
Ferguson, Henry George (Harry) xiv, xx, xxiii, 142–9
Ferguson, James 142
Ferguson, Joseph Bell (Joe) 142, 143, 148
Ferguson, Mary Adelaide (Maureen) (*née* Watson) 148
Ferguson, Mary (*née* Bell) 142
Ferguson–Brown Company 145
Fermilab, Illinois 255–6
Festival of Britain 204, 206
Feuerbach, Ludwig 64
fibre optics 65
Fine Gael 226, 227, 228–9, 230–1
First World War 157
Fisher, R.A. 129, 130
Fitzgerald, Anne Frances (*née* Stoney) 70, 93
FitzGerald, Garret 230–1
Fitzgerald, George Francis xiv, xx, 70–3, 91
   Scientific writings 71, 72
Fitzgerald, Harriette May (*née* Jellett) 70

FitzGerald, Joan 230
Fitzgerald, William, Bishop of Cork (later Killaloe) 70, 93
flavonoids 208, 209
Fleming, Alexander 66
Flight 142
fluorescence 77–8, 82
fog signals 65
folates and folic acid 236–9
Foley, J.H. 36
Food and Agriculture Organisation of the United Nations 187
Food Safety Authority of Ireland 238
food science xxiii, 186–7
Foras Talúntais, An 241, 245
Forbes, James D. 60
Ford Company 147
Ford Ferguson tractors 146
Ford, Henry 144, 146, 147
Ford, Henry II 147
Ford Model T cars 144
Fordham University, New York 102
Fordson tractors 144, 145, 146
Fortnightly Review 64
Forum Club, Grosvenor Place 158
Foster, Norman 179
Fourier, Jean-Baptiste Joseph 18, 34
Fournier D'Albe, E.E. 72
Francis, Martin 179
Francis, William 60
Frankland, Edward 58, 59, 60–1
Franklin, Rosalind xvi, xvin5, 203
Fraser, Revd Alexander 135
Fraunhofer lines 78
French Academy of Architecture 180
French Society for the Encouragement of National Industry 180
Fresnel, Augustin Jean 28, 29, 30
Froebel kindergarten pedagogy xvi, 198
Frost, E.B. 103
Fuchs, Klaus 174

G

Galapagos Islands 245
Galvani, Luigi 9
galvanisation 12
Gamow, George 196
Gandon, James 95
geodesy 76
Geological Society of Dublin 55
Geological Society of India 56
Geological Society of Ireland 54
Geological Society of London 54, 55
geology 52, 53, 55
germ theory 65–6
'Gibbs–Wilbraham phenomenon' 18
Gifford Lectures 80
Gill, David 86
glacial flow 52
Glasnevin Cemetery 44, 185
Glass, I.S., *Victorian telescope makers* 123
Glazer, Mike 205
Glenstal Castle, County Limerick 42
Golders Green 108, 161
Gordon, Lewis 98
Gosset, Agnes Sealy (*née* Vidal) 127
Gosset, Colonel Frederic 127
Gosset, Thorold 133
Gosset, William Sealy (Student) xx, xxii, 127–30
  'Application of the law of error to the work of the brewery, The' 127
  'On the error of counting with a haemacytometer' 128
  'On the probable error of a mean' 128–9
  'Probable error of a correlation coefficient, The' 129
Gough, Ellen (*née* Dunne) 169
Gough, Lizzie 169
Gough, Mary (St Mary de Lellis; Maggie) xx, xxi, xxii, xxivn16, 169–72, 224

'On the condition for the existence of triangles in-and-circumscribed to certain types of rational quartic curve and having a common side' 171, 224
'Representability of a number by an indefinite binary quadratic form, The' 170
Gough, Walter 169
Government Code and Cypher School (GC&CS) 158
Government Communications Bureau 159
Government School of Mines, London 75
Graham, Victor 247
Grassmann, Hermann 22
Grattan Bridge, Dublin 94, 95, 96
Graves, Charles 16
Graves, Robert Percival 26, 33, 34, 35
gravity 71, 76
Great Saltee Island 183
'greenhouse effect' 62
Gregory, Duncan 15
  Examples of the process of the differential and integral calculus 15
Gregory, Sir R.A. and Hadley, H.E., *Class book of physics, A* 13
Griffith, John Purser 95
Groningen University, Netherlands 132
Grubb, Eleanor (*née* Fayle) 121
Grubb, Henry Thomas 124
Grubb, Howard xix, xx, 75, 106, 118, 122, 124, 125–6
Grubb, Mary Hester (*née* Walker) 125–6
Grubb, Sarah (*née* Palmer) 124
Grubb, Thomas 121–4
  Great Melbourne telescope, The 123
Grubb, William 121
Gustavus Adolphus College, Minnesota 200

H

Haddon, A.C. 138
haemoglobin 79
Hahn, Otto xvin5
Hahnemann, Samuel 20
Halpin, George, Jnr 94
Hamilton, Archibald (d.1819) 24–5
Hamilton, Archibald 36
Hamilton, Arthur 26
Hamilton, Lord Claud 68
Hamilton, Francis 24
Hamilton, Helen (*later* O'Regan) 36
Hamilton, Helen Maria (*née* Bayly) 33, 36
Hamilton, Hugh, Bishop 189–90
Hamilton, Isabella 189, 190
Hamilton, James, 1st Duke of Abercorn 68
Hamilton, Revd James 25–6, 35
Hamilton, Sarah 24
Hamilton, Sarah (*née* Hutton) 24
Hamilton, William 24
Hamilton, William Edwin 36
Hamilton, Sir William Rowan xx, 22, 24–36, 49
  Essays on a general method in dynamics 30–1
  Lectures on quaternions 33
  mathematical papers 191
  'Theory of systems of rays' 27
Hamilton, Sir William 191
Handbook of the Napier tercentenary celebration 112
Harmony Hall, Hampshire 58
Harrington, T.C. 110
Harry Ferguson Limited 143
Hartlib, Samuel 2
Harwood, John T., *Early essays and ethics of Robert Boyle, The* 7
Hasenöhrl, Friedrich 31
Haslam, Louisa 44
Haughton, Revd John 74
Hayes, Edward 97

Haynes, Euphemia 171
Health Research Board 236
Heaviside, Oliver 71, 73
Heineman Prize 175
Helmholtz Medal 81
Henry, Françoise xvii, 224
Henry VIII, King 189, 190
Herschel, Caroline 88
Herschel, John 88, 105
Herschel, Sir William 77, 88, 115
Hertz, Heinrich 71
Hewish, Antony xvi
Hinton, Charles Howard 131
   New era of thought, A 132
Hirst, T.A. 61
Hitler, Adolf 151
Hodgkin, Dorothy 203
   'Kathleen Lonsdale' 168
Hodgkins Trust 87
Holden, Edward 86
Holland, John 101
Holland, John Philip xiv, xx, xxii, 101–4
Holland, Julia 104
Holland, Margaret (*née* Foley) 103–4
Holland, Mary (*née* Scanlon) 101
Holland, Michael 101, 102
Holland I (submarine) 102
Holland VI (submarine) 103
Holloway Prison 166–7
homeopathy 20
Homer 88
Hooke, Robert 3
Hooker, J.D. 61
Hopkins, Michael 180
Hoppe-Seyler, Ernst 79
Horton Award 227–8
Hosking, William 98
Hovestadt, Heinrich, *Jena glass and its scientific and industrial applications* 136
Huggins, Margaret Lindsay (*née* Murray) xv, xvii, xx, 86, 105–8
   articles in *Encyclopaedia Britannica* 107
   biography of Sir William 108
   monograph on Maggini 107
   On the spectrum, visible and photographed, of the great nebula in Orion 106
   Photographic atlas of representative stellar spectra 107
   Proceedings of the Royal Society, research papers in 107
Huggins, Sir William 86, 105–6, 108
   Collected scientific papers of Sir William Huggins 107
   On the spectrum, visible and photographed, of the great nebula in Orion 106
   Photographic atlas of representative stellar spectra 107
   Proceedings of the Royal Society, papers in 107
   Sketch of the life of Sir William Huggins, A 108
humanism 63
Humphreys, Joe 155
Hunter, Michael, *Robert Boyle by himself and his friends* 7
Hunter, Michael and Davis, Edward B., *Works of Robert Boyle, The* 6
Hunter, Michael et al.
   Boyle papers, The: understanding the manuscripts of Robert Boyle 6
   Correspondence of Robert Boyle, The 6
   'Work-diaries of Robert Boyle, The' 6
Huxley, T.H. 61, 63, 66
Huygens, Christiaan 29
hydrodynamics 75–6
hydrology xxvi, 226–8, 229
Hygeia 207
'Hypercircle', method of 192

I

'Iceland spar' 29
Imperial College, London 177, 247–8
  Department of Physics 218, 219–20
Incarnate Word College, San Antonio 170, 171
induction coil 10–11, 12–13
Industrial Development Authority (IDA) 250
information and communications technology (ICT) 249, 250, 251
infrared analysis 62
Institute for Advanced Study, Princeton 224
Institute of Chemistry 133
Institute of Chemistry of Ireland 208, 209
Institute of Civil Engineers of Ireland (ICEI) 227, 228
Institute of Electronic and Electrical Engineers 222
Institute of Food Science and Technology 187
Institute of France 81
Institute of Physics 175, 176, 221, 222
Institution of Civil Engineers (ICE) 52–3, 54, 55, 56, 94, 95, 233
Institution of Civil Engineers of Ireland (ICEI) 55, 94, 96
Institution of Mechanical Engineers 55, 119
Institution of Naval Architects 95
International Association of Hydrological Sciences 229, 230
International Business Machines (IBM) 113, 248
International Commission on Water Resources Systems 230
International Conference on Water and the Environment (ICWE) 232
International Council for Science 230
International Federation for Information Processing 251
International Journal of Food Science and Technology 187
International Meteorological Organisation 232
Irish Builder 96
Irish Council for Bioethics 245
Irish Farmers' Journal 183
Irish Film Society 226
Irish language 68, 211, 226
'Irish logarithms' 112
Irish Mathematics Teachers' Association 172
Irish Naturalist 139
Irish Republican Army (IRA) 210
Irish Science Journalists' Association 243
Irish Society of Civil Engineers 54
Irish Times 155, 242, 243, 251
Irish Volunteers 210
irradiation of food 187
Iveagh, Lord 72

J

Jacobs Award 184
Janus Advertising 183
Japan, Emperor of 103
Japanese Navy 103
Jellett, John Hewitt 70
jellyfish 139, 140
Jerrard, Joseph Henry 74
Jevons, W. Stanley, *Principles of science* 17–18
John Gabriel Byrne Computer Science Collection 113, 250
John P. Holland Torpedo Boat Company 103
Joly, John 72
Journal of the American Medical Association 237

Journal of General Relativity and Gravitation 192
Journal of the Science of Food and Agriculture 187

K

Kant, Immanuel 31–2, 34, 63
   Critique of pure reason 32
Keating, Justin 184
Keating, Seán, RHA 155
Kelly, John B. 211
Kelvin of Largs, William Thomson, 1st Baron *see* Thomson, William (Lord Kelvin)
Kelvin unit of temperature 90
Kernan, Anne xi, xx, xxii, xxiv, 253–7
Kernan, Annie (*née* O'Connor) 253
Kernan, Frederick 253
Kerry Archaeological Magazine 140
Kerseboom, Johann 6
Kevans and Son 111
Keynes, John Maynard, *Treatise on probability theory* 19
King, Alexander Hyatt 161
King, Harriette (*née* Lloyd) 47
King, Revd Henry 47
King, Mary *see* Ward, Mary (*née* King)
King's College, London 98
Kirchhoff, Gustav Robert 78
Knoblauch, Heinrich 59
Knott, Eleanor xvii, 224
Knowledge 8
Knox, Dilly 159–60

L

Laing Art Gallery 119
Lalla Rookh (yacht) 92
Lambert, Johann Heinrich 17
Lambton College, Canada 175
Lancet 237
Landy, Aubrey Edward 170–1
Lardner, Dionysius 105
Larmor, Sir Joseph 71, 83, 91, 135, 157
laser research xiv, 218–21
Lassell, William 107
Lawrence Berkeley National Laboratory 175, 254, 256
Lawrence Radiation Laboratory 254
Lawson and Mansergh 97
Le Fanu, William 45
Lederle Award 240
Leeds University 164
Leibniz, Gottfried Wilhelm 17
Lemass, Seán 200
Letterkenny Institute of Technology 214
Lick Observatory, California 86
light
   conical refraction 29, 30, 35
   double refraction 28–9, 78
   electromagnetic theory of 71, 82, 91
   wave theory of 29–30, 77
   wavelength of fluorescent light 82
'light-pipe' 65
lighthouses 68, 75, 94, 95
Lilienthal glider 72
Lille TGV Station 179
Linnean Society 140
Lister, Joseph Jackson 66
Liverpool Mercury 57
Lloyd, Bartholomew 26, 29
   Analytical geometry 26
Lloyd, Humphrey 29–30, 123
Lloyds Building, London 180
Lockyer, Joseph Norman 86
Lodge, Oliver 71, 72
logic 15–16, 17–18, 22
London College of Music 159
London Gazette 160
London School of Medicine for Women 20, 133
Lonsdale Club, Hampstead 158

Lonsdale, Jessie (*née* Cameron) 163
Lonsdale, Kathleen (*née* Yardley) xv, xvi, xvii, xx, 163–8
　International tables for X-ray crystallography 165
　Is peace possible? 167
　Simplified structure factor and electron density formulae for the 230 space groups of mathematical crystallography 165
　'Tabulated data for the examination of the 230 space-groups' 164
Lonsdale Student Prize 168
Lonsdale, Thomas Jackson 164
'lonsdaleite' 166
Lord's Cricket Ground, Mound Stand 180
Lorentz, Hendrik 71
Lorentz–Fitzgerald contraction 70–1
Loughry College of Agriculture and Food Technology 186
Lubbock, John 61
Ludgate, Alfred 110
Ludgate, Alice 112
Ludgate, Frederick 112
Ludgate, Mary (*née* McMahon) 110
Ludgate, Michael 110
Ludgate, Percy Edwin xii, xiv, xxiii–xxiv, 110–13
　'Automatic calculating machines' 112
　'On a proposed analytical machine' 111, 113
Lyle, T.R. 72
Lynden-Bell, Ruth 205
Lyric FM 242

M

McColl, Hugh, 'Calculus of equivalent statements, The' 19
McCormick, William 40
MacEntee, Margaret 152–3
MacEntee, Seán 152–3
McHale, Desmond 133
McIntosh, J.J., *Boyle on atheism* 7
Macneill, Sir John 93
McNulty, Anne (*née* Nelis) 210
McNulty, James 210–11
McNulty, Kathleen Rita (Kay) xii, xiv, xviii, xx, xxii, 210–15
Maddison, R.E.W., 'Portraiture of the Honourable Robert Boyle, The' 6
Maggie Gough Competition 172
Maggini, Gio Paulo 107
Magnetic Observatory, TCD 123
magnetism xiii, 9, 53, 60, 90
Magnus, Gustav 59
Mahon, Lady Jane (*née* King) 49
Mallet, Anne (*née* Pike) 51
Mallet, Cordelia (*née* Watson) 55
Mallet, Frederick Richard 56
Mallet, John 51
Mallet, John William 54, 56
Mallet, Mary (*née* Daniel) 56
Mallet, Richard 51
Mallet, Robert, Snr 51
Mallet, Robert Trefusis 56
Mallet, Robert xiii, xix, xx, 51–6
　Great Neapolitan earthquake of 1857, The: the first principles of observational seismology 54
　'On the dynamics of earthquakes' 53
　Robert Mallet FRS 1810–1881 (Cox) 56
　'Volcanic energy' 54
Mallet, Thomasina 51
Mallet, William 51
Mallet–Milne lectures 56
Manhattan Project 198
Marburg University 59, 157
March, Arthur 151
March, Hilde 151, 152
Marcombes, Isaac 1
Marconi, Guglielmo 71
marine biology 138–41

Marine Station, Plymouth 139
Maritime Institute of Ireland 104
Mark, Herman 203
Mars, Stokes Crater 82
Marseille Provence Airport 179
Martin, Richard 43
Mary Mulvihill Association 246
Mary Ward Centre, Ferbane 50
Massey-Ferguson Company 147–8
Massey-Harris 147
mathematics xiv, 14–20, 26–7
   algebra 15, 16, 22–3, 31–2, 36
   differential equations 19–20
   French mathematicians 14, 15, 34, 89
   quaternions xii, 22, 31–3, 36
   see also Boole, George; Gough, Mary; Hamilton, Sir William Rowan
Mauchly, John 213–14
Maunder, Annie (*née* Russell) 135, 243
Maunder, Edward Walter 243
Mauretania, RMS 118
Max Planck Medal 154
Maxwell, James Clerk 71, 91
May Street Motors, Belfast 143
'Maynooth' battery 11
Maynooth College *see* St Patrick's College
Maynooth University 12, 168
Medaglia Matteucci 154
Megaw, Annie (*née* McElderry) 202
Megaw, Helen Dick xv, xvi, xx, 202–6
   Crystal structures: a working approach 205
   Ferroelectricity in crystals 205
Megaw Island, Antarctica 205
Megaw, Robert, KC 202
Megawite 205
Meitner, Lise xvi, xvin5
Meitnerium xvin5
Melbourne Observatory, Australia 122, 123, 124
Melloni, Macedonio 61–2

Mer de Glace, Chamonix 52
Met Éireann 245
meteorology 61–2, 76
Methodist College, Belfast 135, 195, 200, 202
Michelson–Morley experiment 71
microbiology xiii, 66, 186
microscopes 47, 49, 123
Mineralogical Society of America 205
Minkowski, Hermann 191
Monck, W.H.S. 71
Monge, Gaspard 27
moon 82, 88
Moore School of Electrical Engineering 211
Moran, P.F. 68
Morawetz, Cathleen Synge 190
Morrison, Elizabeth (*née* Martin) 186
Morrison, James Stewart 186
Moss, Stirling 148
motorcars 142, 143, 144, 148
Mount Jerome Cemetery 35, 95, 113, 124
mountaineering 66–7
Mozart, Wolfgang Amadeus 158, 161
Mulvany, George 41
Mulvany, John Skipton 44
Mulvihill, Joe 241
Mulvihill, Mary Rita xviii–xix, xx, 241–6
   Chopped, pickled and stuffed 242
   Drive like a woman, shop like a man: greener is cheaper 245
   Ingenious Dublin 244
   Ingenious Ireland: a county-by-county exploration of Ireland's marvels and mysteries 244, 246
   Lab coats and lace: the lives and legacies of inspiring Irish women scientists and pioneers xviii, 243
   Maunder, Annie (*née* Russell), article on 243

Pedals and pebbles 242
Perfect pint, The 242
School of Cosmic Physics, history of 245
Science@Culture newsletter 243–4
Stars, shells and bluebells: women scientists and pioneers xviii, 139, 243
Time, please 242
Up'n'atom 242
Washed, peeled and dried 242
Mulvihill, Maureen (*née* McGrath) 241
Murray, Helen (*née* Lindsay) 105
Murray, John Marjoribanks 105
Murray, Robert 105
Murray, Robert (d.1934) 105
Museum of the History of Science, Oxford 123
Museum of Irish Industry xxi
Musicians Benevolent Fund 161
musicological research 158, 160–1

N

National Academy of Sciences 35
National Association for the Mentally Handicapped of Ireland 209
National Botanic Gardens, Dublin 242, 244
National Committee for Commemorative Plaques in Science and Technology 246
National Education Office 110
National Froebel Union 198
National Gallery of Ireland 40, 41
National Institute of Higher Education 242
    see also Dublin City University (DCU)
National Institutes of Health (NIH) 235, 238, 239
National Inventors Hall of Fame 214

National Museum of Science, Technology and Industry, Paris 179
National Physical Laboratory 137
National Portrait Gallery, London 68, 119
National Science Council 209
National University of Ireland 154, 193
    Seanad Éireann panel 231
    travelling studentship 223
natural habitats in Ireland 183, 185, 244
Natural History Museum, Dublin 141, 242
Natural History Museum, London 138
natural philosophy 2–5
Nature 63, 86, 111, 112
Nature Genetics 239
Navier, Claude-Louis 76
Navier–Stokes equations 76
navigation system 133
nebulae 93, 106, 116
'nebulium' 107
neural tube defects (NTDs) 236–9
New England Company 5
New York Harbour Board 102
New York Sun 102
Newman, Francis 74
Newton, Sir Isaac 28, 77, 80, 90
Nineteenth Century 64
Nobel Prize
    chemistry (1944) xvin5
    chemistry (1964) 203
    physics (1933) 151, 224
    physics (1951) xxii, 200
    physics (1974) xvi
    physics (1984) 255
    physiology (1962) xvin5
'non-locality theory' 174–5
Nore viaduct 52
North Bull Lighthouse 94, 95
North Wall, Dublin 94–5

Nova Aurigae (T Aurigae) 107, 136
Nuclear Energy Board 209
nuclear physics 153, 196–7, 199–200, 224
nuclear weapons 199
Nuova Cimento 175
nutrition, biochemistry and xxiii, 235–6
Nutrition Society 187

O

Observatory Lane factory 125, 126
Observatory, The 86, 107
O'Connell Bridge, Dublin 95, 96
O'Connor, Valentine O'Brien 43
O'Donovan Rossa, Jeremiah 102
Office of Public Works (OPW) 227
O'Gorman, Fergus, *Irish wildlife book, The* 185
Oh Kay computer (documentary) 214
Ohio State University 192
Oldenburg, Henry 4
optical instruments 118, 121, 137
Optical Society of America 221–2
optics 27, 28–30, 36, 136, 137
optoelectronics 62
Ó Raifeartaigh, L., *General relativity* 193
Order of the British Empire 160, 166
Order of Merit (British) 90, 119
Order of Merit (German) 161
Ordnance Survey 57–8
O'Regan, John 36
O'Regan, John, Archdeacon 36
orofacial clefts, biobank of DNA 239
Orpen, Sir William 119
Osaka Airport 180
Oulton Park Gold Cup 148
Our Boys 185
Overend Gurney (bankers) 43
Owen, Robert 58
Owens College, Manchester 98

P

pantographic machine 123
Parnell, Sir Henry 37, 38
Parsons, Sir Charles Algernon xiii, xix, xx, xxii, 116–19
Parsons, Clere 116
Parsons Foreign Patents Company 118
Parsons, Katharine (*née* Bethell) 119
Parsons, Laurence, 4th Earl of Rosse 116
Parsons Marine Steam Turbine Company 118
Parsons, Mary (*née* Field), Countess of Rosse 48, 50, 116
Parsons, William, 3rd Earl of Rosse xix, xx, xxiii, 12, 47, 48, 50, 93, 115–16, 122
particle physics 253–6
Pasteur, Louis 65–6
pasteurisation 66
patents 117, 118, 145–6, 213
Paterson Museum, New Jersey 102
Pauli, Lüders and Wolfgang 174
Pearson, Karl 128
Peel, Robert 58
Peierls, Rudolf 174
Penicillium 66
Penrose, Sir Roger 193
Perry, John 135
Philbin, Eva Maria (*née* Ryder) xv, 207–9
Philbin, John (Jack) Madden 207, 209
Philbin, Revd William Joseph 207
Philips Lamps Ltd 203
Phillpotts, Marjory Surtees (*née* Gosset) 129
Philosophical Magazine 10, 60, 70, 90, 156
Philosophical Transactions of the Royal Society 4, 78, 79–80, 164
photochemistry 62
Photographic Society of Ireland 123
photographic spectroscopy 106

photography 105, 106, 116, 123, 124, 136, 183, 205, 214, 243
Physical Review 72
Physical Society of London 70, 136
Physics 174
Piano, Renzo 179, 180
Pickering, E.C. 86
Pierce Malone Scholarship 226
Pike, William 51
Planck, Max 151, 154
Plücker, Julius 59
Plunger (submarine) 103
pneumothorax apparatus 133
Poggendorff, Johann Christian 59
Polytechnic Institution, Regent Street 137
polytopes xvii–xviii, 20, 132–3
Poolbeg Lighthouse 94, 95
Pour le Mérite 81
Power, Christina (*née* Cunniffe) 223
Power, Michael 223
Power, Sheila (*later* Tinney) xvii
Practical Mechanic's Journal 54
Praeger, Robert Lloyd xxvi
Prager, William 192
Preston, Thomas 72
Price, James 189
Prince Philip Medal 232
Princeton University 151, 152, 191
prison reform 167
probability theory 18–19, 127–8
Proceedings of the Royal Irish Academy 95, 123, 138, 154
Proceedings of the Royal Society 107, 174
Prussian Academy of Science 81
Pugwash movement 167, 199
pulsars xvi
Purser, Sarah 36

Q

quakers 58, 121, 124, 166, 167
quantum electrodynamics 224
quantum field theory 174
quantum mechanics 31, 151, 153, 173–4, 175
quantum physics xxvi, 174, 175
quantum theory 36, 107, 150, 153, 174–5
quantum-wave mechanics 151
Queen's College, Barbados 157
Queen's College, Belfast 98, 135, 205
Queen's College, Cork (QCC) 16, 20, 21, 98, 131
  see also University College Cork (UCC)
Queen's College, Galway 98, 156, 157
  see also University College Galway (UCG); University of Galway
Queen's College, London 131, 133
Queen's Colleges xxi–xxii, 98
Queen's University Belfast (QUB) 135, 175, 177, 193, 200, 202, 222
  Bell, John Stewart and 173–4, 176
Queenwood College, Hampshire 58, 59–60

R

racing cars 148
radiation 61–2
radio transmission 71
radioactivity 107
railways 39–40, 41–2, 43, 52, 58
  viaducts 39, 52, 93–4
Rambaut, Arthur A. 82
Ranelagh, Katherine Jones (*née* Boyle), Viscountess 4, 6
Reader 64
Reality Foundation Prize 175
Regent Street Polytechnic 137
relativity, theory of 70–1, 151, 174, 193
  Synge's investigation of xiv, 191, 192

religion xxii, 1, 7, 80
  science and 5, 8, 63–4, 199
Renner, Karl 154
Reynolds, Annie Charlotte (*née* Wilkinson) 100
Reynolds, Charlotte (*née* Chadwick) 100
Reynolds, Jane (*née* Hickman) 97
Reynolds, Revd Osborne 97
Reynolds, Osborne xiv, xix, xx, 97–100
'Reynolds equation' 100
'Reynolds number, the' 99
Rice Francis Ritchie (RFR) Design Engineering 179
Rice, James Patrick 177
Rice, Maureen (*née* Quinn) 177
Rice, Peter Ronan xx, 177–80
  Verre structurel, La (*Structural glass*) 179
Rice, Sylvia (*née* Watson) 178
Riley, John 6
Ritchie, Ian 179
roadbuilding 38–9
Robinson, Thomas Romney 28, 53, 82, 121–2
Roebling Medal 205
Rogers, Richard 179, 180
Roman Catholic hierarchy xxii, 44, 68
Romantic Movement 34
Ross, Andrew 47
Ross Limited 118
Rowan, Archibald Hamilton 24–5, 35
Royal Academy of Engineering 232, 233
Royal Artillery 59
Royal Astronomical Society 49–50, 87, 108, 124, 125
Royal Belfast Academical Institution (RBAI) 89
Royal Dublin Society (RDS) xxi, 40, 45, 73, 95, 111, 123, 125, 225
Royal Engineers 59, 127
Royal Geographical Society 163
Royal Holloway College 217, 218

Royal Institute of British Architects (RIBA) 180
Royal Institute of Chemistry 208
Royal Institution (RI) 60, 64, 68, 87, 107, 164, 165
  Low temperature research at the Royal Institution 1893–1900 87
Royal Irish Academy (RIA) x, 27, 54, 68
  bicenentary history 208
  Cunningham Medal 35, 55, 125, 222
  Dooge, James (Jim) and 230, 232
  Gold Medal 232
  Grubb, Howard and 125
  Grubb, Thomas and 124
  Hamilton, William Rowan and 27, 35, 191
  Mallet, Robert and 53, 54
  Philbin, Eva Maria and 208
  Schrödinger and 154
  Scott, John Martin and 239
  Stoney, Bindon Blood and 95
  Synge, John Lighton and 193
  Tinney, Sheila (*née* Power) and 224
  Walton, Ernest and 200
  women admitted to xvii, 224
  see also Dictionary of Irish Biography (*DIB*); *Proceedings of the Royal Irish Academy*
Royal Navy 118, 125
Royal Observatory, Cape of Good Hope 86
Royal Observatory, Greenwich 50, 86, 122, 136
Royal Philharmonic Association 161–2
Royal St George Yacht Club 45
Royal School of Mines 64
Royal Society of Arts 148
Royal Society of Canada 193
Royal Society of London
  Baconian lectures 62
  Boole, George and 21–2, 23

Boyle, Robert and 4, 6
Boys, Sir Charles Vernon and 111
Bradley, Daniel Joseph and 221
Copley Medal 80, 90
Davy Medal 166
Davy Prize 107
Everett, Joseph David and 135
first female fellows 166
grants from 60
Grubb, telescopes supplied by 124
Grubb, Thomas and 124
Huggins, Margaret, pension awarded to 108
Huggins, William and 106, 107
Hughes Medal 175, 200
Lloyd, Humphrey and 30
Lonsdale, Kathleen and 166
Mallet, Robert and 53–4
Parsons, Charles and 116, 119
Parsons, William and xiii, 47, 116
Royal Medal 15, 35, 70, 221
Rumford Medal 78
Schrödinger, Erwin and 154
Stokes, George Gabriel and 79–80
Stoney, Bindon Blood and 95
Synge, John Lighton and 193
Walton, Ernest and 200
women and xvii
see also Biographical memoirs of fellows of the Royal Society; Philosophical Transactions of the Royal Society; Proceedings of the Royal Society
Royal United Kingdom Beneficent Association 161
Royal University of Ireland (RUI) 135
RTÉ 184, 225
RTÉ Radio 1 242
Rubbia, Carlo 255
Ruhmkorff, Heinrich 12
Rutherford, Ernest xxii, 196, 197
Ryall, John 20, 131
Ryan, Thomas, RHA 201
Ryder, George 207

Ryder, Kate (*née* Donegan) 207
Ryle, Martin xvi

S

St George's Church, Dublin 52–3
St James's Hospital 238, 240
St Mary's University College, Belfast 216
St Patrick's Cathedral, Dublin 6
St Patrick's College, Maynooth 9, 12, 152
St Paul's Cathedral, London 108
Salmon, George 15, 21
Sands, William (Willie) 143, 144
Sapienza University, Rome 9
Saturday Review 64
Scheele, Carl Wilhelm 62
Schoute, Pieter H. 132
Schrödinger, Annemarie (Anny) (*née* Bertel) 150, 152, 154
Schrödinger, Erwin xxii, 31, 150–5, 166
  Meine Weltansicht (My view of the world) 154–5
  Nature and the Greeks 154
  What is life? 153–4
  'Schrödinger's wave equation' 151
Schrödinger, Georgine Emilia Brenda (*née* Bauer) 150
Schrödinger, Rudolf 150
Schrödinger, Ruth 151, 152
Schwarzschild radius 192
Science 71
science, religion and 5, 8, 63–4, 199
science journalism 242–6
Science Research Council (SRC) 220
Science@Culture newsletter 243–4
Scientific Proceedings of the Royal Dublin Society 111
Scott, Anthony 247
Scott, Clare (*née* Doran) 235
Scott, Isabel (*née* Finnegan) 240

Scott, John Martin xx, xxiii, 235–40
　'Folate levels and neural tube defects. Implications for prevention' 237
Scott, Martin 235
Scully, Reginald, *Flora of County Kerry, The* 140
sea anemones 140
Seanad Éireann 228, 229, 230–1, 232
searchlight mirrors 118
seaweed research 207
Second World War 147, 159–60, 182, 198
　Hungarian diplomatic codes 159–60
　Italy and 159
seismic experiments 53–4
seismology 54
seismoscope 53
Semple, George 95
sexual abuse 152–3, 155
Shannon, Claude xiii, 23
Sheridan, Cormac 244
Simon, Francis 203
Simpson, Maxwell 164
Single European Act (1987) 232
Sinn Féin 210
Sisters of Charity of the Incarnate Word 169, 172
Sisters of the Sacred Heart 43
Sloane, Robert 173
Snow, C.P. 198
Society of Earthquake and Civil Engineering Dynamics 56
Society of Friends 167
Solar Physics Laboratory 80
Somerville, Mary 50
Sommerfeld, Arnold 31
Soroptimists International 254
South East Technological University (SETU) 172
South, Sir James 122
spectroscopy xiv, 59, 62, 79, 82, 105–6, 217–18
Spencer, Herbert 17, 61

Study of sociology, The. 17
Spottiswoode, William 61
Stadio Nuovo, Bari 180
Standard Motor Company 146
Stanford University, Linear Accelerator Centre 254
Stansted Airport 179
Stapp, Henry 175
Starkey, George (Eirenaeus Philalethes) 2
statistics xiv, 128–30
steam engines 115, 117
steam-powered road locomotive 50
STEM xi–xii
　communicators xxiii, 47–50, 182–5, 243–6
　family backgrounds and xx–xxi
　gender disparity xxvn17
　socio-economic status and xx
　women and xv–xviii, xixn11, xxv
Stephenson, Marjorie 166
sterilisation 65–6
Stevenson, Hilary (Mary Hill) (*née* Morrison) xx, xxiii, 186–8
　Detection of irradiated food – current status 187
　Food irradiation and the chemist (co-editor) 187
Stevenson, Noel 188
Stokes, Arthur Romney, 2nd Baronet 83
Stokes, Elizabeth (*née* Haughton) 74
Stokes, Gabriel 74
Stokes, Revd Gabriel 74
Stokes, George Gabriel, 1st Baronet xiii, xiv, xix, xx, xxvi, 23, 68, 74–83, 124
　correspondence with Thomson (Lord Kelvin) 83, 91, 92
　Burnett lectures 80–1
　Conditional immortality: a help to sceptics 81
　Natural theology 80–1
　'On the change of the refrangibility of light' 78

'On the effect of the internal friction of fluids on the motion of pendulums' 75–6
'On the theories of the internal friction of fluids in motion, and of the equilibrium and motion of elastic solids' 75
scientific papers 83
Stokes, Mary Susanna (*née* Robinson) 82–3
'Stokes line' 82
'Stokes parameters' 82
'Stokes phenomena' 78
Stokes Programme (SFI) 81–2
'Stokes shift' 82
'Stokes's law' 82
'Stokes's solution' ('Stokes's reagent') 82
Stokes Summer School, Skreen, County Sligo 81
'Stokes theorem' 78–9
'stokes' unit of kinematic velocity 82
Stokes, William 74, 81
Stoneman, Walter 119
Stoney, Anne (*née* Blood) 93
Stoney, Bindon Blood xx, xxiii, 93–6
  Strength and proportions of riveted joints 94
  Theory of strains in girders and similar structures, with observations on the strength and other properties of materials, The 94
Stoney, George Johnstone 70, 93
Stoney, Susannah Frances (*née* Walker) 96
Stott, Leonard Boole 133
Stott, Walter 20, 132
Stuart, Sir William 189
Sturgeon, William 10
Sturgeon's Annals of Electricity 10–11
submarine telegraphy 91
submarines 101–3, 125
suffrage movement 156

sun 78
Sun Advertising, Dublin 182–3
sunshine hours, measurement of 78
Swift, Jonathan 25
Sydney Opera House xxiii, 177–8
Sylvester, J.J. 15
Synge, Edward 189
Synge, Edward, Archbishop of Tuam 189
Synge, Elizabeth Eleanor Mabel (*née* Allen) 190
Synge, Ellen Frances (*née* Price) 189
Synge, John Lighton xiv, xx, 189–94
  General relativity: papers in honour of J.L. Synge on his 75th birthday (Ó Raifeartaigh) 193
  'Gravitational field of a particle' 192
  Kandelman's Krim 193
  'On the geometry of dynamics' 191
  'On the tightness of the teeth, considered as a problem concerning the equilibrium of a thin incompressible elastic medium' 192
  'Relativistic hydrodynamics' 192
Synge's theorem 191–2
Synge, John Millington 190
Synge, K.C. 189
Synge, Thomas Millington 189

T

t distribution xiv, 129
Taisce, An 184
Tait, Peter Guthrie 33, 90
  Treatise on natural philosophy 90
Taubes, Gary 255
Taylor, Edward 21
Taylor, Sir Geoffrey Ingram 21, 132
TE (Tractor England) models 146
Teagasc 245

Tebbutt's Comet 106
Technology Ireland 242
Telefís Éireann 183–4
  see also RTÉ
telescopes 105, 106, 118, 121–5
  Birr Castle and 12, 48, 93, 115–16, 122
Television Society 137
Telford Medal 55, 95
Telford, Thomas 38, 39
theology 5, 63, 80–1
thermodynamics 90–1, 99
Thomas Young Medal and Prize 221
Thomson, Frances Anna (*née* Blandy) 91
Thomson, James (d.1849) 89
Thomson, James (d.1892) 60, 89
Thomson, J.J. 71
Thomson, Margaret (*née* Crum) 91
Thomson, Margaret (*née* Gardner) 89
Thomson, William (Lord Kelvin) xix, xx, 16, 23, 60, 72, 73, 78–9, 89–92
  correspondence with Stokes 83, 91, 92
  Treatise on natural philosophy (Thomson and Tait) 90
Tinney, Ethna 225
Tinney, Hugh 225
Tinney, Mary Catherine 225
Tinney, Sean 224, 225
Tinney, Sheila Christina (*née* Power) xxi, 223–5
Tisdall, Juliana 190
Titanic, RMS 163
Todd Memorial Scholarship 202
Tolansky, Samuel 217
Tory Medal 193
Townsend, J.S.E. 72
Transactions of the Royal Society of Edinburgh 48
transatlantic steamers 42
tribology 99–100
Trignometrical Survey of India 75

Trinity College Dublin (TCD) xxi, xxii, 93, 116, 175
  Andrews Professor of Astronomy 27
  Boole's paper (MS 2398) 23
  Bradley memorial bench 222
  chair of civil engineering 98
  chair of computer science 248
  chair in experimental nutrition 235–6
  chair in optical electronics 221
  computer science, undergraduate degrees in 249
  'Computing through the ages' (exhibition) 251
  Department of Computer Science 248–51
  Diploma in Computers in Education 249
  Diploma in Systems Analysis 249
  Erasmus Smith chair 70, 191, 198
  finances 198
  Fitzgerald Building 72, 201, 222
  Fitzgerald Medal 72
  information and communications technology (ICT) 249, 250
  J.L. Synge prize in mathematics 193
  J.L. Synge public lecture 193
  John Gabriel Byrne Computer Science Collection 113, 250
  John Scott fellowships 240
  McCullagh prize 196
  manuscript library 201
  Physics Department 197, 198, 199–200
  Provost's Award 240
  reform 26–7
  scholarships 190, 195
  School of Biochemistry 239
  School of Engineering 247, 248
  School of Medicine 239
  Schrödinger and 153–4, 155
  Scott elected to fellowship of 239
  student hardship fund 251

Synge as honorary fellow of 193
Walton as a fellow 197
see also Dublin University;
 University of Dublin
Trinity College Library 36, 251
Trinity House 68, 75
Trouton, Frederick 72
tuberculosis 133
turbines 117–18, 119
Turbinia (steamship) 118
turbo-alternator 117
turbulence 99
Tyndall, John, Snr 57
Tyndall, John xiii, xx, xxvn17, 57–69
  Apology 68
  Belfast address 63, 64, 68
  'Cometary theory, A' 62
  Contributions to molecular physics in the domain of radiant heat 61
  'Dust and disease' 65
  Essay on floating matter of the air in relation to putrefaction and disease 66
  Faraday as a discoverer 60
  Forms of water in clouds, rivers and glaciers 67
  Fragments of science for unscientific people 64
  Glaciers of the Alps, The 67
  Heat considered a mode of motion 65
  Hours of exercise in the Alps 67
  Lessons in electricity 65
  Mountaineering in 1861 67
  New fragments of science 64
  'New series of chemical reactions produced by light, A' 62
  Notes of a course of juvenile lectures on heat visible and invisible 65
  Notes of a course of nine lectures on light 64
  Notes on a course of seven lectures on electrical phenomenon and theories 65
  Notes of a course of six lectures (adapted to juvenile auditory) on ice, water, vapour and air 65
  Notes on a course of six lectures on the motion and sensation of sound 64
  Notes on electricity 65
  On light 65
  'On the scientific use of imagination' 63
  On sound: a course of nine lectures 64
  Researches on diamagnetism and magne-crystallic action 60
  'Science and man' 64
  Six lectures on light. Delivered in America 65
  Sound: a course of eight lectures 64
Tyndall, Louisa Charlotte (*née* Hamilton) 68, 69
Tyndall, Sarah (*née* McAssey) 57
'Tyndall blue' 62
'Tyndall scattering' 62
tyndallisation (sterilisation) 66

U

Ulster Folk and Transport Museum 143
Ulster Volunteer Force 143
ultraviolet (UV) rays 77, 78
United Irishmen 25
United Kingdom
  Department of Health Expert Advisory Group 238
  Medical Research Council 236
United States Army
  Aberdeen Proving Ground 211, 213
  ENIAC, development of 211, 213
United States Army Air Force 191
United States Department of Energy 255, 256

United States Military Academy 122
United States Navy 101, 103
UNIVAC 213
Universidad San Pablo, Madrid 240
University of Berlin 151, 157
University of California, Berkeley 254
University of California, Riverside 254, 255, 256
University of Cambridge xvi, xxii, 14, 18, 80, 97, 157
  Analytical Society 14
  Cavendish chair 89
  Clerk Maxwell scholarship 197
  Conservative MP, Stokes as 80
  Girton College 135, 202, 204, 206
  Library 23, 68, 83, 90
  Lucasian chair of mathematics 75
  Pembroke College 74–5, 81, 83
  Peterhouse 89
  Queens' College 97
  St John's College 116
  Smith's Prize 74, 89
  Trinity College 196, 197
  tripos examinations 79, 97, 135
  see also Cavendish Laboratory
University College Cork (UCC) 23, 227
  see also Queen's College, Cork (QCC)
University College Dublin (UCD) 207–8, 226, 228, 233, 253–4, 256
University College Galway (UCG) 156, 157, 162, 207, 232
University College, London (UCL) 23, 128, 164, 165, 168
University of Dublin 95, 148
  see also Dublin University; Trinity College Dublin (TCD)
University of Edinburgh 80, 223–4
University of Galway 162
  see also Queen's College, Galway; University College Galway (UCG)

University of Ghent 154
University of Glasgow 89, 98, 135
  Library 23, 89, 135
University of Graz 151
University of Iowa 227
University of Limerick 81, 168
University of London 80, 163, 164, 216
University of Madrid 151
University of Manchester 100
University of Oxford 16, 21, 22
  Clarendon Laboratory 203
  Magdalen College 115, 151
  New College 127
  Wadham College 2
University of Pennsylvania 211
University of Rochester, New York 253
University of St Andrews 193
University of Strathclyde 186
University of Texas 170
University of Toronto 190–1, 193
University of Ulster 149, 200, 222, 238, 240
University of Vienna 150, 154, 203
University of Zürich 151, 152
USS Holland 103
Utzon, Jørn 177, 178

V

Valentia Island 138–9, 141
van der Meer, Simon 255
van Gelderen, Gerrit xxii, xxiii, 182–5
  Telefís feirme series illustrated by 184
  To the waters and the wild series 184
  Irish wildlife book, The 185
  To the waters and the wild: adventures of a wildlife film maker 185
van Gelderen, Johannes Gerardus 182
van Gelderen, Lize (Lies) (*née* Henderson) 183, 185
van Helmont, J.B. 2

Vassar College, USA 136
Vega (star) 106
Venn, John
  Mind 17
  Symbolic logic 17
Victoria and Albert Museum 206
Victoria Institute 80
Victoria, Queen 24, 41, 50, 83, 108
Victoria University of Manchester 98
Vignoles, Charles 39
vitamin B12 research 236, 239
volcanoes 54
Volta, Allesandro 9
von Guericke, Otto 3
von Neumann, John 175
von Spreckelsen, Johann Otto 180
Voynich, Ethel Lilian (*née* Boole) 20–1
  Gadfly, The 20–1
Voynich, Wilfrid 20

W

Walker, John Francis 96
Wall, R.H. 74
Walsh, William, Archbishop of Dublin 11
Walter Premium 52–3, 55
Walton, Anna Elizabeth (*née* Sinton) 195
Walton Causeway Park, Dungarvan 200
Walton, Dorothy Letitia 195
Walton, Ernest Thomas Sinton xx, xxii, 195–201
Walton, Freda (*née* Wilson) 197–8
Walton, James Kirkwood 195
Walton, Revd John Arthur 195
Walton, Mary Elizabeth (*née* Kirkwood) 195
Ward, Edward, Viscount Bangor 48
Ward, Harriett 47
Ward, Henry William Crosbie 48
Ward, Jane 47

Ward, John Gilbert 47
Ward, Mary (*née* King) xv, xx, xxiii, 47–50
  article on natterjack toads 48
  Entomology in sport; and entomology in earnest 49
  Microscope teachings (*The microscope*) 49
  Sketches with the microscope 49
  Telescope teachings (*The telescope*) 49
  Windfall for the microscope, A 49
  World of wonders revealed by the microscope, A 49
Ward, Seth 2
water management 232
water waves 76–7
Watkins, Michael xvin5
Watson, Adam 148
Watson, James xvin5, 154
Watts, William (Bill) 221
Weir, Donald G. 235, 236
Wellesley College, USA 108
Welsh, Elizabeth 135
Wessely–Moser rearrangement 208
Westminster Abbey 90
Wexford sloblands 43, 44
Wheeler, Thomas Sherlock 207, 208
Whitaker, Andrew 176
Whitaker, T.K. 200
Whitehead, A.N. 22
  Treatise on universal algebra, A 22
Whitney, Mary 136
Whittaker, Edmund 152
Whitworth engineering laboratories 98
Whymper, Edward 67
Wigham, John 68
Wilbraham, Henry 18–19
Wilde, Lady (Speranza) 34
Wilde, Oscar 34
Wilkins, John 2
Wilkinson, Revd H. 100
Willis, Thomas 2
Wilson, Annie (*née* Elliott) 198
Wilson, Revd Charles 197–8

Wilson, David B. 83
Wolf-Rayet stars 106, 107
Wollaston Medal 55
women
   discrimination against 243
   gender constraints 49
   STEM and xv–xviii, xixn11, xxv
   university scholarships and 135
Women in Technology Hall of Fame 214
Women in Technology and Science (WITS) 243
Women's Army Auxiliary Corps (WAAC) 157
Wordsworth, William 34
World Climate Impact Studies Programme 230
World Health Organization (WHO) 237
Wren, Christopher 2
Wright, William 248

X

X-Club 61, 66
X-ray crystallography xvin5, 164, 165, 202–3, 204, 205
X-ray machine 133

Y

Yardley, Fred 163
Yardley, Henry Frederick 163
Yardley, Jessie (*née* Cameron) 163
Young, Thomas 28

Z

Zalinski, Edmund L.G. 103
Zalinski (submarine) 103
Zuse, Konrad 113